Venus
After Forty

❧VENUS❧
AFTER FORTY

Sexual Myths, Men's Fantasies, and Truths About Middle-Aged Women

Rita M. Ransohoff, Ph.D.

NEW HORIZON PRESS
Far Hills, New Jersey

Distributed by
MACMILLAN PUBLISHING COMPANY
New York

Library of Congress Cataloging-in-Publication Data

Ransohoff, Rita M.,
   Venus after forty.

   1. Middle aged women—Sexual behavior. 2. Sex
(Psychology) 3. Menopause. I. Title.
HQ29.R36 1987   306.7'0880564   87-12233
ISBN 0-88282-034-6
New Horizon Press

For Joan and Joey

Interview with Lillian Gish:
You know when I was making films, Lionel Barrymore first played my
father, and finally he played my husband. If he had lived, I am sure I
would have played his mother.

The New York Times. December 31, 1982.

Interview with Charles Panzer, 82, a retired postal clerk and
steady patron of the Roseland Ballroom for 60 years:
"I like my partners to be light and have rhythm, like I've got.
But not of my age bracket, naturally. I mostly choose women 25 or 30
years younger."

The New York Times. January 29, 1980.

Contents

10

The Narcissistic Woman: Women Who Buy the Myths

PART III   OPTIONS

11

Couples Who Make It

12

Single, Female, and Over Forty

13

The Sensual Older Woman

Preface

This is a subject that has lived with me for a very long time. I am grateful to Dr. Joan Dunphy and Margaret Russell of New Horizon Press for making it possible for it to leave my study and join the world. I want especially to thank Elaine Markson, my literary agent, and her assistant, Geri Thoma, who believed in the importance of this material. I will always be indebted to the Union Graduate School, where this work first began. Thanks, too, to Romy Franklin, who is not only a superior typist, but kept finding wonderful evidence to use in this book.

Introduction

News Item:
Definitely a man who knows how to enjoy his golden years,
Dr. Christiaan Barnard—who has given up heart transplants
because of arthritis in his hands—spent the summer on
the French Riviera with Karen Setzkorn, who is young enough
to be his granddaughter. They had so much fun they plan
to get married. Karen, a model barely in her twenties (he's 61),
got approval of the match from her parents in England. No
date yet, but Barnard, who now runs a clinic on the Greek
island of Cos, is ready, having divorced his wife Barbara in
1982. "Young girls like me because of my name," the doctor
explained, "and I like young girls because they are prettier
than old ones."

New York Post. October 15, 1984

. . . How unwanted a woman is who has passed the age of
sexual attractiveness . . .

Charles Simmons, in
Wrinkles, A Novel

It is close to three decades now since I first began working as a psychotherapist, and in that time I have witnessed great changes in the lives of my female patients. I have seen the effect of sexual freedom on their personal lives, of diet and exercise on their physical well-being, of jobs with greater power and responsibility on their self-esteem, of husbands participating in the rearing of children on their family life. These changes have radically altered their lives. What many of them have learned is how to create a balance between their intellectual, their maternal, and their sexual selves.

Yet, for all these advances, there is still one group that does not feel that their lives are appreciably better. They are the middle-aged women—or those approaching middle age. Like younger women, they have been able to enter professions that were previously closed to them, enjoy better health, look better, and even, in many cases, start families. Yet, as a group they do not feel good about themselves. Their self-image is vulnerable; their sense of self-esteem is shaky. The problem is that middle-aged women, living in a culture obsessed with youth and sex, inevitably know that they are potential sexual rejects.

I wonder how many people who have not had to face this threat realize how devastating it is to have your hard-earned sense of mastery, control over your life, feelings of pride and well-being challenged or actually taken away. I say this because even though a woman in her forties or fifties may be successful professionally, her identity as a whole person includes her sexuality. If a woman can no longer attract a man, what is she to do with her sexual needs, her ability to give and to receive pleasure, to nurture, and to create that sense of wholeness, without which life may seem to be reduced by half? What is she to do with all of these qualities which she has developed over her lifetime?

But women who find themselves alone at midlife and beyond face additional obstacles. Not only is there loss of sexual identity, but there is a real drop in status. In our culture, a significant part of a woman's identity comes from the fact that she is married, or coupled, and from her partner's status. Widowed or divorced, not only does she lose her sex life and her status, but her economic security as well. This often happens at a time in her life when she is less employable or may, at best, have a substantially lower

Introduction

earning capacity than her former partner. The statistics that I have found show that, looking ahead to the years after sixty-five, it is estimated that women alone have a sixty percent chance of being destitute.[1]

These are the real anxieties of middle-aged women. But the overriding fear is the threat of loss of sexual attractiveness. It is so pervasive that I even hear women in their late twenties and early thirties bemoan approaching birthdays. Women in their forties and fifties who have never married, or who are divorced or widowed, often come to me preoccupied or obsessed with finding a man. They come to my office depressed—bright, educated, self-supporting women. Too many are "grayed out," desperate to find men. Some go to "adult weekends," take courses in which they hope men will be enrolled, or put seductive ads in "Personal" columns. Too many settle for proverbial crumbs, waiting at the telephone for the voice of a married man, feeling hurt, abused, angry, helpless. Soap opera? No: real life. The sum total: loneliness, depression, lack of self-confidence and self-esteem. To help middle-aged women transform this image of themselves is one of the most difficult therapeutic problems I face.

Perhaps the most corrosive part is the anger. One woman, recently widowed, who has lived in a small community all of her adult life, tells me: "A close married friend invited me to dinner. I said I was busy and was very sorry I couldn't come. After a pause, she said, 'Well, that's just as well. If you came there'd be two single women and the men wouldn't like it . . .' "

Why not?

I counsel a bright, attractive woman in her forties who has become so preoccupied with finding a man she can speak of nothing else. She has become an uninteresting human being.

A student of mine said in wonder and indignation,

"You know, when I told them at my office I was leaving to get married for the first time, start a brand new professional career, and celebrate my fortieth birthday, the only response I got from the guys was, 'What! You're not really going to be forty!' "

In recent years my practice has increasingly been filled with women who fear that they are becoming "invisible." Some have given up after having waited a long time for a man to divorce his wife; others have just left men who have raised their own families and who suddenly refuse to "allow" them to have a child of their own. They resemble all those women who have achieved professional success; they have acquired and furnished a pleasant home, but they live in it by themselves. These women, instead of enjoying their maturity, feel punished by it. When they find themselves single in a couple-oriented society, they develop a sense of personal failure, as if they are somehow defective.

One of the best early descriptions of this problem appears in a 1972 article by Susan Sontag called "A Double Standard of Aging."[2] In it she underscores the familiar fact that mature men, especially those with a degree of power and influence, remain sexually attractive to women, including women much younger than they. That the situation has not changed is illustrated by a story about Marcello Mastroianni at sixty. His face is described as "a touch jowly"; in the film version of Pirandello's "Henry IV" we are told there is a nude scene which exposes his paunch. Yet it appears to be entirely credible that when he is visited in exile by an early love and her grown daughter it is the latter who falls madly in love with him.[3] Such an event could happen to a fairly ordinary man.

Sontag pointed out that there are some women who are treated like Mastroianni, but that they are, for the most part, not ordinary women, but those with the power

Introduction

that comes from their public lives: actresses, film stars, television personalities, and the like. And even though *Vanity Fair's* 1984 Hall of Fame declared that "fifty is hip," the women they singled out were Gloria Steinem, Sophia Loren, and Shirley MacLaine. It is vastly encouraging that women can acknowledge fifty as a birthday and that *Vanity Fair* finds these three women extremely attractive. Yet for women as a group, the double standard of aging is still a fact of life, given credence by the weight of culture and history.

Women still in their forties understand what I mean: it is in the very air that they breathe. A friend tells me that she went to a new doctor for a check-up. Inquiring about the status of her menstrual cycle, he asked in a bantering tone, "Are you still a woman?" Is the implication that she is doomed to become an androgynous figure after the menopause?

Here it is again: An attractive middle-aged woman told me about her flight home from a ski trip in Colorado:

> I got on the airplane feeling great and looking good. Next to me was a man my age and next to him a younger woman. He immediately turned to her and for three hours I could not avoid overhearing his conversation. Every subject he touched was an area of interest and excitement to me, certain books, parts of the world I knew intimately and loved, art, theater, food. It was a shock to discover that it was as if the seat I sat in was unoccupied. I realized that no matter what I might have been able to share with this man, it was all irrelevant to him. Clearly his interest was in the other woman because she was young. And without sex appeal, all of a sudden, I felt dead, dead as a woman.

Any of these women can tell you how hurtful it is to be the recipient of unprovoked hostility from a man, but, worse than that, the recipient of his profound indifference. I can't count the number of times when I have given lectures at which women in the audience have told me how they felt when at a certain moment of time they realized that no man looked up when they walked by. It is as though the sexuality of the older woman is taboo: "Hands Off!" "No Man's Land!"

Clearly, the media is partially responsible for the perpetuation of these attitudes. For the past twenty-five years, at least, since Joe Kennedy discovered he could sell his son for the presidency "like soap flakes,"[4] we have bought products—whether organic or inorganic—that reflect the advertising industry's notion of what will sell. George Gerbner, Dean of the Annenberg School of Communications at the University of Pennsylvania, has studied sexual roles on television since 1967. He notes that "In their depiction of women, that now instead of lagging thirty years behind the times, the networks may be only twenty or fifteen years behind." Dr. Gerbner is referring to the honest reflection of women's roles in the workplace.[5] From the point of view of the physical attractiveness of mature women, the media is beginning to acknowledge that women as beautiful as Linda Evans of "Dynasty" is in her early forties. Blake Carrington, her husband, is played by John Forsythe, a man in his late sixties. But we can see how far we still have to go when we come across a news item such as the following: A Miss Carter, waiting for a modelling audition, said, "I've had good success in Cleveland. . . . You can get away with not being quite tall enough or slightly too old in other cities, but in New York you have to be absolutely perfect—5'-8" to 5'-10" tall and fifteen to twenty years old."[6]

Do we understand the reason why the dichotomy between youth and age is so particularly hard on women? Why do they lose their sex appeal? And what's more, why do such attitudes even exist? It is certainly time that

Introduction

someone stopped and asked. Men, of course, had no reason to ask, and women, dependent as they have been on men, have been afraid to. The Women's Movement of recent years has challenged much of the power and sexual arrangements between the sexes. But the problems generated by men's attitudes towards older women remain. With a great increase in the number of women between forty-five and sixty-five who are single, widowed, or divorced, the issue is urgent. There are almost six million women in these categories, according to the 1980 census. Their prospects are:

• Men in first marriages marry women two to three years younger.

• Men in second marriages marry women five or more years younger.

• If a man remarries in his forties, the woman is ten or more years younger.

• If a woman is divorced in her twenties, she has a 76 percent chance of remarriage.

• If divorced in her thirties, she has a 65 percent chance.

• If she is in her fifties or older, she has less than a 12 percent chance.

• In 1980, 94 percent of men in their fifties were married.

• In 1978, there was an increase of 50 percent in the divorce rate of people between forty and sixty-five.[7]

There are important historical reasons underlying the current attitudes that these statistics reflect. One is the fact that up through the nineteenth century men outlived women, and as has been recently pointed out, this is still true in many parts of the world.

In the Western world in 1900 women's life expectancy was forty-eight. By 1920 women outlived men by two years—to about age fifty-six. By 1984 women's life expectancy had increased to age eighty, eight years longer than men's.[8]

It was only a short time ago that there was no middle age for women. Many died in childbirth. After multiple pregnancies and poor gynecological care, women were left with post-partum infections or with permanent damage to the uterus or vaginal area. By the time they reached the menopause they *looked* and *felt* old. Moreover, because of the high rate—world wide—of infant mortality, a post-menopausal woman in many cultures accepted the fact that in order to have enough live hands for work a second or third wife would have to supplant her.

In eighteenth-century France, for example, of every ten babies born, two or three died before their first birthday and four or five died before the age of ten.[9] But today, with vastly improved medical care, and fewer pregnancies, women live one third of their lives after their childbearing years are over. They can be dynamic, energetic, sexual beings. And while such a drastic alteration should have profoundly affected the mental set and expectations people had when women died early, a lag exists in our culture: men have not caught up with the new reality. It is as though a woman's sexuality is still tied to child bearing. In spite of middle-aged women like Jane Fonda and Gloria Steinem, who are in the forefront of the attempts to change this image, middle-aged women are still treated as though they are sexually "used up." The notion and others like it are not only artifacts from the past. They are the creation of men's fantasies about women. If we are to understand why older women are viewed as sexually over the hill, we must look for the reason in the psychology of men. The well kept secret is that *men turn away from older women because of anxieties they themselves experi-*

ence in middle age. The causes of the double standard of aging lie hidden within the emotional life of men.

In proving this thesis, my first task was to get a broad sample of data about men. Many researchers collect information by sending out questionnaires or by conducting a series of interviews. But responses given in this way have limitations; people can only tell you what they know. It is difficult, if not impossible, for them to probe the inner reaches of their minds and tell what they do not consciously know, what is hidden—even from themselves. To get such information in a clinical setting takes a considerable length of time. In order to gather material quickly and to have a broad enough sample, I had to find ways of collecting data that were as rich as that which one gets in a consulting room. I had to find resources that were spontaneous, unself-conscious, off-guard expressions of men's thoughts and fantasies about older women. I found there were ready sources of men's fantasies lying around unnoticed. I found them in ancient and modern myths, in fiction, in the media, and, perhaps best of all, in the wonderfully rich store of jokes and cartoons. Freud recognized decades ago that humor is a rich source of fantasy, and that it expresses, within the context of the joke, deep-seated fears and anxiety as well as persistent wishes.

An experience of mine that illustrates exactly what I mean about the use of humor as a source of men's fantasies happened while I was taking a brief Caribbean vacation at a lovely little guest house. It was run by an American family on an old sugar plantation overlooking the sea, and was idyllic. Every evening the guests gathered at a little bar for drinks before dinner. One evening I went to use the bathroom just off the bar. I was in a peaceful, far-away mood and not at all prepared for the sight that awaited me. Someone had decorated the "john," which

Introduction

was used by both men and women, with nudes from *Playboy* magazine. The walls, from floor to ceiling, and the ceiling, were papered with every possible shape and size of breast, aureole, and nipple, all of them staunchly and persistently firm, over which glowed hundreds of smiling young faces.

But above the toilet was one lone cartoon; a joke. Out on the Great Plains stood a covered wagon surrounded by Indians. Obviously, the men, their bullets spent, had failed to save the day. The Indians were closing in for the kill. At this crucial moment an old woman burst out of the covered wagon, her pendulous breasts exposed. One look and the Indians turned and ran for the hills!

Imbedded in this cartoon are fantasies of the awesome power of the older woman. She is pictured as ugly and totally repellent. What's more, she is horribly denigrated: her place of honor is over the toilet. The cartoon offered me a clue: in this fantasy the older woman is given power over life and death. Why, I wondered, was such power given to an older woman and not to a young one? It was this question that started me thinking about the dichotomy in men's minds between younger and older women. When I got home, I began to look around for more expressions of such attitudes that were spontaneously expressed in humor. They were not hard to find. Example from an anthology of jokes:

> *What do you do with a wife of 40?*
> *Take her to the bank and change her for two twenties.*

On a "decorative" plaque found for sale at a flea market:

> *A woman is as old as she looks.*
> *A man is not old until he stops looking.*

Introduction

Using humor is an acceptable way of expressing uncomfortable ideas and feelings. You can always deny the meaning of what you are saying by insisting, "It's only a joke." Joke-telling is a social institution, for jokes are told to a group. Other people join in. The audience encourages the teller. One joke leads to another. Within the group anything goes: subjects that are generally censored, including sexual adventures of every kind from pederasty to incest are allowed. Even the most casual one-liners, and some of the old chestnuts that we tend to dismiss because they are so familiar, contain a hidden message, like the joke:

> *What's wrong with being a grandpa?*
> *Having to sleep with grandma.*

If you examine such jokes about older women, the hostility is obvious. What is less apparent is the tendency of these jokes to blame the older woman. The man says, "I have no problems with sex and aging. *She does."*

Joking is a marvelous human invention through which we domesticate fantasies and daydreams and make life more tolerable. Jokes are significant expressions of fantasies. They contain assumptions that underlie many popular attitudes. They share their importance with the fantasies that we find everywhere we turn: in the media, in advertising, and in everyday conversation. They cannot be dismissed. When it comes to the fantasies about women in their forties and older, they are simply waiting to be understood. But when jokes get so aggressive, when they attempt to destroy the object of the wit, they lose their adaptive function as safety valves and become weapons of attack.

I spend a great deal of my time looking for the sources of people's behavior. Psychotherapy, in essence, is a process of examining the effects of repeating old patterns, of coming to the same conclusions, of finding ourselves caught again and again in destructive situations of our own making. If we apply this dynamic to social and group behavior, we can see how we are dictated to and become prisoners of popular attitudes. The beliefs expressed in the fantasies are so widespread that they are generalized into popular myths which have taken on a life of their own. They become accepted truths. One such myth is that older women are not sexual beings. It is sad to see the effects of such a myth on some women, especially when they begin to mock themselves. Many women have so internalized the culture's myths about them that they almost believe that they are true. The following example illustrates what I have in mind:

> I walk into a friend's bedroom. She is a vital and handsome woman and happily married. She is in her fifties. On her dressing table mirror she has taped a cartoon typical of the ones that I have found. It shows two middle-aged women, fat and ugly. "The only nudity that can shock me," says one woman, "is my own."

Behind her attempt to make a joke out of her own physical maturity lies her acceptance of the myth that her body, like those of other older women, is sexually unappealing. Myths of this kind inhibit us from enjoying one another. It makes a man I know say, in considering his malaise at midlife, that he no longer wants to look up old friends. He doesn't want to see how they have changed— especially if they are women. We are not permitted to mature. Why can't we appreciate one another's middle-aged presence—our middle-aged bodies? We seem to be stuck for a lifetime with a twenty-year-old's image of beauty. Maybe one day both sexes will have the wisdom of a Colette, who could deal with time and change. She knew that a woman with self-esteem would not feel negative about ". . . a day when beauty in its fading must have recourse to grace."[10]

What do we mean by middle age anyway? Unlike adolescence, it is not a moment with precise biological landmarks. Rather, middle age is a series of moments. In some cases it is a time when one realizes that birthdays are counted in years yet to live. We enter this period through many doors—sexual, social, and familial. If middle age must be given a chronological peg, it could be said to begin roughly in the forties. Even though a woman's longevity has significantly increased, she still knows that in her forties her childbearing years will be ending. For men, the forties can be the time when they realize that they have reached a plateau in their professional and business life, and that they must come to terms with their own limitations. Anthropologists used to define middle age as having grown children. Today this is no longer a valid measure, since many couples have delayed having children until their late thirties or early forties.

I would suggest that middle age is a state of mind, and that it begins when one becomes internally aware of *being* middle-aged. The moment of awareness can come gradually or may catch you by surprise as it did the woman in the airplane, already quoted, and as it did William Attwood, when he was newly appointed Ambassador to Kenya. After his first diplomatic function he considered inviting to dinner an attractive young woman he had met there. She asked if his family was in Nairobi, and he told her that his wife and children would soon arrive. "Oh," she said, "I hope you have a son my age! There is no one for me to date here."[11] Since not all men are treated like Marcello Mastroianni by young women, experiences such as this have made me focus on many men's vulnerability in middle age and their responses to an awareness of decline in their own sexual attractiveness. For it is at such

moments that some middle-aged men stop wanting to be
seen with middle-aged women.

A man's disenchantment with his wife of many
years is a popular theme in current literature. Philip Roth
celebrated the alienation of a middle-aged man from a
woman who is his peer in his novel *The Ghostwriter.* Other
novels with this theme, intent, and mood are Bernard
Malamud's *Dubin's Lives,* John Updike's *Rabbit Is Rich,*
Joseph Heller's *Something Happened,* and John Cheever's
short stories, "Oh Youth! Oh Beauty!" and "The Swimmer."
The protagonist in Roth's novel is E. I. Lonoff, who is fifty-
six, a writer living in a remote New England farmhouse.
Everything about his life seems frozen, an obsessive ritual
of reading and work. His wife spends a great deal of time
in the kitchen. On Sundays she accompanies her husband
on walks. She talks; he is silent. The young visiting writer,
Nathan Zuckerman, describes her: she is made to appear
unattractive and aged, "used up."

> . . . a smallish woman with gentle gray eyes and
> soft white hair and a multitude of fine lines criss-
> crossing her pale skin . . . I just couldn't believe
> that she looked so worn from living alongside
> E. I. Lonoff while he wrote stories for thirty years.

Their sex life is practically non-existent, since for a
long time Lonoff has come to bed obsessing about the
revisions of his stories. The charm and the challenge of
The Ghostwriter is, in reading Roth's maze-like construc-
tions, to try to figure out what has happened in the young
writer's imagination of a mature writer's life, and what has
actually taken place. The story revolves around the pre-
sumed love affair between Lonoff and a student his daughter's age. His wife feels the deadness of the marital relationship and tries to leave. She begs her husband to chuck
her out.

Lonoff voices his disillusionment to the young visitor: "If your life consists of reading and writing and looking

at the snow, you'll end up like me. Fantasy for thirty years." Lonoff knows his work is not exceptional enough to win him immortality. His particular middle-aged fantasy is to be living in a villa in Florence with a woman of thirty-five:

> She would make life comfortable and beautiful and new . . . At the breakfast table she would wear long feminine nightgowns under her pretty robe. They would be things I bought for her in a shop by the Ponte Vecchio . . . There would be flowers in a vase. She would cut them and put them there. . . .

The fantasied solution, the protagonist's defense against the winter cold, is a magical escape, a daydream that will offer a cure for his own depression. Lonoff has ceased to negotiate for change in his married life. He has settled for daydreams—the dream that only a young woman can restore him.[12]

Since one of the best sources of attitudes to women of middle age can be found in myths and fantasies, Part One of this book looks at a number of them. They seem to fall into discrete categories, which I describe. I then take up the relationship between them and the psychology of men. Part Two offers facts about the sexuality of women of middle age which the myths effectively hide. It also describes some men who have escaped the stereotypical behavior to which so many succumb. And it deals with the consequences for men and women who live by the myths and become obsessed with staying young—including men who desert mature wives for young women.

The last third of the book is concerned with new options for middle-aged women. This includes the significantly larger number of women choosing to remain single, younger men/older women relationships, and later first marriages as well as those women choosing to remain in marriages of long duration.

Introduction

Drawing on history, on my clinical experience, and on talks with colleagues and acquaintances, I discuss some older women who feel good about themselves, their bodies, and their sexuality, women who have full and exciting relationships with men. Then I write about men and women with enduring friendships, and couples, married or not, who have surmounted painful crises at midlife with insights which have enhanced their ability to love one another.

I feel very strongly about the second and third parts of this book. They are a long overdue antidote to all the propaganda about middle-aged women and the "expected" responses of middle-aged men. If we look back over the centuries, we can see there has been progress in the age-old battle of the sexes. We have debunked some of the myths and superstitions about the frightening power of women. Men no longer believe that women are witches, or that their menstrual blood is so magical and dangerous that having sex with a menstruating woman can drive a man mad. Our middle-aged numbers are increasing. The forty million children born in the postwar baby boom of 1947–1957 are reaching their forties.[13] It's time to challenge the myths surrounding the sexuality of women after forty, because women are sexual all of their lives. And it is high time we challenge the cultural imperative that asserts that to stay young, to maintain his masculinity, a man of middle age must turn into a satyr and chase every nubile girl through the computer forests of the workplace.

Men *and* women should have the right to the passion, the beauty, and the comfort of expressing their sexuality—both in response to individual differences in their needs and to change over the life cycle. Sexuality could then become what it has always been meant to be: not a commodity of exchange, but the closest form of human intimacy.

Part One

MYTHS AND FANTASIES

1

The Evidence: Ancient and Modern Legends About Women Over Forty

Unexamined myths, wherever they survive, have a subterranean potency; they affect our thinking in ways we are not aware of, and to the extent that we lack awareness our capacity to resist their influence is undermined.

Evelyn Fox Keller.
Reflections on Gender and Science, 1984.

A woman of middle age does not have to turn to the personal ads in the magazines to realize that middle-aged men feel free to take on a young woman while she has to struggle to maintain her sexual appeal. Women are forever telling me anecdotes like this one:

I was having lunch with a friend of forty-eight who was complaining bitterly that he could not

3

> find a woman who would make a commitment to
> him. I asked about the ages of the women he was
> dating, and he said they were from twenty to
> thirty. I suggested he might find a woman ready
> to join him if he started dating one closer to his
> own age. "Oh," he said, "but you know she
> wouldn't be able to keep up with me!"

Anecdotes like this one filter through our culture like light refracted through a prism. They are reflections of unexamined myths and fantasies, automatic, unaware, perhaps for the most part not even consciously hostile. They have their own psychological reasons for existence.

All of us have fantasies. They have a normal adaptive function. When we suffer a humiliating personal defeat we make ourselves feel better by imagining an exquisite revenge, even though we know that in reality we'll never carry it out. Through fantasy we test out new ideas, arrive at solutions, find comfort and solace, and escape from all sorts of painful feelings. Sometimes fantasies fail to lessen anxiety. When there are too many pressures, when a person is upset, when feelings become painful, fantasies may trigger a different set of reactions that even distort his picture of reality. In the case of this middle-aged man, for example, fantasies have colored his vision of himself in relation to a wife. The following is taken from the autobiographical sketch in a twenty-fifth college reunion bulletin:

> One Richard B. reported on his life since gradua-
> tion. He had developed a successful consulting
> firm, had a wife and three children, was an avid
> skier and flew his own plane. About his wife he
> wrote only this: "Jane has *her* (italics mine) two
> grandchildren. They give her such pleasure."

One wants to remind him, "They're your grandchildren too. Why don't you say so?" Richard B. does not say so because the idea of grandparenthood is, in all probability, symbolic for him. He is trying to avoid the aging process by making his wife the only grandparent. In Richard's fantasy they are *her* grandchildren. He may be aware of his need to cling to the image of himself as a powerful younger man, but not of his need to do so at the expense of his wife. Would Mr. B be amused by that venerable anti-older woman joke, already quoted:

> *What's wrong with being a grandpa?*
> *Reply: Having to sleep with grandma.*

Both Mr. B.'s note to the alumni magazine and the joke contain an expression of a wish, a daydream, a fantasy. This is why you will find me turning to jokes like a compass pointing north; they are such a rich source of experience. All of them contain a message.

Gershon Legman, one of our great chroniclers of jokes, has written three substantial volumes analyzing dirty jokes and limericks.[1] He studied more than two thousand jokes in the English language. The basic themes he discovered are as old as the hills. They deal with ancient anxieties that do not change but simply put on modern dress. Legman proved that, by and large, jokes are the invention of men. Since men are their inventors, even when the joke is bitterly anti-male or anti-old man, with the lines placed in the mouth of a sarcastic woman, the uneasiness expressed is his, the jokemaker's. Here is one of Legman's examples. The theme will become a familiar one, a man's dissatisfaction with his own sexual performance:

> *A fireman told his wife, "From now on we're gonna do things right, by bells, like we do at the station. One bell means you meet me at the door with a big kiss. Two bells mean you head for the bedroom, three bells mean we undress. Four bells mean we hit the sack, ready for action."*

> *Things went well, except suddenly she rang the*
> *bell five times.*
> *"What does that mean?" asked the fireman.*
> *"That means," said his wife, "for you to reel out*
> *more hose—you're not close enough to the fire."*

And a sarcastic joke about the sexual potential of an old man with a young woman:

> *Note in a society column: After his wedding to*
> *Mary Smith, age thirty-five, John Jones, age*
> *seventy, presented his wife with a gift of an*
> *antique pendant.*

Even when the content of the joke appears to give no solace to the storyteller, he is still appealing to the sympathy and support of his audience. By universalizing his worries, he reduces the anxiety they cause him.

Reliable statistics about jokes were collected by Erman Palmore, Leland J. Davies, and Joseph Richman, three experts on humor and aging. They actually tallied up the jokes in the joke books. Their findings substantiate what we already may have guessed: that anti-older women jokes greatly outnumber those that denigrate older men.[2]

Fantasies, whether expressed in jokes or in a variety of other forms, are often simply wishes come true. As long as we dwell in the fantasy, we feel at ease, our problems laid to rest. For example, visualize, in light of a man's concern about his sexuality, a Greek painter circa 500 B.C. painting rows of satyrs running around the circumference of a vase, each one with his penis happily and eternally erect. A lovely bit of wish fulfillment—and a typical representation. But the figure of the satyr itself is a creature of myth. As necessary as fantasy is to the life of the individual, so, too, are myths essential to the well-being of a group. There are many and complex definitions of myths, whether as revelations, as archetypes, or as rooted in historical events. For our purposes it may be useful to take as a hypothesis that myths are fantasies based on anxieties so urgent that they are generalized and shared by a culture. As fantasies serve an important function in the life of the individual, myths serve equally essential functions for the well-being of the group. They lend causality to such mysteries as the origin of the universe, of life and death. They explain natural disasters such as floods, disease, and famine.

Myths have always been social lubricants, helping people live communally. They institutionalize rules, determine good and evil. Myths attempt to explain human suffering and offer ritualized ways of dealing with anxiety. They are invented as a means of controlling the uncontrollable. Daniel M.A. Freeman, an authority on the Apache Indians, has demonstrated that myths arise to meet the needs of society at various stages of the life cycle. In Apache culture not only do the myths address such familiar topics as that of the young man about to leave home to seek his fortune, but how to become a responsible elder in the "grandparent stage."[3] You may already have begun to suspect that contemporary mythology is not so obliging to the male elders of this society.

Joseph Campbell notes that myths are a picture language, which, like fantasy and the dream, must be read in order to be understood. Although folk tales and fairy tales contain many themes of mythology, they were meant to be a form of entertainment. But because they contain the same elements, he believes their symbols, too, can be read.[4]

Myths endure because they contain something for everyone. They embody the hopes and wishes, the magical expectations, of every man, woman, and child. But in a patriarchal world the *epic myths* are male creations and are used pedagogically to institutionalize the interest of the powerful, the Divine Right of Kings. As Marta Weigle, the anthropologist, says in her book *Spiders and Spinsters, Women and Mythology,* "As generally understood and undertaken, mythology—the study of sacred symbols, texts, rites, and their dynamic expression in human psyches and societies—concern *men's* myths and ritual. Most extant documents, field data and interpretations come from male scribes, scholars and artists and 'informants.' "[5] Such messages as contained in epics permeate the culture from folk tales to nursery rhymes. Whether it is Ulysses, a knight at the time of the Crusades, or even the story of "The Three Little Pigs," traditionally males have gone out to seek their fortunes and their Penelopes have remained in place at home. So I would add an additional definition of mythology because of its particular relevance to the subject of this book. It is that a myth is "One of the fictions or half-truths forming part of the ideology of society (example: the myth of Anglo-Saxon superiority),— a notion based more on tradition or convenience than on fact."[6] Myths thus defined lose their purpose of serving the entire group and are used politically to control minorities—and that includes women.

It is both the irrationality and the adhesiveness of the myths about older women that have been such a source of pain and bewilderment to them. They have had a devastating effect on women's self-image and self-esteem.

Certain myths have been around, essentially unexamined and unchanged, at least since ancient Greek civilization, and they have caused the same feelings of helplessness in mature women throughout the ages. For example, Hera, the wife of Zeus, wanted a full sex life as part of her marriage. Even though she was revered as the protector of marriage and of married women, she had terrible marital problems of her own, we are told. Although their married life started out promisingly enough—Robert Graves notes that their wedding night

lasted three hundred years—Zeus soon began philander-
ing—with Maia, Lato, Semele, Europa, Leda, Danäe, and
Niobe—and others too numerous to mention. After a
while, he was forever off on amorous adventures, leaving
her angry and frustrated. Like many a mortal wife, Hera
kept trying to maintain her marriage. She even borrowed
the love goddess Aphrodite's magical girdle to arouse her
husband's passion. But this effort, too, proved futile.
Hera, the Goddess of Marriage, the myth would have it,
was unable to keep her husband's sexual interest.[7]

You may wonder as you read through this discussion of myths about middle-aged women why you will find
so many negative references to wives and to *old* women.
They originate in what I see as "The Hera Position": shortly
after a woman becomes a wife, men's fantasies about her
begin to change. If you can bear to read through the
volumes of jokes and quotes "written for every occasion"
which toastmasters, speakers, and stand-up comics seem
to cull, you will find that *old wives* in fantasy, are equated
with mature women, as opposed to *brides,* who are
thought to be young, innocent, open, and sexually inviting. Wives are supposedly frigid, inhibited, and boring.
Henny Youngman, the well-known stand-up comic on television, often starts his act with "Now take my wife—
PLEASE." Another wife joke, told by a group of blue collar
workers during a lunch break, is:

> *What is the difference between a wife and a cup
> of tea?*
> *Answer: When you are finished with the tea you
> can throw away the bag.*

Only a young woman is pleasing and sexually appealing.
An old woman is a hag. A look at *Webster's Dictionary*
reveals that a hag is "an evil and ugly old woman endowed
with supernatural powers." But when you look into a

dictionary of slang you will find that "hag" is a term used to describe middle-aged women as well![8] Unfortunately, you won't find such a definition confined to the dictionary. Robert M. Butler, M.D., the world-famous authority on aging, remembers that when he was a medical student older people of both sexes were referred to as "crocks," *but so were middle-aged women!*[9]

I doubt if any writer has topped Joseph Heller's fantasy of the physical unattractiveness of a middle-aged woman. In his novel, *Something Happened,* the fiftyish hero is reminiscing about a former girlfriend:

> . . . She'd be older than I am *now* (italics mine) and probably a pest: She would be stout and wrinkled and suffer from constipation, gall stones, menopausal disturbances and bunioned feet, and I more than likely would not wish to see her.[10]

When Heller's hero says, "She'd be older than I am *now,*" he expresses his own fantasied wish that a woman ages more than a man. He has given her the physical problems of both middle and old age. Clearly, *she* has become sexually undesirable because the man does not want to consider his own aging process. Heller's hero is like Richard B., who gives his wife the grandchildren. Men have convinced themselves that they can avoid aging if they can avoid *her*—the middle-aged and older woman.

Although myths, like fantasies, are rooted in a variety of men's concerns, all have the same effect: they put mature women into "The Hera Position." Myths as a whole fall roughly into four categories.

First, there is the ancient myth of the voracious woman. For example, the Empusae in Greek mythology were said to be filthy female demons with the haunches of asses. They were sexually greedy and insatiable, capable of the deception of turning themselves into beautiful

young maidens. The power of transformation from a repulsive crone to beautiful maiden is assigned to many a
legendary older woman. The tales end happily—for male
readers—when she is made powerless or punished for her
sexual desires. In every situation the old woman is considered evil. The message is clear. Her sexuality is taboo.

Fairytales take up the theme of the sexually aggressive and repulsive older woman. The "Desart (sic) Fairy" in
the tale of "The Yellow Dwarf" is described as ". . . a large
old woman at whose Age and Decripitness (sic) they were
not so much surprised at as her Ugliness: She leaned upon
a Crutch . . . (her clothing) all in Rags . . . holding a lance in
her hand . . ." She loved to kidnap and seduce young men,
particularly if they were handsome and virile princes. At
the nuptial of the princess "All Fair," the terrible fairy
appears, captures the Prince, and carries him off to her
lair, where she holds him captive. She also transforms
herself into a beautiful nymph. She insists that the Prince
marry her as a condition of his freedom. To achieve a
happy ending the Desart Fairy, a typical personification of
evil, must be frustrated by the forces of good.[11]

Of course, young women, too, can be depicted as
sexually dangerous to men: the Delilah myth, the Sirens,
or mermaids who lure men to their doom. They can snare
and entrap men, but their sexuality is generally not dis-
tasteful and forbidden.

Witches in the Middle Ages were believed to be
sexually voracious. The tales of their obscene rituals—of
the Witches' Sabbath, the lewd dances around the Devil in
the form of a goat, the sexual orgies with demons lodged
in the bodies of animals—are well known.

Myths about the sexually aggressive older woman
appear to have been brought to America in the folklore of
every immigrant group. No longer a figure of antiquity,
she had become by the nineteenth century the woman

who lives next door. Folks in the Ozark Mountains brought Anglo-Saxon beliefs about witches with them into the area. This recycled medieval tale was believed as fact and reported as a news item in a local paper just after the Civil War:

A Confederate Army veteran sent in a story that Albert Pike, a well-known Arkansas poet and editor, had made a covenant with the Devil. He said that he had found Pike enthroned while naked witches danced around him during the night. When sufficiently aroused, they indulged in sexual orgies. The most striking aspect of this tale was that some of the witches were the wives of Pike's best friends.[12]

Another tale with a similar ring is told in our own century. This story turned up in Chicago, where it had travelled from the South. The narrator had a hair-raising confrontation with his prospective mother-in-law. At the time of the story, he was engaged to be married to Lucy Ann. His beloved's mother was just approaching middle age. She appeared to the young man, as he was saying good night to her daughter, transformed into the shape of her own black cat. What better portrayal of the so-called evil woman's sexual need could there be than this paragraph:

> The black cat had a candle burning in her belly and came walking straight at me on her hind legs. She was playing the fiddle and singing, "great big house and nobody living in it." Every step she took toward me made her grow—bigger than a cow—bigger than an elephant. Then she became truly terrifying. She said (the fire now coming out of her nose), "I forbid you to see Lucy Ann anymore. I love you myself. You are to be my partner at the witches' dance tonight."[13]

When an older woman is sexually aroused, is "on fire," wants someone to "inhabit her house" and makes these needs known, in the minds of the creators of these tales she is turned into a caricature of a woman. She becomes frightening to men.

Today, for all our sexual enlightenment, the fantasy of the sexually-obsessed older woman hasn't altered at all. We find her in situation comedies on television in which she is fat and unattractive, or doddering and senile. The joke is that she wants sex and no one wants her. We seem embarrassed by her interest in sex and reject it with humor and scorn. Even in those instances where the older woman is attractive—for example, Joan Collins in *Dynasty*—we find that her sexuality is so overdrawn that she still becomes a caricature: an evil woman, a vampire. This is why jokes about the sexually-voracious older woman are still very much in circulation:

> *In World War II the Germans took over a French*
> *village and were about to rape the women.*
> *Young girl: "Do anything you want with me, but*
> *spare my grandmother!"*
> *Grandmother: "Hush, child! War is war!"*

The jokes are especially funny, it seems, if they are about "mother superiors" and "old maids":

> *Two spinsters were walking through the Greek*
> *sculpture gallery of an art museum.*
> *First spinster: "My, doesn't that statue of*
> *Hercules have large testicles?"*
> *Second spinster: "Yes, and so cold too."*

Even Peter Arno, that master cartoonist, used to love the salacious old woman routine. One of his middle-aged women sits watching a baseball game. She has a gleam in her eye as she scrutinizes two young players. The manager is telling her: "We do sell them sometimes, lady, but only to other teams."[14]

There is a second myth about the older woman: She is a warlike creature, well-armed; she is, in fact, a regular battle-ax. She is so powerful that she has control over life and death. (The old woman in the cartoon in the Caribbean bathroom, already described, was one such creature.) Her capacity for acts of violence against men have a long history. In "The Bacchae" by Euripides, women in a state of alcoholic and religious ecstasy tear Penteus, the King, to pieces. They are led by a battle-ax who happens to be Agave, no less a person than the Queen Mother.[15]

The Erinyes, better known by their Roman name, The Furies, are imagined as horrifying old women. Aeschylus, in "The Eumenides," gives this description of these aggressive women: "repulsive and they snort with breath that drives one back . . . these grey and aged children with whom no mortal man, no God or even beast will have to do. . . ." They are assigned power over life and death. They enforce a kind of primitive justice. Their task is to seek out and wreak vengeance on murderers, particularly if the guilty one has killed a blood relative.[16]

When we come across this powerful woman in fairy tales, legends, and folk tales, we find more evidence that these ugly women are interested in control, whether they are on the side of life or death, or of good or evil. Dame Ragnell, in the King Arthur legend of "Sir Gawain and the Green Knight," is a prototypical hag, yet she alone in all of Arthur's realm has the power to rescue him. At the final moment, with King Arthur's life hanging in the balance, it is Dame Ragnell who tells Sir Gawain the answer to the riddle that will save the King.[17]

The witchcraft frenzy in Salem, Massachusetts in 1692 is a familiar piece of our history. Just as familiar is the fact that although a few young women were accused of witchcraft at the trials, most of the accused were mature women. But what is not generally known is that in seventeenth- and eighteenth-century America people were convinced that ordinary women could become witches and acquire power over all sorts of daily events. Witches were blamed when a woman had a spontaneous abortion, or in the case of infant crib death. They were thought to be responsible for disease and epidemics, crop failure, or the death of farm animals. They were feared by sailors since they could cause storms and shipwrecks. Witches reigned all along the Eastern seaboard, big-headed, tangle-haired, and long-nosed, capable of giving anyone the Evil Eye. These wicked, subversive old women never seem to disappear. Not so long ago when the historian Carl Carmer was wandering through the Hudson Valley not far from the Catskills in New York State, he came across a family who lived just a few yards off the paved highway, and who complained to him that the state troopers were useless in ridding the area of a witch because they didn't have a silver bullet with which to kill her. The witch, Carmer learned, had been bothering the family for some six years, and, according to them, had been turning herself into a cat, throwing shoes in the dark, spoiling the milk, and spreading manure over the food.[18] An old dame of such evil intent, if not controlled, it was implied, could starve a family to death.

Current humor is explicit in expressing the fact that the fantasy that a wife has control over life and death is still very much around. Buck Brown, well-known *Playboy* cartoonist, created telling illustrations on the theme of the battle-ax.

Third, there is a persistent and wholly contradictory myth still floating through our culture that mature women are neither belligerent nor sexually voracious. They are, on the contrary, benign and asexual creatures, *totally* without interest in sex. They project a positive maternal image, but if attention is ever paid to their sexuality, it is defined in negative terms. This woman is not without

Gladys, is it really you?

some power, but she is passive. Like the Spider Woman in Navajo Indian myths, you may find her waiting patiently in her hole underground until she is needed. When called upon she imparts her knowledge in the interest of the next generation: for example, she tells the young twin War Gods how to make their way safely on their perilous journey to the home of their father, the Sun. In this incarnation, the older woman is permitted to be interested in and supervise the sexual development of the next generation. She is the Queen Mother of the fairy tale trying to find a suitor for her daughter. The Brothers Grimm treated the subject of the mature woman as guardian and mentor in the fairy tale "The Goose Girl at the Well." The older woman lived in the mountains caring for her animals, in close touch with time and the rhythms of nature. She knows that the young man who comes her way will not be prepared for love and marriage until he has learned to be responsible for his own actions. She knows, too, that the girl must be sheltered until she is mature enough to be in touch with the beauty of her own body and its sexuality. She teaches both of them that time cannot be hurried; she is the one who is able to judge the moment of their readiness.[19] She is, of course, the mother we celebrate on Mother's Day, a woman not without power in her family, but a totally post-sexual being. As this day approaches, the ads and store windows are filled with lingerie for her—nightgowns, bathrobes, and negligees in pastel colors, full of dainty eyelet embroidery. There is not a red satin or black lace nightgown in the bunch.

In modern fantasy, these women are occasionally permitted a sex life. When they are, however, we are told they are a turn-off in bed. Besides the terrible jokes about wives as "cold potatoes," the myth has crept into places where it does not belong—in psychiatric literature, for example. Dr. Alex L. Finkle, writing about sex in the second half of life, says, "In truth, many aging wives would prefer to forget the whole thing. Perhaps most of the time an aging wife makes herself available to or responds just to please her husband." The writer notes, however, that most of the research on sexual activity in the second half of life has been "directed to the male."[20] In all fairness to the psychiatric profession I would say that I do not believe that Dr. Finkle's article, published a decade ago, would be written today. The fantasy has not disappeared in the minds of men, but it is being challenged by the findings of research into sex in the second half of life.

The myth of the asexuality of the older woman, even of her active disinterest in sex, bears some relationship to the fourth myth about older women: that their bodies are unaesthetic, physically unsatisfying, in fact, that they are in terrible shape for sex and are beginning to decay. The myth is quite specifically cruel. Men attach aversive fantasies not only to the bodies but even to the genitals of these older women and project onto them all of their own fears of physical decline. On a decorative plaque in a souvenir shop I found inscribed the so-called "Seven Ages of Women." Two are:

> *At forty she's like America: less technically competitive than she used to be.*
> *At fifty she's like Lebanon: devastated.*

The myths have evolved until the older woman has become the personification of death itself. The popular Fellini movie, "Amarcord," opens with lyrical scenes of almond trees bursting into bloom, their blossoms drifting across the bare landscape. They herald the birth of spring, of warmth and life. Then comes the reenactment of a seasonal ritual. A huge bonfire is kindled in the village square. An effigy of an old woman is thrown upon it. Winter and death disappear in the heat of the new season. Two young men, aroused by the scene, grab a young woman and toss her rhythmically up and down in the air—up and down in a symbolic imitation of intercourse. The old woman is put to death.

All of these myths are still instrumental. They reveal that in the fantasy life of men there are still only three stages in a woman's life. Whether it was Dr. Butler's experience as a medical student when he found that middle-aged women were called "crocks," or the popular usage of the slang term "hag" to designate a middle-aged woman, the anti-wife jokes, or the self-protective daydreams of Joseph Heller's hero, they add up to this simple all-inclusive fantasy: *There is no difference between a middle-aged and aged woman.* And in making the distinction between middle-aged and aged woman, I am in no way subscribing to the negative image of *old* women. I firmly believe that women are loving and sexual beings all of their lives.

But what a waste it is, and how sad, to see how many midlife women still buy the "hag" image.

But what about midlife men?

My colleagues and I frequently discuss the problems of men in midlife who have all the outward attributes of success—prospering careers, money, children who are on the way up the proverbial ladder. Many of these successful men feel restless, concerned, or frightened about their futures. Many cast about for quick or magical solutions: drugs, alcohol, and/or young women.

My focus has been on the negative fantasies about the older woman, fantasies of her power and sexuality that appear as a threat to men. We must not forget, however, that there are also warm and loving aspects to fantasies about her: woman as the source of life to which men return in death. She is the Earth Mother who holds her children. Michaelangelo's *Pieta* in St. Peter's Cathedral is so moving because the mother cradles the dead body of an *adult* man in her arms.

Women can personify the wholeness of life. They are the Three Fates; Clotho, who spins the thread of life; Lachesis, who measures the growth and work of a man; and Atropos, a symbol of death, who cuts the thread of life. (Men, too, can be personified as Death. Pluto is the chief God of the Underworld and Father Time is a symbol of death. But more often, woman, in her loss of fertility, is equated with aging and dying.) They are ancient moon goddesses, the three phases of the moon: the new moon, the maiden of springtime; the full moon, the mature goddess of summer and fecundity; and the old moon, the crone goddess of winter and the end of life. The Three Fates, however, link the image of women to only three seasons: spring, summer, and winter, and leave no room for the ripeness and fullness of maturity that is personified by women after their childbearing years are past. I believe the human imagination has room for a new image—a fourth season—a true picture of a middle-aged woman.

The psychological sources of the myths about older women are understood in only the most general way. Men may make a joke about the strength of a Margaret Thatcher and call her an "iron maiden," but are they aware of the psychological meaning of the comparison of a woman to a medieval instrument of torture? They are only aware of a need to deride and devalue a mature woman of such apparent strength. The precise sources and the specific meanings of such fantasies lie hidden, their roots formed in early childhood.

᪥2᪥

Out of the Nursery: Evolution of the Fantasies

There is a William Steig cartoon which is the frontispiece for his book, *The Agony in the Kindergarten*. It shows a woman's face, all mouth, teeth, and piercing eyes. She is yelling, "Willie!" Willie, looking scared, is precariously hiding in the cave of her open mouth.[1] With this single image, Steig has landed us dead center in the middle of the fantasy life of the little boy, and of the ambivalent feelings he has toward his mother. The cartoon expresses his wish, his need for a safe, warm place that is protected from the world, that is close to mother— back in the original cave of the womb. But how safe is this refuge? Willie is afraid of being destroyed, of being swallowed up. He is worried that he will never get away. The woman's threatening mouth is filled with teeth—one of the classical defenses, the "displacement upward," of the fantasy of the vagina with teeth that can injure or castrate. (The so-called "vagina dentata" is a fairly common fantasy

Willie!

among boys that creates anxiety about mother's anatomy. It can be one source of a man's fear of women. The little boy's thinking is very concrete. If mother's vagina looks like a mouth, it follows that it must have teeth. This makes it a dangerous place where the penis can be damaged or bitten off.) And Steig does not forget the angry eyes of the intrusive mother. Willie is convinced that mother sees everything; she is so magical and powerful, she can even read his thoughts. Punishment will follow!

Willie is still a very little boy, with the fears of a two-, three-, or four-year-old child. He's getting enough scary ideas in his head to keep him on the run from women all of his life. But he is not as helpless as he seems. His ego has been developing ever since he was born; he is becoming able to defend himself against the anxiety generated by his fantasies. He is acquiring the ability to repress some of his feelings, along with the ideation—the fantasies that became attached to them. Although the act of repression pushes some of the most troublesome of these fantasies out of consciousness and relieves him of anxiety so that he can go on with the business of growing up, he is not yet home free. The fantasies, still attached to memory, even though they are underground—in his unconscious—may continue to affect him. For example, if an adult man treats sexual intercourse as if it were a battle, his behavior may be related to a childhood fantasy, no longer recalled, that in intercourse father was attacking mother. In addition, it is not just that behavior may be motivated by *unconscious* fantasies, but, at any moment in a lifetime, *repressed* fantasies can return to full awareness and once again become a conscious source of anxiety. The women in his life will be the recipient of his ambivalent feelings.

In infancy, the sources of anxiety are the same for both sexes. Freud's theories of child development are so well known that we readily recognize his hypothesis that the infant in the first year or two of life is primarily motivated by his biological need to satisfy hunger and to avoid discomfort and pain. From alternating experiences of gratification and frustration, the child develops an image of the "good mother"—the fairy godmother, who feeds him, and the "bad mother"—the witch, who weans him. Every culture I have examined contains this dual image of the benevolent mother who feeds and protects the infant and the malevolent cannibalistic witch who is capable of destroying him.

While Freud's hypothesis of the oral origins of the fantasies of the good and bad mother are still useful, in the past few decades, with the introduction of the theories of ego psychology and with findings based on direct observation of children, new models of child development have been put forward that enrich the old ones.

Edith Jacobson[2] and Margaret Mahler[3] are among the most recent writers who suggest that the child, as he develops memory and cognition, slowly internalizes images that are tied to feeling states of comfort and discomfort, of gratification and frustration. The infant does not yet know the difference between inside and outside. Images of himself and his mother are still fused. In normal development, as differentiation takes place, the child begins to recognize himself as separate. But in this stage he is not yet able to grasp the idea that the image of the loving and giving mother comes from the same person who gets angry and frustrates him. The picture of her is split. This presents him with a kind of internal "double vision," which is normal for an infant from roughly six to eighteen months.

Between eighteen and twenty-four months, if a toddler's development goes well and he gets a healthy mix of gratification and frustration, the internal images of himself as good and bad begin to fuse, and so do the double images of his mother. He begins to be able to tolerate his own mixed feelings and to recognize that the mother who is nice and smiling is the same as the one with the angry face. This synthesis is necessary, we find, for the development of trust; without this basic ingredient, a child cannot go on to build friendships nor learn how to love another person. It should be noted, however, that the research of Daniel N. Stern, M.D. on infant development in the first year of life is beginning to alter the view that the earliest representatives of "self" and "other" are fused. Stern believes that on a cognitive level, a child can distinguish himself from another person in the first six months of life. His emphasis is on normal development and does not address the origins of pathology in the development of relationships. His findings are impressive and no doubt will have an effect on our developmental hypotheses.[4]

Although the theoretical debate about the origins of the child's view of the "good" and "bad" mother may continue, I am convinced, on the evidence from myths and fairy tales, as well as from human pathology, that the phenomenon remains a crucial one in human psychology.

There is a second development in the emotional life of the infant during the first two years. It flows from his growing awareness of the difference between himself and his mother. In infancy there is pleasure and safety at being "at one" with her: being held, comforted, and sharing in her protective power. Sometime in the second year, as the child begins to get an internal picture of himself as a separate person, as his mastery of walking and talking propels him toward independence, he becomes torn between two contradictory imperatives, two wishes, two needs that are life-long. The first is the wish for passive dependency and gratification. Opposing this wish is the drive for autonomy, as the child of ten to eighteen months develops the power of locomotion, and is stimulated by his growing ability to explore his world.

Although at this age his sense of autonomy has been growing, he is still very dependent on mother to take care of him. He is presented with a further dilemma: it is not safe to feel angry toward someone he still needs so much. The common early defenses of denial and projection are brought into play. The child in fact believes: "I am not angry at her! *She* is the bad one; she's the one who's angry! I wouldn't hit her, but she might hit me, might even bite me!" In fantasy, mother is personified as the cat with claws, the creature of the nightmare, the wicked witch.

Or, if a child cannot deal with the intensity of his bad feelings toward his mother, he no longer even blames her. He does something more complex: he denies his bad feelings *and* splits them off. He creates a comfortable image of himself and of his mother as "all good" beings.

The vision of the good mother, of the fairy godmother, is now separated from and alternates with that of the bad mother and the wicked witch. The child has performed an important service for his own feeling of security: he has isolated his much-needed image of the "good mommy" from the "bad mommy" fantasies generated by his aggression.

Youngsters with fairly severe emotional problems can use this defense of splitting the image of people into good and bad for the rest of their lives. More often, however, it is a defense that is called on only in times of severe anxiety. We believe that children first resort to splitting during the period between eighteen and twenty-four months, a period which is particularly crucial. Margaret Mahler stresses the fact that it is in this period that the child becomes more aware of things as they really are. He is frightened by this new knowledge which tells him he is not omnipotent, that he is indeed still a helpless creature. The youngster who has been blissfully exploring his world becomes conscious of his separateness and his lack of control over the world. He regresses and begins to whine and cling. Mothers are confused by this sudden return to babyishness, do not know that it is normal and transient behavior, and often respond in a negative manner.[5]

I have said that the *needs* of both sexes are identical at birth, and boys and girls face the same early tasks: to begin to separate from mother, to establish an internal image of her and of themselves as both good and bad, to pursue autonomous development and to learn how to trust. But differences in gender have important developmental consequences. From the outset the girl is treated differently from the boy. Parents do not have the same expectations for the two sexes. The boy's autonomous growth is promoted much more enthusiastically than is the girl's.

I believe that it is at the sensitive period between

eighteen and twenty-four months, when a child normally regresses and begins to cling, that dependency is especially frowned on in the male child. He is told, "You already know how to do that for yourself." "Don't cry like a baby!" "No, I won't carry you. Big boys know how to walk!" Boys get the message that independence is a highly approved form of behavior.

This period marks a significant divergence in the development of gender identity in boys and girls. We tend to think of a boy acquiring a sense of himself as male in identification with his father. But he has a particular task to perform before he is free to. A boy's earliest identification is with his mother. He must deny his initial identification with this most important "other" who has so many warm qualities he admires, whom he loves—who is female. If he does not, or, if, for a variety of reasons, he cannot, he is going to have trouble with his sense of himself as a man, with consequences for his behavior toward women. Part of his need to demean and devalue women may stem from his ongoing struggle against his early feminine identification, his perception of his mother's power, and his need to deny his envy of her.

Because boys have to move so decisively away from their identification with mothers, their drive toward autonomy is more urgent and pronounced than girls'. They define themselves in terms of their degree of separateness, the sharpness, incisiveness, and clarity of their sense of themselves and their freedom from dependency. And because girls identify with the person from whom they must individuate, they never become so uniquely autonomous. Maturity in men therefore comes to mean independence; while for women maturity is more defined by closeness. In her book, *In a Different Voice*, Carol Gilligan points out, "Each sex perceives a danger which the other does not see—men in connection, women in separation."[6] The contradictions persist for a lifetime.

Between the second and third year, or even earlier, the boy becomes aware of the difference between his anatomy and that of a woman. This knowledge is the source of concern about the safety of his own sexual equipment. To deny his anxiety, he creates the fantasy of the mother with a penis, sometimes a very small one, hidden from sight, but a penis nonetheless. It is normal for little children to repress such images. Evidence from the dreams and fantasies of boys and adult men, however, makes it safe to say that the fantasy is ubiquitous. We have already seen it expressed symbolically in the cartoon in Chapter 1 of the wife as executioner with a halberd in her hand. Fantasies of this nature can render a man extremely passive in his relations with women or, alternatively, he may sexualize these fantasies and find pleasure in doing battle with or being aggressively dominated by them.

The fantasy of the "mother-with-a-penis" may be elaborated on in the mind of a little boy to help him feel secure about the safety of his own genitals: if she hasn't lost *hers*, I can't lose *mine*. But he pays a price for this reassurance. Mother is big and strong; if she is equipped like father, she must be manly and powerful, and can overwhelm him, castrate him, destroy him. The image of the powerful and destructive woman in Eugene O'Neil's "Strange Interlude" is a good example of this image.

The fantasies I have written about focus on the interaction between the child and his mother. Writers such as Dorothy Dinnerstein[7] and Ethel Spector Person[8] believe that if the father were to be significantly involved in the care-taking of a male child, there could be a moderating effect on the child's feelings toward women. Currently, although fathers are spending more time caring for their children, shared parenting has not become a widespread practice. Chief responsibility remains with mothers and mother substitutes. We do not know if, or to what extent, primitive fantasies about mothers could be modulated if fathers spent equal time both giving to *and* frustrating their babies. But there are two unalterable differences between men and women that have an inescapable effect on the boy's fantasy life. Changes in parenting cannot alter the *psychological* effects of the differences between the sexes. It cannot change the fantasies created by the fact that he is borne by a woman, that he has developed within a womb and emerged from the birth canal, and although the vagina will later become the goal of his sexual desires, fantasies about that dark, mysterious place that so attracts him may remain as one source of his ambivalence toward women—ambivalence which finds ready reenforcement in our culture in the aversive myths about mature women.

From the age of three to five, the little boy, in spite of all his fantasies, loves his mother, wants to replace his father, and must solve the conflicts of the well-known Oedipal period. He has to come to terms with his sexual thoughts and wishes in relation to his mother who is so wonderfully appealing. In fantasy, she is, after all, like "The Desart Fairy," who is capable of transforming herself from mother to seductive maiden and carrying the young prince off to her lair. Even though he says he wants to marry her when he grows up, he feels he cannot compete with his father: visual evidence convinces the child that he is woefully inadequate for the job. He fears, too, that his father would be envious and punishing—and ultimately castrating.*

---

*I will be using the word "castrating" a great deal in this book. I use it in a figurative or metaphorical sense: to mean the way a man feels threatened or emasculated by a more powerful man—or woman. Castration anxiety, as it is understood currently, can contain within it and act as a mask for even more profound fears that arose at earlier stages of development: fears of loss of love, of abandonment or annihilation.

No wonder that all of this can be too much for a child to sort out and that once again the defensive maneuver of repression is called upon. Memories of this period are pushed out of consciousness and replaced by the ubiquitous fantasy of the middle years of childhood: the asexuality of parents, especially mothers. There's the old joke that comedian Sam Levenson used to tell. When asked if he thought his parents ever had sex, he'd answer, "My father, maybe. My mother, never!" This is the force that leads to the idealization of women, who, in fantasy, become good, asexual fairy godmothers or the pure and virginal mother of Jesus Christ.

All of a sudden a boy's voice begins to change, body hair appears, his genitals start to grow and behave in a mysterious fashion. Peter Blos, who has done the classic psychoanalytic research on adolescence, believes that the onset of the powerful biological processes of puberty provokes *normal* regressive behavior on the part of the boy. He becomes sloppy in his dress, is always in motion, and loves bathroom humor. Blos states that it is through this regressive pathway that the young adolescent has an opportunity to rework some of the problems of the first five years of his development, among them, issues of activity versus passivity, of dependence versus independence.[9] His dependent wishes arouse the same fears and fantasies he had as a small child: of the power of his mother to take over, to control, and to emasculate him.

One day I unavoidably kept an adolescent male patient waiting a few minutes at my door. When I opened it, *he* apologized. I wondered why, since the fault was clearly mine. He said, "Oh, it's 'cause I feel every woman is so overwhelming—almost like she's as big and dangerous as an elephant!" One day he reported a dream about me. He was a little boy, crouched naked in one corner of my office. When he looked up he saw I had grown a mustache, had hairy legs, and was wearing big military boots. His dream was not unlike the fantasy of another adolescent who pictured himself in my office as sitting in a dentist's chair—and I was the dentist with a drill.

In mid-adolescence, from fourteen through sixteen, as the boy matures sexually, Oedipal wishes in relation to mother are reawakened. He must give up his feelings toward her and find his way to an appropriate female. Although his conflicts may be at their height in this period, this can be an optimal time for solving them. There are many reasons for failure. A boy may be intimidated by his mother's managerial qualities, or by his profound pleasure in relying upon her. He may be frightened by what he believes to be her seductive behavior or immobilized by his conviction that she disapproves of his attempts to move toward girls his own age. At any phase of adolescent development, when emotional feelings become too intense a boy may fall back on the early defense of splitting. Then fantasies of the good and bad mother reappear. A number of outcomes are possible. Women can be over-idealized or attitudes of distrust and misogyny can take over. Fears may be overcome by counterphobic behavior—a repetitive campaign to conquer and subdue women—that can persist for a lifetime. Or there can be a permanent split in a man's fantasies. When this is the outcome, he will look upon his wife as a pure, good, asexual creature and only be able to find sexual freedom and pleasure outside his marriage, with "bad" women.

Whatever his fears and conflicts, the adolescent boy is propelled on his path to sexuality, however, by his physical needs. His penis has grown; he is now capable of erection and ejaculation. He feels a great sense of urgency to see if his equipment "works." I remember seeing a documentary film at a conference on adolescent development. A group of teenagers were discussing sex. The boys were talking about their sexual exploits and comparing notes about "scoring," while the girls, looking very embarrassed by the male talk, were speaking to one another about what they liked about their boyfriends. The adolescent girls were explicit in indicating that they were sexually active, yet they did not talk about intercourse. Their definition of themselves as sexual beings was as much involved in various aspects of the relationship with the boys as it was by the act of intercourse per se. The boys, however, were showing the essence of what it meant to them to be men.

Over a lifetime, the act of intercourse is a proof to a man that his masculinity—his genitals—is intact. According to Ethel Spector Person, men's sexual performance is "a mainstay for a man's gender, in a way that it is not for women." She feels this is "the single most telling distinction between male and female sexuality." A woman's sense of gender does not depend on her being orgasmic *in the same way* that it does for men (italics mine).[10]

At the end of adolescence a young man should be well on the road to maturity, with a sense of who he is and what he wants to become. His gender identity should be securely in place and he should be capable of heterosexual love and intimacy. This is a so-called normal or optimal picture. But of course no one grows up problem-free.

Normal development requires a fair mix of genetic endowment and good parenting. By that I mean a mother who is adequately tuned in to her infant's signals, who can supply a fair balance of indulgence and limit-setting, who is neither overly intrusive and seductive in her relationship with the boy, nor cold, isolated, and uncaring. He needs a father to share in his caretaking and who is available to lure him away from his dependence on mother and with whose masculinity he can identify. He needs parents who care about each other at least to the degree that the child has a model of a relationship to go on. These are the basic factors that help a youngster to grow up liking women, and they are not always in place. So there are pitfalls in the way of development. That all of these pitfalls are not avoidable is clear. It is true, nonetheless, that when a man is unable to modulate his earliest fantasies, he can grow up with a life-long fear of women. It is more than likely that he will have to live with an enduring ambivalence toward them, subject to the alternative lures of dependency and freedom, of closeness and avoidance.

Mixed feelings are at their lowest point when a man is newly in love. His woman is idealized. She is the "all good" figure he has always dreamed of. A man looks for a person who will complement him, whose presence will make him whole. He wants his wife to become the wished-for good mother, a caring, nurturing presence, but one who may be desired sexually—without feelings of guilt. In the complementarity of love, the fantasies of coupling abound: she is the hearth, he is the flame; she is the anvil, he is the spark; he is the warrior, she keeps the candle burning in the window lighting his path back to home and safety.

The fantasy of the all-good mother who asks nothing for herself is embodied in the idealized image of "the little woman." For all our current repudiation of the image of the masochistic, self-denying woman (Hans Christian Anderson's "Little Mermaid," or Eleanora Duse playing the self-sacrificing wife in D'Annunzio's "La Gioconda,") the fantasy still remains in the minds of men.

It reappeared recently in modern dress in a popular film, "Tender Mercies," directed by and starring Robert Duvall. In it Duvall played a middle-aged Country and Western singer, a down-and-out alcoholic, who had obviously made a mistake that destroyed him. As a young man he married a "bitch," a woman who competed with him and established a highly successful singing career of her own. In the film he is saved when he finds an "all-good" mother in a beautiful young widow and is restored by her selfless love. She sits at home when he goes off on a binge. In fact, she irons his shirts while she waits up for him. Even though she has a lovely voice, she will only sing in the church choir, because she will not compete with her man. She asks for nothing but his love.

There is one variant of this fantasy that has different roots. Its source is a man's identification with his mother's role and functions. When this fantasy is played out, a man wants his wife to be his baby and he will be an all-good mother to her. He will take her as his child, teach her, and tell her what to wear, what to do, and make her into the image of what a female child of his would be. In the Greek myth, in Shaw's "Pygmalion," and in Lerner and Loewe's musical adaptation, "My Fair Lady," he educates, trains, actually "creates" her. His lady is "fair" because he has made her so. She is his possession; he identifies with her perfection as does a mother with her child. Popular songwriters have loved this theme for years since "Yes Sir! She's My Baby!" "My Baby Just Cares For me," and "Baby Doll."

These have been primary fantasies of men in working out their wish to find in their wives an idealized "all-good" mother. Traditionally this fantasy fit the needs of women who were cast in the role of the sex who needed protection, yet who were capable of summoning up the last ounce of their strength on a man's behalf. Of course I am not speaking of the changes in women's roles brought about in the last twenty-odd years or of the accommodations that these changes have inevitably wrought in the relationships between the sexes. But the traditional role of women as the weaker sex bolstered a man's feeling of masculinity. I emphasize this aspect of a woman's role because changes in the balance occur in middle age. But historically, even when women faced the same hardships as men—trekking across the Great Plains in covered wagons, confronting hostile tribes of Indians, or settling down in profound isolation in sod houses in Nebraska—when times got tough a man could deny his own anxiety by rationalizing, "I must deal with the dangers ahead because *she* isn't able to." An example of such casting of women into the role of "sponge" for men's anxiety occurs in *Giants in the Earth.* O. E. Rolvaag writes about a small community of Norwegian settlers trying to establish themselves on the prairie. A bunch of rough and drunken Irishmen come and threaten to evict them from their land. Per Hansa says to the Norwegian men, "Don't breathe a word to Kjersti [his wife] about how things are! . . . If the women ever get hold of this, they'll die of fright."[11]

Such are men's dreams of a perfect woman, and, I repeat, whatever his conflicts, his ambivalence is at its lowest point when he is newly in love and in the thrall of his fantasies of her perfection. But even on the eve of a wedding, the stag party takes up the negative theme. In essence, it is that a man is giving up his freedom for "a ball and chain," a woman who will control him, and hold him hostage.

Hostility toward mothers-in-law, even in the form of joking, drains off some of the negative feelings toward wives as marriage becomes less honeymoon and more reality. The arrival of children can provoke a crisis, however, as a man must begin to share the caring and attention he receives from his wife with his offspring.

By and large the energies of young men in our culture are preempted by the pursuit of a dream and the validation of masculinity that comes from the attainment of success and power. When a man reaches the midpoint of his life and looks into the future, however, he faces a threat to the homeostasis he has achieved as a young adult. With it can come some profound questions about power and masculinity. There are consequences for his attitudes toward mature women. The old ambivalence he has felt toward mother once more becomes a central issue, providing more fuel to the cultural brush fire—the persistent myths about older women.

3

The Downside Of The Curve: The *Angst* Of the Middle-Aged Man

Walk loose and jangly. Never look back. Something may be gaining on you.

Satchell Paige, baseball star.

. . . The manhood game is never finished . . .

Leonard Kriegel,
On Man And Manhood.

The simple fact of the situation is the arrival at the midpoint of life . . . The individual has stopped growing up and has begun to grow old.

Elliott Jaques

In terms of aging, everything about the downside of the curve is negative. It is associated with slippage, decline, loss. Yet as a form, an abstraction, the whole of a curve is beautiful, and its symmetry is impaired if it is cut off or incomplete. Our grief is greatest when a young person dies before he or she can experience the fullness of life. So why do we so denigrate the second half of life? In our gerontophobia, Alex Comfort writes, we create "a rejection of our own coming selves."[1]

In his seminal article, "Death And The Mid-Life Crisis," written in 1965, psychoanalyst Elliot Jaques pointed out that eminent writers, painters, and composers like Dante, Michelangelo, and Goethe, quite suddenly in their late thirties became aware of the passing of youth and the inevitability of death. Jaques found that this awareness was followed by a period of depression and then a normal but often painful reordering of priorities in preparation for the second half of life.[2] This direct confrontation with aging and mortality helped the artists create their great mature works. But in our culture at this moment of time there is quite a different response. As soon as we become aware of our transience we immediately turn ourselves around and walk backwards into the future. We so desperately want to avoid aging that we inhabit a vacuum of our own making.

My argument is that this response has a profound effect on the behavior of men. One of the consequences is reflected in attitudes toward mature women that have become ingrained in the culture.

As a people we are not given to the reflection necessary to question our reactions or to reorder our priorities for the second half of life. But at middle age, certain happenings cannot be readily denied. They are the typical, well-publicized problems: the physical changes, the onset of a chronic illness, the children leaving home, a husband's response to his wife's taking up a postponed career. And there are the more elusive problems: a growing sense of limitations, or the boredom and ennui that can set in from years of work at the same tasks.

We can push thoughts of mortality out of our minds

just as we do awareness of the lethal possibilities of nuclear destruction. It's just that it's harder to do as we grow older. Ernest Becker, in *The Denial of Death,* spoke of man's "quest," his "dreams of glory," his attempts to "make it big" in life as an effort with great symbolic meaning. Becker felt that men were searching for immortality: through their great achievements they would be able to deny transience, to avoid thoughts of death.[3]

For the relatively few highly successful men, the power and authority they command well beyond middle age may indeed have this effect. But the vast majority of men know by the time they are in their mid-forties or fifties that they have reached a plateau. They are aware, not only that they will not receive the Nobel Prize, but that they will not even get the next promotion. In fact, they know they face a future in which they become a supernumerary.

The psychologist Daniel Levinson, in his study of middle-aged men, finds that, for the most part, when faced with this reality, men are able to give up their dreams of greatness and accept their limitations. They shift into new roles in middle age by becoming mentors of younger men and by allowing the more interpersonal, affiliative aspects of their lives to develop.[4] I would agree that such a resolution of the challenge of transition from young adulthood to middle age is possible for some men. But I do not think it is an outcome that is easy to achieve in our hyper-competitive culture where "Winning isn't everything; it's the only thing!" I believe that a man's sense of identity is so intimately tied to his drive for power that if he acknowledges his limitations his self-esteem is threatened. Did not Willy Loman's son in Miller's "Death of a Salesman" offer this as his eulogy of his father, after he had died a failure and a suicide: "Even so, Willy Loman did not die in vain. He had a good dream. It's the only dream you can have . . . to come out number one man."[5]

For a Willy Loman the limits imposed by his failure

led to depression and death. But the ordinary man who has even been moderately successful still has to deal with the limits of his power. The psychoanalyst/psychiatrist Gregory Rochlin observed that at every stage of life men need reaffirmation of their masculinity. Middle age, he says, is a time of "enclosure." So he asks:

> What is the impact of these constraints on a man's commitment to prowess, performance and the pursuit of achievement exhibited in every previous period? What substitutes, alternatives, exchanges and new dimensions will be assigned to masculinity in the middle years?[6]

Another psychiatrist, Arnold J. Mandell, asked the same question in unequivocal tones. In his book, *The Coming Of (Middle) Age,* Mandell tells us that by the time he reached forty, he was the head of a department of psychiatry in a medical school, the author of five books and some two hundred scientific papers. He was married, the father of two children and an accomplished semi-professional jazz musician. Then he was suddenly hit in close succession by two life-threatening illnesses. Mandell summed up his crisis in this single question: "What do you do after a life of fighting and fucking?"[7]

Generally, our society offers no new definitions of masculinity for middle age. Rather, it says, "Do more of the same." The world measures a man by what he does. In fact, I have known many men, who, as they faced their limits of achievement at work, turned more and more to the sexual aspects of their lives for confirmation. It was the sociologist Norman Storer, who pointed out to me how crucial the motto (already quoted) is for a man:

> *A woman is as old as she looks.*
> *A man is not old until he stops looking.*

This is a core anxiety for men in middle age. To "stop looking" is to become passive. That is what he is afraid of.

An acquaintance who had been in the Korean War told me that he had always had two fantasies that defined his sense of himself as a man. One was the challenge he felt when his company went into action and he faced death; the other, of equal importance, was the way he felt when he approached an attractive woman socially and, in the first few minutes, had to engage her interest.

Men do not habitually speak of their concerns about decline in sexual power. Yet when a man does speak freely, the threat to his sense of identity is explicit. The novelist, Charles Simmons, writes:

> As a boy he and his friends urinated in arcs to see whose would go higher . . . In his fifties occasionally in the morning he will wonder if he could urinate out the chest-high window above the toilet bowl in the bathroom: he will not try it although he will at times slowly retreat from the bowl to see what thrust is left to him . . . At a certain point—he will think it is when he can no longer organize his gray and thinning hair into a conventional form—women on the streets and in shops will discard him in quick looks just as he had discarded unattractive women all his life . . . and before he gives up sex he will pride himself that he had never been impotent while sober.[8]

With his usual eloquence Norman Mailer explains the inexorable tie between a man's sexuality and his masculinity:

> . . . that the primary quality of man was as assertion . . . that one had to alienate oneself from nature to become a man . . . be almost as if opposed to nature . . . if the calm of the seas is seen as the basic condition of nature, *that man was a spirit of unrest who proceeded to become less masculine whenever he ceased to strive.* (Italics mine.) The phallus was the perfect symbol of man since no matter how powerful a habit was its full presence, it was that one habit that was always ready to desert a man . . . The phallus

erect is nothing less than grace under pressure.
. . .[9]

Passivity becomes equated with the ultimate loss of power—sexual failure—the impotent man. The following joke illustrates this:

> *Susan and Edward decided to celebrate their Golden Wedding Anniversary by spending the night at the same hotel to which they had gone on their honeymoon. Edward reported the event to a friend: "We not only went to the same hotel, we even had the same room."*
> *"How was it?" his friend asked.*
> *"Oh," said Edward, "everything was exactly the same. We went up to the room at the same time. The room looked the same; the bed looked the same. . . . Only this time I was the one who went into the bathroom and cried."*

A middle-aged man thought this was a funny joke. He could identify with the situation, but could avoid his own anxiety by having the problem be that of a considerably older person.

Another anecdote leads us further along a trail that reveals additional meanings to the fear of passivity in men. A middle-aged foursome had been playing golf together for many years. They were very competitive and ribbed each other mercilessly. When one of them missed a putt, the others feminized his name: Robert became Roberta; Louis, Louise. When a man fails to put it "in the hole," he not only is a loser with women, he is no longer a man—he is a woman. The men are trying to veil their anxiety through the bantering.

Bobby Kennedy, as a member of the Senate's McClellan Committee, was unremitting in his investigation of corruption in the Teamster's Union. The Union could not get him off their backs. One of their counter-strategies was to spread rumors about Kennedy in the hope of totally discrediting him. One of the rumors said that when Bobby was a child, he had dressed in girl's clothes. [10]

In order to understand the psychological underpinnings of this aspect of the fear of passivity, we strike out over well-known yet complex theoretical ground. The twin threats of loss of power in the eyes of the world and of decline in sexual performance open up old struggles—struggles that had temporarily been laid to rest in the active, driving, exploratory phase of young adulthood. I speak of the lure of, the pleasure in, the powerful *appeal* of passivity. The very *fear* of passivity hides its flip side: the *wish* to be passive. Not only do men have to hide full awareness of their wish to be dependent on women, but they must suppress even more forcefully their wish to be taken care of, to be taken over by men. What a man *can* experience, especially at middle age, is his vulnerability in relation to other men.

The theory of which I speak is the other half of the Oedipal "epic," the source of a man's passive sexual wishes in relation to another man. It is a hypothesis that is hard for us to accept in our culture. Heterosexual men in America are not comfortable being physical with one another. Two Bedouins walking hand in hand in Saudi Arabia are expressing a friendship. In America such behavior smacks of homosexuality. And for all the advances made by the gay community, we are still a homophobic society. Calling most men "fag" and will demonstrate this clearly.

There are only a few exceptions to the "hands off" policy men practice with one another. One of these is visible during a game of football, when players hug or give each other a pat on the buttocks. I would guess that this contact is made permissible by the competitive tension and the camaraderie the game induces.

Fear of sexual surrender to a man develops during the period of a boy's life when he is from three to five years old. During the boy's passage through the Oedipal phase, his feelings seesaw back and forth, finding attraction, then danger, in closeness to one parent or the other. I do not wish to oversimplify a complex, dynamic process, one that is never identical for any two people. But when, for instance, a boy feels his mother is too close to him, too controlling or seductive, he may look for a safe escape. He feels that Dad will rescue him. What will make Dad love him? The answer: being like Mom—that is, by conforming to his small boy's view of how mother behaves with father. The fantasy surfaces in the analysis of men's dreams when we find men in competition with women in trying to attract a man. Why? In dreams a man clearly wants to escape from his feared mother and win the love and protection of a powerful man.

There is danger here too. There are the boy's competitive thoughts in relation to his father and the wish to get rid of him, to replace him. These notions make the boy afraid that father may take his revenge—get rid of him— castrate him. A solution to this conflict, too, can be found by avoiding danger and becoming passive and submissive to father. But these possibilities must be confined to the disguise provided by the dream or the casual bantering of the joke, because such thoughts would imply a wish to give himself to men, a resolution that is ultimately most damaging to his sense of masculinity.

Most men deny or repress their fantasies about wanting this passive solution over the course of a lifetime. I am not speaking of the adaption made by men who, for many complex reasons, choose a homosexual way of life. Most men in our culture are deeply afraid of their homosexual wishes and defend themselves against them with great passion. The denial of their own passive wishes leads to the equating of passivity with femininity—and a further devaluation of women. Does not the Orthodox

Jewish man begin each day with a prayer (as he "submits" himself to God the Father) "Blessed art Thou, Lord our God, King of the Universe, who has not made me a woman"?[11]

In his fascinating book, *Phallos: A Symbol and Its History in the Male World,* the Danish psychoanalyst Thorkill Vanggaard describes the vigilance with which the men in his clinical practice fend off their passive wishes in relation to other men. He turns to Greek history for cultural validation of his thesis. There was no shame, he notes, when a grown man seduced a young boy in ancient Greece. Rather, the man was in a dominating position, acting as teacher and mentor of the youth whom he took on as a companion on the battlefield. He was, in fact, initiating him into the world of men. If a boy did not grow up to marry and have children but, rather, engaged in homosexual behavior with other adult men, then he was viewed with scorn.

Vanggaard also points to the Near-Eastern practice of anal assault on the part of the victor in the final humiliation of a vanquished enemy, the ultimate rape of his manhood, a theme on which Norman Mailer wrote extensively in his novel, *Ancient Evenings.*

Vanggaard concludes that this is true for all men: in a state of disturbed potency, or at a time when feelings of manhood are wavering, a man feels he will be scorned and attacked, not just by women, but by other men. This is poignantly illustrated in his chapter on the feminization of Gustav Von Aschenbach, a man in his fifties, in Thomas Mann's story, "Death in Venice."

Submitting to the scorn of other men: I do not think I have to stress that I speak of this problem in a symbolic sense. The victorious in the Western world do not rape the vanquished. They take him out to lunch, give him a gold watch, and tell him to "step down." I do speak to the feelings a man experiences when he must submit to more powerful men, the feelings connected to the psychological substrate of his early years in relation to his father, that make him feel so vulnerable.

I have described some of the anxieties men experience in middle age to bring us to the epicenter of the issue. It leads to the connections between the *angst* of the middle-aged man and his emotional responses. It leads to an understanding of the connection between his emotional responses and his fantasies about the middle-aged woman.

Many men will say they don't feel any different at all in middle age. They deny that they have experienced any change. Most men are not so successful in warding off feelings about getting older.

Anxiety creates tension. At times of stress it is harder to fight fears and keep them out of consciousness. It is harder to fend off disturbing fantasies. We do everything we can to restore the old equilibrium. We call out all the troops. Among them are defenses we have not used in a long time. The reemergence of old fantasies and the employment of old defenses have a profound effect on men's attitudes toward women who are their contemporaries. They are at the root of the myths about the sexual unattractiveness of the older women.

Fantasies that originated in infancy have to be laid to rest once in childhood and once again in adolescence. In middle age, fantasies about the bad and dangerous mother reemerge and are reinvested with strong feelings. The old defense of splitting is called on. As the psychoanalyst Peter Blos writes: "We know that originally the 'good' and 'bad' mother is not the identical object in the mind of the child." Dr. Blos goes on to talk about the process whereby the two images become fused. He continues, *"The potentiality that this process becomes reversed un-*

der stress is never totally extinguished during life: It must be considered part of the human condition." (Italics mine.)[13]

Once more in men's fantasies we are dealing with two images of women. The myths of our culture stand ready to offer them credibility. The young woman is equated with the beautiful fairy; the middle-aged woman is the bad mother, the dangerous witch.

I add a second key dynamic to this complex psychological brew. Dr. Hans W. Loewald had this to say about the Oedipus complex:

> . . . no matter how resolutely the ego turns away from it and what the relative proportions of repression, sublimation and "destruction" might be, in adolescence the Oedipus complex rears its head again, *and so it does during later periods of life, in normal people as well as in neurotics.* (italics mine.)[14]

For many years psychiatrists have talked about how Oedipal feelings can be aroused in middle-aged men. They refer to the fact that a man may have incestuous feelings toward his daughter when she turns into a sexual teenager, or that he has the same competitive feelings toward his son he once felt toward his father. But these writers have not spoken about Oedipal feelings that may resurface in relation to a wife. Even if he has made it fairly well through the early days when he wished to marry his mother and had to deal with his fear of his sexual feelings toward her, it is possible that his struggles in relation to her are not permanently out of the way. A middle-aged woman usually has raised a family; she has exercised her maternal functions toward her children. Even if she has not had a child, still she has acted in a maternal fashion toward her husband. A woman of fifty does not have the body of one half her age; in most cases, it has "ripened," matured. I've heard many a long-married man call his wife "Mom." In middle age, a man can develop sexual conflicts in relation to his wife that have their origin in early feelings toward his mother.

In defense against such feelings, a man will turn away from his wife: he avoids her. Or he projects his bad feelings onto her and blames her for his problems. He may look elsewhere for sexual satisfaction.

When these early fears of the powerful mother and fantasies about her sexuality become operative again, and, in some measure, emotionally "real," then a man begins to relate to older women as though they were weeds, thorns, or faded blossoms. Ugly images, to be sure, but they help him close his eyes to what is happening within himself. They are the images in three of the myths about older women that we are about to explore.

❧ 4 ❧

Weeds, Thorns, and Faded Blossoms: Delilah, Battle-Ax, or Whistler's Mother

---

A little boy is shouting at a very old, deaf and bespectacled granny:
"Old woman, old woman, shall we go a-shearing?"
"Speak a little louder, sir, I am rather hard of hearing."

"Old woman, old woman, shall I love you dearly?"
"Thank you, kind sir, I hear you very clearly."
Whereupon the old lady jumps up, looking both eager and spry, and proceeds to chase the little boy, who runs away in alarm as fast as his legs can carry him.[1]

This nursery rhyme is an echo of the ancient "Delilah myth" about woman's sexual voraciousness and the power of her sexuality. According to the myth, older women are obsessed with sex, their appetites insatiable, their behavior aggressive in the extreme. This sexuality is to be

49

"Old woman, old woman, shall we go
a-shearing?"
"Speak a little louder, sir, I am rather
hard of hearing."
"Old woman, old woman, shall I love you
dearly?"
"Thank you, kind sir, I hear you very
clearly."

From W. H. Smith and Sons, Ltd. London 1976:
Bedtime Story and Nursery Rhyme Book.

feared; it can sap the strength of a Samson. And I have found that of the three images of middle-aged women included in this chapter, this, the fantasy of the voracious woman, is the one that men find the most threatening.

The Bible tells us that when Delilah cut off Samson's hair she took away both his strength and his masculinity. She had already castrated him symbolically when she delivered him shorn to the Philistines. They made doubly sure he was unmanned and powerless by putting out his eyes. There are, of course, logical and obvious sources for this fantasy of the woman as voracious. They begin with the differences in the physiology of men and women. Unlike other mammals, women do not have periods of sexual activity (in animals popularly known as "heat," or, to use the more formal term, "estrus") which alternate with periods of quiescence. Physiologically, women are always capable of sex. What's more, a woman can have intercourse repeatedly, while a man must rest for varying lengths of time before becoming aroused again.

Why should a woman's availability lead to the belief that her appetite is voracious? Here the fantasies of child-hood, which we talked about earlier, come into play. The little boy is fascinated by the mysterious changes that take place in the size of his penis, changes that are not under voluntary control. It is possible that he has been an ob-server of intercourse between humans or animals and has some awareness that the penis of an adult can change markedly in size. He may have seen his father urinate or have seen him with an early morning erection. Whatever the experience, fantasies about what causes the penis to change so much are sure to exist. They undoubtedly merge with troubling questions about the size of mother's vagina and its ability to engulf him. And, since a child's thinking is very concrete, a boy may get the notion that, since the penis becomes smaller after intercourse, the woman is responsible: something happened when the penis was inside her to take away the strength of a man.

The myth has not disappeared. I do not know if coaches still tell athletes not to weaken themselves by having intercourse the night before a game. But I did come across this advice being given to opera stars. Writing in *The New York Times Magazine*, Terry McEwen, currently Director of the San Francisco Opera, insisted on absti-nence for male stars:

> When he becomes famous he has to observe rigid sexual control. I can hear, for example, if a singer has sex before a performance. It takes the guts out of his voice and weakens the middle sound.[2]

The same fantasy is expressed in this joke:

> *A very retarded man was a patient on a hospital*
> *ward. He had a very large penis, and since he*
> *masturbated a great deal, it was often erect. The*
> *nurses were fascinated.*
> *One day one of them insisted that the man have*
> *sex with her.*
> *"Well," she asked, after they were finished, "how*
> *did you like that?"*
> *"You took away my bat!" he said. "I want it back!"*

And in the words of one of my male patients, "A powerful man is 'full of juice.' A woman sucks him dry."

A woman's genitals are part of the mystery of her sexuality. A woman functions in the dark places of her body, in secret, at unknown depths. And while part of the pleasure and the challenge in the arousal of a man can be contained in this mystery of the unseen—exemplified, for instance in the Dance of the Seven Veils, where Salome slowly reveals herself or in the mounting excitement of a male audience during a skilled striptease act—a man also may have the fantasy that the very fact of sex with a woman can weaken him. Her mysterious internal genital functions can create anxiety. How can a man *know* if he has sufficiently "pleasured" a woman, whose anatomy is so alien and mysterious? Her responses are so different. She is capable of an indeterminate number of orgasms. How can he know when she is sated? If she is not, will she, with her readiness for sex and her orgiastic capacity, look elsewhere, and thus shame him, "take away his strength" symbolically, by making him a cuckold?

The ever-present availability of a woman, the mystery of her hidden genitals and of her sexual response, have given rise to the fantasy that she is lewd, promiscuous—a wanton. This fantasy is fueled by the fact that men are eternally unsure of their control over women. Did not a child's own mother, that fantasied asexual creature, betray him by producing brothers and sisters? For centuries men have tried to control women's bodies and their sexual functions. A man could never be certain if his wife was faithful or if a child was his own progeny, his rightful heir. Thus, the creation and use of chastity belts in medieval Europe, and the death penalty for adulterous women in China and the Near East.

It follows that women have been blamed when men, so responsive to visual stimuli, and whose sexual arousal is not voluntary, become excited. Certain cultures take elaborate precautions: Moslem women are veiled, their bodies hidden, their lives confined. Orthodox Jewish wives have their heads shaved; they wear wigs and modest, long-sleeved dresses so as not to stimulate men. Our culture operates under similar assumptions, exemplified by men's insistence that women "ask" to be raped. Part of the current opposition to abortion is based on men's fear of their inability to control a woman, as they used to, when they could "keep her barefoot and pregnant."

After the menopause a woman is freer to be sexual. A man can no longer keep her pregnant or tied down by infants. He still feels he is not a man if he is not able to control her sexuality. Men in Mediterranean cultures tried to solve this "problem" by insisting that widows not remarry and that they identify themselves by wearing black for the rest of their lives. When the widow in Kazantzakis' *Zorba The Greek* defied the rules by having intercourse with a young Englishman, the men in the village stoned her to death.[3] And were not upperclass Hindu widows convinced, by the mores established by men, that they should put themselves "out of business" by throwing themselves on their husbands' funeral pyres?

Why should the sexuality of a mature woman be such a threat to middle-aged men that it requires extraordinary measures to keep it under control? *Because at a time when the men are experiencing changes in their own sexual arousal patterns, women appear to be unchanged and unchanging.* The most comfortable masculine response to this is to say, "My sexual staying powers are unchanged. It's just that she's gotten more demanding and harder to satisfy." A man of fifty-five and his new wife, who was at least ten years his junior, were overnight guests in my house. At breakfast the next morning he teased her about her sexual appetite. "You are Glinda the Witch," he said. Now Glinda is a good witch in *The Wizard of Oz*, but she is nonetheless a witch. That he let me overhear his remark was partly a sexual boast that he could take care of her. But he was expressing more than that: we all know that the use of teasing and humor is a way of expressing anxiety under the cloak of banter. Witches are creatures who cannot be controlled. They are given to all-night sexual revels. They are related to Lilith, Delilah, Morgan La Fay, and to Greek matrons who participated in Dionysian revels, aggressive sexual orgies which were highly dangerous for men. Clearly my friend was worried about his ability to satisfy and control this woman.

Isaac Bashevis Singer wrote a short story about a rich widower in Miami Beach. He was not flattered by the women who pursued him; he was overwhelmed. "The town is full of widows," he said, "and when they heard that I'm alone, the phone calls and the visits started. When the females turn so wanton, the men become like frightened virgins."[4] Men's worst fears revolve around the fantasy that they are not adequate enough to satisfy a woman. The fear of inadequate performance is masked by the myth that says the problem is her voraciousness.

The second aversive myth about mature women I call "the myth of the battle-ax." The battle-ax has as much power as the voracious woman. She is bossy, angry, and unfeminine. No soft, warm spots on this lady! She is mostly too preoccupied with running things to be interested in sex. Until recently, the wife as "ball and chain" was a staple of popular humor. Even as talented a man as Richard Pryor used extraordinarily hostile anti-wife jokes in his nightclub act, and just the other day, while waiting for a receipt in a furniture store, I overheard one salesman tell another one of them: "Bob said when he got married he'd be boss or know the reason why. He got married and now he knows the reason why!".

At a sophisticated restaurant in Southampton, Long Island, I was handed a cocktail napkin printed with cartoons and "funny" messages for men: "Get rid of ugly fat. Divorce her." "Behind every good man is a woman: his secretary." In this one, the "good man," is being chased by an enormous middle-aged wife brandishing that obsolete weapon, a rolling pin, while the "good" woman, the young secretary, hides behind him.

The battle-ax is that thoroughly charming middle-aged creature, overwhelming in size and strength, or bitingly sarcastic in speech. (A William Hamilton cartoon: "No, Charles, I do not have a cold. What you hear in my voice is contempt.")[5] She controls a man and, what's more, turns him off sexually. Peter Arno captured this aspect of her behavior when he drew two powerful-looking ladies in a movie theater. On the screen, a determined middle-aged man has caught a resisting maiden and clasped her in an embrace. One matron turns to the other and says fiercely, "He'd try that with me just once!"[6] She is a larger-than-life creature, a combative and controlling figure, awesome in size and girth. In a cartoon by Rau, she's "the little woman" no longer. She confronts her husband and declares angrily, "You're wrong and *you* know it, and I'm right and *I* know it!"

Some studies of aging (over sixty) men and women have shown that women do become more assertive, while men tend to become more affiliative in their behavior.[7] I believe that the myth of the powerful and controlling older woman may be reinforced by some of the realities that confront a man at middle age about a woman. She has survived the hazards of childbearing. Her health, in fact, may be considerably better than his. Statistically he knows she will outlive him. She is, in addition, extremely capable of taking care of a man.

But there is no radical shift in a woman's persona at midlife that turns a sweet maid into a termagant. I have known a large number of women who have travelled into and through middle age and I have not observed sudden changes in their behavior. Research indicates that character style is set at least by the age of twenty and does not alter profoundly thereafter. Bette Davis was never cast in roles that were appropriate for Helen Hayes. If a man needs a managerial type of woman to lean on, he chooses her at the outset.

When a man feels threatened by aging, a woman may appear to be very strong indeed. He doesn't want to think about how much he'd like to borrow her strength, which he secretly envies. So, he turns these thoughts and feelings around in a "sour grapes" response—and devalues her. Many men are just as unhappy about their dependency upon her.

Still, why does she appear on stage with a battle-ax? And why in this incarnation is she portrayed as armed with a lance, a rolling pin, or riding a broomstick? Psychologically, we are transported back to the fantasy life of the little boy and the way in which the large and powerful mother is imbued with a penis. The Ozark Mountain folk tale, "Uncle Bill's Story," gives eloquent testimony to this fantasy. Every night Uncle Bill had a dream in which a witch turned him into a pony and rode him to her magic cave, the "riding" is a symbolic expression of intercourse initiated by a woman. In the cave, the witch met some robbers; together they hid the gold she helped them steal. Uncle Bill was not permitted to enter this secret, forbidden place with its precious contents. He was tethered just outside the entrance of the cave to a "small sapling."

The psychological revelations of this story are clear. The injunction against incest kept him from her cave; the little sapling was the mother's imagined penis.[8] According to legend, this "manly" witch with her magical powers could turn someone into a woman. This could explain why Amazons, women who were beautiful and powerful warriors, have been a feature of men's fantasy life since the time of ancient Greece. The ultimate challenge for a man was to conquer such a woman, then "turn her on" sexually. But if he failed, the defeat was dreadful. In Spenser's *Faerie Queene*, the Amazon Radigund captures knights, takes away their weapons, dresses them in female clothes, and puts them to women's work.[9]

Of course, a man does not plan to turn a woman into a battle-ax. But if he is feeling at all shaky about himself at midlife the old fantasies and defenses reappear to protect him, and often she, the battle-ax, is blamed for his troubles. According to such defense mechanisms, she becomes a dangerous woman with an imagined phallus. The battle-ax is no longer even a woman. Graffiti chalked on a wall in Chicago said simply, "You ain't the man your Mammy was."[10]

Fantasies about the power of the middle-aged matron were emphasized for me in one particular cartoon. A man and his wife are out duck-hunting. They sit in a boat; she's in the bow with her back to him. Both are armed with shotguns. You can tell by the gleam in his eye that he's gotten a wonderful idea. He's going to get rid of the old

Venus After Forty

hen by shooting her. But because she is so magical, she can read his thoughts without even looking at him. She turns and confronts him. In the last scene, though, their weapons have equal fire power; he has surrendered. She sits over him like a prison guard, while he looks dejected, depleted, a dog brought to heel. Such jokes seem to indicate that the wife in the cartoon is like the Mom who knows when you've put your hand in the cookie jar, who is stronger than you by far, and armed to boot. You can't get away. She's everywhere, all-knowing, inescapable.[11]

The third myth about the mature woman describes her as all motherly or grandmotherly. She is a faded

Drawing by Claude: © 1957. 1985 *The New Yorker* Magazine, Inc.

blossom. Because she has lost the "bloom" of youth, she has lost interest in sex. She is a good mother, an asexual woman, on the way to becoming Whistler's Mother—a little old lady. You see her in television commercials advertising corn oil for the fried chicken. Then you see her in denture ads. The older woman in this guise reassumes the fantasied image that children have of their mothers: asexual. Countless patients have told me, "I could never imagine my mother doing anything like that." Customs and mores indicate that mothers should be pure, their sexuality hidden from sons. An adolescent patient complained that he couldn't bear it when his mother wore a bikini, although it obviously pleased his Dad. Many boys are staunchly puritanical when it comes to their mothers. And often time this discomfort, this irrationality, lasts.

Stanley Cath, a Boston psychoanalyst who has been involved in research on the sexuality of older people, had a very hard time getting male medical students to interview older women about their sexual behavior.[12] According to Western tradition, a boy must pay lifelong attention to the incest taboo. This results in the admonishment that mothers should not wear bikinis: they should act their age! I recall a middle-aged experience of my own. My husband and I were having a drink at a bar waiting for the end of a nearby movie. After a while he left to buy tickets, and I stayed at the bar to finish my drink. A young man walked in, sat at the far end of the bar, looked me over and asked in an unpleasant tone, "Got your driver's license?" The same attitude is echoed in a cartoon in which an older woman approaches a middle-aged man at a bar, sits next to him and says, "Hello there . . ." He looks startled, amazed. Is she *really*, could she *possibly* be interested in sex?[13]

Contained in this fantasy is the assumption that older women really *should* give up sex. No matter what a man's age, he does not believe an older woman should be sexual. As a consequence, she is punished and banished to asexuality. The Queen in *Snow White* is a wicked step-mother who tries to murder her stepdaughter, her sexual rival. But at the wedding of Snow White and the Prince she gets her comeuppance. She has to dance in red hot shoes until she drops dead. We know that dancing can be a sexual symbol. She must dance till she becomes worked up and overheated; i.e., aroused. It's all right if a middle-aged man dies in a sexual dance. "What a way to go!" men say approvingly. But a middle-aged woman is punished for not surrendering and turning over her sexuality to the next generation.

Many men seem quite comfortable with the notion of the older woman as a faded blossom. She is no sexual threat; she offers no competition; she needs protection. She is the "little woman" grown older. The fantasy extends to the intellectual accomplishments of older women as well. One aspect of the image of the faded blossom is that she is on the way to becoming dim-witted. In the nine-teenth century men insisted that if women used their brains it would affect their "maternal organs." Bryn Mawr, always a college that attracted highly intelligent women, used to be called "a man's college for women." The "blue stockings," women writers, were caricatured mercilessly by artists like Honoré Daumier, who pictured them as deserters of the home and of infants.[14] Suffragettes got the same treatment in the early twentieth century, and so have contemporary women leaders.

We've recognized for a long time that women have been afraid of success for fear of being labelled "mascu-line." Women without intellectual "parts" can be a comfort to men's traditional sense of identity, leaving the realm of the mind their exclusive preserve. Many men have been

Adieu mon cher, je vais chez mes éditeurs. . . .
je ne rentrerai probablement que fort tard . . . ne manquez
pas de donner encore deux fois la bouillie à Dodore. . . .
s'il a besoin. . . . d'autre chose. . . .vous trouverez ca sous le lit.
. . .

Honoré Daumier. *Lib Women, Blue Stockings and Socialist Women.*
Leon Amiel, Publisher, Paris, New York, 1974.

making adjustments to women's achievements, as one after another of those areas marked "For Men Only" are opened to women. Even so, they are still able to consign the older woman to her place. She's a "faded blossom" who is foolish, irrelevant, and given to making pronouncements about the obvious. Only a short time ago, she was a stock ending for feature stories in which a bit of humor was needed to lighten a sad tale. Nicholas Gage, for example, wrote an affecting story about a sixty-two-year-old American photographer who returned to Athens with terminal cancer to photograph the Acropolis one last time. Because of the pollution, taxis were not permitted to drive close to the site. The sick man's final wish went unfulfilled. He was not strong enough to climb the rocky path. Our interest and sympathy were caught by the plight of the older man. Why did Mr. Gage have to bring on the post-menopausal clowns?

> A portly matron in a double-knit pants suit struggled to the high point of the Acropolis and clutched her companion's arm. "Oh, look," she cried out, pointing dramatically. "From here you can see the Hilton."[15]

With the myth of the faded blossom, men have still another means of projecting their fears of aging onto the older woman. She loses her physical attractiveness and her sexual power while his remains unchanged. What's more, his mental competence is not at risk, but the old girl never had it, or is well on the way to losing it.

There is clinical vignette that gives an "insider's" view of the fate of a man who failed to solve his conflicts with his mother and struggled with these myths at middle age. He lived out his fantasies by finding a woman who met his needs for the "perfect" non-threatening woman. The Boston psychoanalyst/psychiatrist Gregory Rochlin writes about a man he calls "Cooper," an attractive and success-ful person who married, had children, and then divorced after fifteen years. He had been single for ten years when he entered psychotherapy because of persistent insomnia and occasional nightmares. He could not become re-attached to any woman because of his fear of being controlled by her. Cooper recalled how dependent he was on his mother, how he allowed her to do everything for him, but how helpless this made him feel. He experienced her closeness as seductive. Cooper felt he had to walk away from her. He thought marriage would be a solution, but he brought his conflicts into the marriage, and espe-cially into the sexual area. His wife made him feel like a victim, made him feel weak.

After his divorce, he found that he enjoyed one-night stands with young women, "foreign-looking, with big breasts and big mouths . . . the sort you see in porno magazines and high fashion magazines . . . They have their mouths wide open. All they need is a big penis shoved into them." He had these aggressive thoughts because he felt these women were Delilahs—after him because of *his* power. He fantasized that they liked to be overpowered and hurt by him. Sex was a battle: the woman an enemy to be conquered. If he saw them only once, he was not threatened by their voraciousness.

Cooper had always loved his children and felt no fears in relation to them. He was free of symptoms when they visited. He loved to take care of them and cook for them; he actively assumed a caretaking role.

Rochlin reports that while therapy helped his pa-tient with his insomnia, he found "a way out" of his problems rather than "solving" them. To remain close to a woman Cooper had to find one who was sexually unde-manding. This was a source of reassurance to him. He met a divorcee ten years his junior with three children. She was feminine, motherly. He avoided his fears of the bad mother, the powerful, controlling woman, the battle-ax. He identified with his fantasy of the good mother, an idealized and asexual madonna. In his love for children, he himself became an "idealized indulgent mother" figure. He would maintain his earliest identification with her. His wife became the "little woman" who needed his protection, who did not rouse his fears and conflicts about her power to weaken and control him. She became, in his fantasy, what he would be if he were an older woman: a non-sexual being, a faded blossom.[16] In this way, Cooper managed to work out his destiny as a middle-aged man. We don't know exactly how many men are successful at this. But we have evidence, in the fallout from myths, fantasies, images, and "humor" regarding middle-aged woman, that many, many men are not.

There is yet another area of masculine insecurity, this one related to sexual prowess. It is another source of the unfortunate sexual image of the woman over forty. I have called it "The Myth of the Small Vagina."

❦❦ 5 ❦❦

"Your Feet's Too Big": The Myth of the Small Vagina

In the days of the Egyptian Empire, just before the invasion of
the Persians, around 570 B.C. or so, it is said, a wealthy
Greek merchant who lived in a city not far from the mouth of
the Nile bought a beautiful young Greek slave girl at an
auction. Then, we are told, he fell in love with the maiden.
He gave her a house and slaves of her own to serve her.
    One day she was bathing in the marble pool in her
garden. Her slave girls held her robe, her jewels, and her lovely
rose-red slippers. Suddenly a falcon, a messenger sent
by the Sky-god Horus, swooped down and seized one of the
slippers in its talons. The bird flew south, carrying the slipper,
straight to the capital at Memphis where the Pharaoh,
Amasis, was holding court. He dropped the slipper right
into the Pharaoh's lap. Amasis was so taken by the tiny size
and beauty of the slipper that he vowed to find the owner.
    He sent forth messengers throughout the land.
They found the girl and the matching slipper. The Pharaoh
made her his Queen and they lived happily together
for the rest of their lives. [1]

The Cinderella story, of course. Variations of this fairy tale appeared in China as early as the ninth century, A.D. It was known in Europe for about a thousand years before the story was written by Perrault in 1679 in the form in which we recognize it today. The Cinderella story has had such universal appeal because it touches on the dreams of generations of children. It tells of the transformation of a young girl into a beautiful maiden who is discovered by a "princely" man. Not only does she go from rags to riches, but in the process frustrates her bad stepmother and triumphs over her siblings.

In addition, the story appears to be a never-ending source of symbolic meaning. Not long ago Colette Dowling used it as a parable of the learned helplessness of women in *The Cinderella Complex*.

But an aspect of the fairy tale has been neglected. One rarely encounters a question about the meaning of the small size of the beautiful slipper and why the right woman for the prince is identified by the perfect way in which a shoe fits Cinderella's foot. The meaning of this part of the story is crucial, I believe, to an insight into the fantasy wishes of small boys and the psychology of men.

Note that in the Egyptian tale quoted, the Pharaoh has not even *seen* the maiden: he simply falls in love with her shoe because it is so beautiful, so rosy red, and so small—and vows to marry its owner. In some versions of the story a ring that slips on easily and fits perfectly is the clue to the identity of the perfect woman. In the Chinese fairy tale, the shoe is made of gold, the most precious of metals, its size "an inch too small for the smallest foot." There is an early English version in which the heroine loses a red velvet slipper richly embroidered with pearls. In France, there is some thought that the slipper was originally of fur (*vair*) rather than glass (*verre*).[2] But all the stories stress the small size of the shoe, its beauty, and the perfect way it fits on Cinderella's foot. Perrault's tale ends this way:

> The prince's messenger . . . asked Cinderella to sit down, and drawing the slipper upon her little foot, he saw it went on easily, and *fitted the foot like wax.* (Italics mine.)[3]

Both the ring and the valuable tiny red shoe are symbols of the female genitals. The "perfect fit" a symbolic way of indicating that it is the Prince's penis that will fit so perfectly.

The admiration of Chinese men for women with exceedingly small feet is well known. The cruel and primitive practice of foot binding was carried on in China well into the twentieth century. The women's tiny feet were rarely seen in their deformed state: rather, they were bathed, perfumed and hidden in tiny embroidered shoes. The mutilated feet were actually "thought to enhance a woman's sexual powers." They were a source of sexual excitement for men.[4] The symbolic meaning of foot size is clear.

Fantasies and myths of this nature have by no means disappeared. A modern musical version of Cinderella that was performed by a group in Harlem had as its theme song Fats Waller's unforgettable "Your Feet's Too Big." It is about a man who hates his girlfriend because of her oversized feet. Here are some of the lyrics:

> *Who's that walkin' around up there?*
> *Sounds like baby patter . . .*
> *Baby elephant patter . . .*
> *Your feet's too big!*
> *Don't want you 'cause your feet's too big,*
> *Can't use you 'cause your feet's too big!*
> *I really hates you 'cause your feet's too big.*
> (emphasis mine.)[5]

The symbolic equation of foot size and sexual attractiveness is not confined to the Cinderella story and Chinese foot-binding practices. Perhaps the ultimate example of the connection turned up in an exhibit shown at the Museum of Contemporary Crafts in New York in 1978. The show was entitled "The Great American Foot," and was sponsored, naturally enough, by a shoe company. In it was an old poster advertising a freak show in Philadelphia. On it stood a young woman in Victorian dress. She had enormous feet. The text read:

> The girl from Ohio, Miss Fannie Mills, who has the biggest feet on earth. She wears a Number 30 shoe . . . Each shoe is large enough to go to sea in. She is a native of Sandusky, Ohio . . . She is a petite blonde, weighs 115 pounds; very pretty, refined and highly accomplished. Mr. Mills, of Sandusky, Ohio, will give to any responsible man who will marry his daughter Fanny, $5,000 and a well-stocked farm . . . Don't let two big feet stand between you and wedlock tinged with fortune.[6]

Apparently this girl's big feet frightened men away; they had to be bribed to even consider approaching her.

Without insight into its meaning to men, women have always wanted small feet. A friend recently recalled that she always bought shoes a size too small, and I have heard that story echoed by a number of women I know. The model shoes on display in stores are always size five, which perhaps gave rise to the joke:

> *There's a woman who suffers for her beliefs.*
> *Why, what does she believe?*
> *She believes she can wear a size five shoe on a size seven foot.*[7]

In their wish to be physically attractive to men, women have not only been defensive about the size of their feet but want just as much to be small and slim all over. (Breasts are the exception. They can be large, of course, because of men's profoundly pleasurable associations with the nursing experience.) Kim Chernin wondered why women try so hard to be thin. In her book, *The Obsession: Reflections on the Tyranny of Slenderness,* she says that women hide their power by reducing the size of their bodies in their eagerness to please men.[8] Models wear size six dresses. "The Forgotten Woman" is the name of a store that caters to large women.

It is true that men often have a negative association, from childhood, between the size and power of their mothers in relation to their smallness and relative feelings of helplessness. But, in my opinion, the association goes further. I believe that there is a displacement of a man's feelings about the *part* of a woman's body that most concerns him—her genitals—to her body as a *whole.*[9] The process is explained in a term borrowed from rhetoric, "synedoche," in which we use a collective noun to symbolize a single part, object, or person, as for example, when we speak of "the law" when referring to a policeman.

Here is a male fantasy that has arisen in response to one of men's key anxieties—which, itself, is a source of one of the most virulent myths about the sexual unattractiveness of older women. We have established the small foot-vagina-small body connection, and it is clear that, stripped of disguise, a man's interest in the smallness of feet relates to sexual fit. The meaning of vaginal size comes out from under the wraps of symbolism in the hands of Henry Miller, who is obsessed with things sexual and undeterred by the need for niceties, as for example when he writes, in *Tropic of Cancer,* "The trouble with

Irene, she has a valise instead of a cunt."[10] Why is Miller so vehement? It is because a man worries about vaginal size to the degree that he is not satisfied with the size of his penis.

Few men are entirely satisfied with their genital endowment. They sneak competitive glances at one another in locker rooms, where some men get a reputation for being especially "well hung." In *A Moveable Feast,* Hemingway makes rather catty remarks about F. Scott Fitzgerald's concern with the size of his penis. Hemingway tries to set Fitzgerald straight by explaining that a man only sees his penis from above, so it always looks foreshortened. But in having to offer such an explanation, he reveals his own interest in the subject.[11] Leonard Kriegel describes this concern in some men as coming close to pure obsession ". . . as though men are born with tapemeasures in their heads."[12]

I have heard the fear that their penises are too small to satisfy women expressed by many of my male patients. As noted in Chapter Two, the fear of genital inadequacy has its genesis in the small boy's competitive feelings about his father. He also knows that babies come from inside his mother, but is confused about her anatomy. The baby grows "in her tummy" and comes out of her "bottom." The vagueness of his knowledge about the inside of his mother's body helps to create the fantasy about the vagina as an unfillable space. The following joke combines two male anxieties: the size of female genitals, and the Oedipal theme—another man (father?) has gotten there first.

> *A man lost his condom during intercourse. He picked up his flashlight and set out to find it. The man walked down a long corridor and saw a light at the end of it. There he discovered another man searching for his condom.*

When a man is anxious about penis size he may use two common defenses which arise almost automatically: Displacement: it's not my problem, it's hers; and Projection: I'm not worried, she is.

Feelings about the inner space of a woman merge with early, primitive fantasies, which, on an unconscious level, are tantamount to the little boy's fear of engulfment. Dudley Moore, who got his start in this country as a "Beyond the Fringe" comedian, was discussing his adolescent sexual behavior in a *Playboy* interview. He did not, he explained, fully penetrate a woman until the age of twenty-two or twenty-three. Joking or not, he reflects the fears of many men when he said, "I was too afraid of leaving anything as valuable as my penis in that cavern of no return."[13]

It is fascinating how the human imagination can address a subject as sensitive and as anxiety-producing as a man's feeling of sexual inadequacy and then use fantasy as a defense that reverses the problem: in fantasy, instead of being a fearful *subject,* he becomes a sexual conquistador. Take, for example, the myth of the large warlike woman, the Amazon, who could turn a man into a woman, mentioned in Chapter Four. Amazons were believed to inhabit the New World. One of their mythic societies was to be found in the far reaches of the Amazon River, where they reigned over hoards of gold and fabulous jewels. For a real conquistador, an Amazon would yield it all, and become a docile wife. The fantasy says that a *true* man can subdue such a woman. A heroic man is heroically endowed, a superman. The Amazon was the ultimate incentive for Spanish explorers of the New World.[14]

Such a hero in modern dress is Sonny Corleone in Mario Puzo's *The Godfather.* His penis was large enough to subdue a latter-day Amazon, to fill the vagina of Lucy, a girl unfortunate enough to have been born too big "down there."[15] We know that penis size is usually not of much importance when it comes to a man's ability to gratify a woman sexually. But it is often difficult to convince anxious men that they are caught in a fantasy. As a defense mechanism such men attribute the problem to the female with whom they are involved. As a psychiatrist not identified by Myron Brenton in his book, *The American Male*, put it: "She must find ways of making this place of hers attractive for the man."[16] Of course she wants to be attractive, but is the problem hers?

In sum, most men grow up with some feelings of anxiety about penis size. With couples who have children, the husband knows that his wife's vagina has been large enough to permit the passage of an infant's body. So, at middle age, when concerns about possible diminution of sexual potency become anxiety-provoking, men can deny them by a familiar defense: if I can't satisfy her, it's because her vagina is too big. An anecdote related to me by the mother of two teen-agers speaks eloquently to this point:

> One evening I was very late getting dressed. Friends had already arrived for dinner. I was having trouble getting earrings adjusted in my pierced ears, so I went downstairs. A male friend in his fifties volunteered to help. "Oh," he said as he looked at my earlobe, *"The hole has gotten smaller . . . that's good!"*

These examples are the creation of insecure men. The often-told jokes and anecdotes reveal their anxiety. The point usually is: it's her problem; I'm all right; time does not alter me; but when you've got a wife who's got grown-up kids, or even has just been around for twenty years it is difficult to avoid the reality of aging. Some men choose the myth that a younger woman with a small, tight vagina will provide better sex, restore a man's feelings of potency, and make them feel younger. It's not a new idea. An old folk song captures the theme:

> *Yonder comes my pretty little girl.*
> *She's going all dressed in red.*
> *I looked down at her pretty little feet.*
> *I wish my wife was dead.* [17]

We now understand the meaning of foot size; the folk singer need not explain that he is sure the "little" girl has what his wife does not. In case there is any ambiguity, *Playboy* says it without poetic metaphor:

> *"I'll fix you, you tightwad!" screamed the woman. "If you won't increase my allowance for clothes, I'm going on a bedroom strike!" "Go right ahead," responded her husband. "My secretary has the tightest little strikebreaker in town."* [18]

In contrast, *Screw* magazine published an article debunking the restorative anatomical powers of young women. It was called "The Myth of the Tight Pussy." [19]

When a man feels insecure, he often rationalizes by viewing his wife as an "old lady" who has lost her sex appeal. Her genitals aren't "right" for men, she's a turn-off. She gets no points for experience, but his experience makes him better than ever. In this myth, he can outperform younger men, even his own son. The gray-haired intruder who arouses the young wife is a favorite theme of pornographic literature. She's a "sleeping beauty," her sexual passion yet untapped by her callow, inexperienced husband; but when the older man takes over, she is aroused to a pitch of sexual excitement she's never known. In many of Harold Robbins' novels, the older man never loses his sexual prowess. In *The Betsy*, for example, the middle-aged hero impregnates his son's wife. The younger man, totally outclassed in bed, gives up women forever and retreats to a life of homosexuality.[20]

The attitudes discussed in this chapter point to a definition of sex as a form of gymnastics. But meaningful sex can be, and should be, an expression of tenderness, communication, and caring between two people. If we define sex purely on the level of performance, however, just how real is the fantasy that the vagina of an older woman or one who has had children, is a hindrance to pleasure?

I have talked to a number of obstetrician/gynecologists and an equal number of sex therapists about this fantasy.[21] Their answers in sum, are: Vaginal size varies among women, but congenitally oversized vaginas, such as "Lucy's" in *The Godfather*, are exceedingly rare. Some stretching occurs throughout a woman's life: when tampons are introduced, with the first penetration by the penis, and after the passage of a baby's head through the birth canal. Vagina size, however, depends more on muscle tone than on any of these happenings. The vagina is after all, a flexible canal surrounded by the muscles of the perineum, the sling of muscles between the vagina and the rectum. The vagina of a woman who has never had children may feel slack to men if the muscles of this area are weak.

In the days before modern obstetrical care, stretching and tearing of the perineum often occurred during childbirth. There is the veteran obstetrician who remarked, "For twenty years, I supported the perineum; now the perineum supports me," referring to the numerous surgical procedures he performed on woman to repair the muscles of the genital area after the years of childbearing were past. This need has virtually disappeared because of improved obstetrical techniques. For many years a minor procedure known as episiotomy has been performed on hundreds of thousands of women during childbirth. A small cut is made in the muscle to the entrance of the vagina to prevent damage. After delivery the muscle is sewn back together. With the revived popularity of "natural childbirth," even the use of episiotomy is, at times, called into question. Women today deliver with a minimum of intervention and with little or no anesthesia. The mother participates as the perineum is supported and the fetal head is allowed to come out slowly, thus reducing the danger of tearing the muscle. After childbirth, exercises designed to restore tone to the musculature of the perineum are routinely prescribed.

Very few women approach their gynecologists with the complaint, "My husband feels I'm too large for him." And, according to well-known obstetrician George Kleiner, even when this *is* a complaint, it is impossible to rule out psychological factors, including marital difficulties or problems of sexual adjustment.

Reparative surgery on the vagina is usually indicated in the face of specific gynecological problems not encountered by the great majority of women. The procedure is called vaginoplasty. A triangular area of the anterior or posterior portion of the vaginal wall and its underlying musculature are resected and brought closer together, resulting in a reduced vaginal opening. This surgery is performed only if there has been major damage during childbirth. Women in need of this operation complain of a feeling of looseness in the area of the bladder, with some urinary incontinence, and similar feelings in the area of the rectum. There may also be a condition known as prolapse of the uterus, a descent of the cervix and uterus into the vaginal canal. Doctors emphatically discourage surgery for purely sexual reasons. All surgery which involves general anesthesia has its hazards. But there are other complications that may arise from vaginal surgery, including the inability to void spontaneously, painful inter- course, or a recurrence of the original condition.

There have been times when men have recognized their own projections of the "tight vagina" myth. Tom Robbin's novel, *Even Cowgirls Get the Blues,* a wonderful satire on sexual reconditioning, is an example of this. The heroines take over the Rubber Rose Ranch, a Western beauty spa named after a commercially successful douche bag. They enlighten the vulnerable older women about the programs set up to exploit them, "the vagina-tightening . . . super-douche, love rub and nipple-wax training" that are supposed to transform them into women desirable to men once more.[22]

As a therapist I have learned how vulnerable many men are about their sexual adequacy. And I know for certain how hard it is for men in our culture to face aging and sexual change. However, the tragedy is that older women have been asked to absorb and relieve men's anxieties—at their own expense. As the recipients of inse- cure men's projections, they are made to feel responsible, disposable, and without redress. And the myth of the small vagina is the keystone of the undesirable image of older women.

Jackie Collins, author of *Hollywood Wives,* com- mented on the Merv Griffin show, that first wives could be jalopies, but second wives were like Cadillacs, well-de- signed and carefully engineered. Second wives usually did their job well: entertaining for their husbands, dressing well—a substantial, quality product. But as their husbands age, even second wives often get traded in for a new model: a sports car, sleeker, trimmer, faster, smaller, and lower to the ground—a young wife who restores her hus- band's feelings of youth and potency.[23] The myth of the small vagina fits the symbolism: the trade-in of a larger car for a sports car by a man of middle age. Such negative images make some wives do dangerous things such as having Caesarian sections instead of normal childbirth, or searching until they find surgeons who will perform "miracles" on their bodies. Since the real reasons for such myths are embedded in the anxieties of insecure men, women who succumb to their irrational thinking search for cures that can never be found.

If the "tight vagina" is a myth, then what *are* men's real sexual complaints about women? The specialists I consulted agreed that men are most distressed by lack of female responsiveness, which is also the finding of Anthony Pietropinto, M.D. and Jacqueline Simenauer in the survey which appears in *Beyond the Male Myth.*[24] Men universally regard inactivity on the woman's part as lack of interest, hurtful to pride, a turn-off. Physiologically, passivity reduces physical stimulation for the male; it also contributes to a lack of emotional and psychic stimulation. If a man and a woman of middle age share their feelings for one another, and if they cultivate some playfulness and imagination in their sexual acts, they both probably will experience mutual stimulation and pleasurable sex. If serious sexual problems occur, there are many therapeutic treatments for restimulating or cultivating rewarding sexual relations between a couple.

I recall the wonderful sexual relationship of a couple who had met when they were well into their fifties. They came to see me because they had run into problems with her children's rejection of him and her anxieties about attitudes he had about money. But when they talked about their sexual life, I realized what a wonderfully sexually attuned middle-aged couple they were.

Yet how strong cultural fantasies are about the sexual unattractiveness of mature women, and how persistent and insidious is the "small vagina" myth. David Reuben, M.D. in *Everything You Always Wanted to Know About Sex,* which has sold close to ten million copies, writes the following about sex and the middle-aged woman:

> The wife needs sexual rehabilitation, weight reduction (that "tiny body" thing again), estrogen (a whole other story to be discussed later), thyroid and cortisone may also be required. (Is she sick?) In the sexual restoration of women, much more can be accomplished by surgery. Plastic surgery on the vagina to compensate for the stretching and tearing of childbirth can add tremendously to sexual enjoyment. The vaginal cavity and the vaginal opening itself can be made smaller; a woman of fifty-five can have the same vaginal feel to her husband and the same vaginal feeling herself, as a girl of nineteen.[25]

Dr. Reuben goes on to recommend plastic surgery for the face and breasts. He overlooks the possibility that women—and their husbands—might object to the prospect of at least three surgical procedures with the risks involved. Do our myths suggest: Rather a dead wife than a middle-aged one?

❧§6§❧

Menopause: The Myths

---

*It is well known, and has been a matter for much complaint,
that women often alter strangely in character after they have
abandoned their genital functions. They become quarrelsome,
peevish, and argumentative, petty and miserly; in fact, they
display sadistic and anal-erotic traits which were not theirs in
the era of womanliness. Writers of comedy and satirists have in
all ages launched their invective against the "old termagant"
into which the sweet maiden, the loving woman, the tender
mother, has deteriorated.*

Sigmund Freud, 1913

I have such respect for many of Freud's insights
that I hesitated before deciding to use this quotation. Yet,
because of his continuing influence on the practice of
psychiatry (and to illustrate the effects of fantasy on even
such a man) I quote his view of post-menopausal women.
In fact, Freud's "transfer theory" of sexual development—
that clitoral sensation must be repressed and taken over
by the vagina in order for a woman to be "normal" in her
sexual functioning—has caused women much damage.

Many of women's feelings of sexual inadequacy were caused by that error. Freud unwittingly did similar disservice to older women as well.

Not only Freud's but most men's attitudes to the menopause and their fantasies about women after their childbearing functions are over are more responsible for "the double standard of aging" than we have recognized. Until I saw the definition in a dictionary of slang, I did not realize that "bag" is a popular word for the womb.[1] So when a woman is called an "Old Bag," it really means that the menopause has made her old and sexually useless. A cartoon in *Penthouse* Magazine is crudely explicit about this negative view of women when it shows a post-menopausal woman—a woman over fifty, fat, buxom and very ugly—standing with her legs apart, while a man lies on his back between her legs on a rolling dolly, the kind used by garage mechanics to get under automobiles, with both his hands up inside the woman's genitals. The ground is strewn with a variety of tools. He is tinkering with her broken-down parts.[2]

Men's fantasies about the menstrual cycle do not arise *de novo* at the time of the menopause. Anthropologists and folklorists have long since described men's fears and awe of the menstruating woman. They document the numerous rituals that surround her: the taboos, the segregation, and the cleansing imposed upon her before she is readmitted to tribal and sexual life.

Clearly, menstruation can be a strange and disturbing phenomenon. Any form of bleeding can make people anxious. We have only to think how children behave when they injure themselves, or of the anxiety of adults, for that matter, when they accidentally draw blood. The act of bleeding is something out of control: we can literally bleed to death. In fantasy, men sometimes confuse menstruation with injury. One patient called his wife's sanitary napkins her "bandages." Such a projection related in part to his early fears about the safety of his own sexual equipment when confronted with the absence of a penis in a woman.

Enormous powers are ascribed to the menstruating woman and to menstrual blood. In primitive tribes a menstruating woman is prohibited from touching her husband's weapons before he goes on a hunt. Menstrual blood is used in some of the most powerful magical ceremonies. As a consequence of ancient lore, myths about the menses die hard. Already mentioned has been the myth that intercourse with a menstruating woman was believed to be dangerous for a man.

The feelings evoked by the mysterious function of menstruation extend to other female functions—such as pregnancy and the act of childbirth itself. Fears of these processes, which are both strange and powerful, evoke, and can be masked by, feelings of awe. Such affects are expressed in the behavior of many husbands during their wives' pregnancies. Their wives are treated with a kind of reverence. Men approach on tiptoe as if the women are made of porcelain.

These affects reach far back in our civilization. In the Middle Ages the mystery of and reverence inspired by the mother's creative power are most significantly expressed in the worship of Mary, the Blessed Mother of God. The thousands of paintings of the birth of Christ or of the Madonna breast-feeding the Child represent clearly the extraordinary significance of these maternal functions.

Yet the reverence and awe inspired in men by pregnancy and childbirth can be a cloak covering other feelings—including the deeply repressed envy of a woman's ability to have a baby. In certain tribes this envy is overtly expressed. In New Guinea, for example, when a man's wife is in labor, the husband takes to his bed and, in the ritual of "Couvade," goes through an imitation of her labor and delivery. In our own culture, expressions of this longing are rarely discussed and invariably discouraged. Still, some little boys do say they'd like to have babies. They want to play with dolls and stuff their shirts, pretending to have breasts. As adults, some men seem to experience morning sickness in the first trimester of their wives' pregnancies. In my practice I have found men to be more in touch with their envy of their wives' ability to breast-feed than with their wish to give birth to children. The latter, which may become evident in psychotherapy, is generally too threatening to a man's identity, to his sense of masculinity, to be allowed into consciousness. It is not insignificant that this is a subject that has not been widely written about in psychiatry.[3]

Most men feel an eternal ambivalence toward women. However, there are periods of a man's life when this ambivalence is more or less held in abeyance. For all the problems that can arise if a man feels displaced by his wife's preoccupation with her children, there is still something compelling when a woman fulfills her biological and nurturing functions in the gestation and the delivery of a child. I would suggest that whatever the degree of ambivalence, a man feels some awe and respect toward a woman when she is pregnant and nursing her young. But it is only after the menopause, when these functions, or powers, are gone, that many men's competitive feelings emerge. At this time women are devalued for the loss of something a man never had.

And on some level, a man becomes angry at her. This old joke expresses a man's pleasure that his continued need for proof of potency can be met:

A ninety-year old man goes to see his doctor because he is planning to marry a woman of thirty. The doctor says he's in good shape, but it

> *might be a good idea if he took in a boarder to*
> *keep his wife happy. Six months later, they hap-*
> *pen to meet on the street. The doctor asks the*
> *old man how his wife is. "She's pregnant," he*
> *replies. "And how's the boarder?" asks the doc-*
> *tor. "Oh, she's pregnant too."*

After the menopause a wife can no longer supply a man with such evidence of masculinity. What's more, she no longer fulfills her concrete "womanly"—i.e., maternal—purpose. She is no longer capable of feeding, of giving life. Consider the fantasy at the climax of John Steinbeck's *The Grapes of Wrath*. A flood of Biblical proportions destroys the Okies' camp. People are starving and dying. In the midst of this tragedy, Rose of Sharon gives birth to a still-born infant. Although the child is dead, she is still capable of giving life: she offers her breast to a starving man:

> For a minute Rose of Sharon sat still in the whispering barn. Then she hoisted her tired body up and drew the comforter about her. She moved slowly to the corner and stood looking down at the wasted face, at the wide frightened eyes. Then slowly she lay down beside him. He shook his head slowly from side to side. Rose of Sharon loosened the side of the blanket and bared her breast. "You got to," she said. She squirmed close and pulled his head close. "There!" she said. "There." Her hand moved gently in his hair. She looked across the barn, and her lips came together and smiled mysteriously.[4]

The mysterious smile: this is Steinbeck's tribute to the female's power. Such power is denied to the post-menopausal woman. The popular expression "as cold as a witch's tit" captures men's anger at the post-menopausal woman's inability to nurse.

In *The Second Sex,* Simone de Beauvoir makes another connection between menstruation and the menopause for men: The monthly physical function of women reminds men of their own bodies, of their physical nature, of their animal origins.[5] When his partner reaches the menopause, a middle-aged man is sharply reminded of his own mortality. I would suggest that many a middle-aged man pushes away thoughts of dying. I am intact, he says, but the old girl, the "old bag," has reached the menopause. She is aging. Aversive feelings about death and dying are once more projected onto her: she is beginning to decay!

A nasty rhyme from *Hustler* Magazine set to the tune of "Little Jack Horner," conveys this fantasy.

The verse:

Little Jack Horner sat in a corner
Playing with Grandma's twat.
He stuck in his pinky;
Pulled it out stinky
And said, Damn it's
Beginnin' to rot![6]

Numerous jokes recur on this theme. And no less an authority than Wolfgang Lederer devotes a chapter to this subject, "Frau Welt [World], or the Perfume of Decay," in his widely quoted book, *The Fear of Women.* Dr. Lederer describes a medieval statue on the south portal of the Cathedral of Worms in Germany. It depicts Frau Welt, a sweet-smiling woman standing with a knight kneeling by her side. Her posterior is nude and in a state of decay; It is in the process of being consumed by frogs and snakes. Frau Welt is a symbol of mortality. In this chapter, Dr. Lederer writes:

I still vividly recall something else about old women—not their appearance but their smell. *Perhaps it is something about post-menopausal*

> *chemistry:* more likely it had to do with a certain physical neglect once physical charms were past. At any rate, what with modern hygiene and modern perfume, I have not noticed it lately; when I still noticed it—for the last time, I think during my medical internship—I could not get away from it fast enough. (Italics mine.)[7]

Here Dr. Lederer is repeating the same fantasy as the one expressed by Freud, quoted at the beginning of this chapter. They both equate a woman's sexual attractiveness ("physical charms") with her ability to have children. In addition, Lederer makes no distinction between middle age and senility. Do women neglect to take care of their bodies after fifty? Stop taking baths? In hospitals and old age homes we know that women and the fewer men who survive into very old age may become incontinent, and in these instances an odor is inevitable. But we are not talking about incontinent old women *or* men. We are looking at the fantasy which equates the post-menopausal woman with decay.

First let's deal with the question of smell. In our evolutionary adaption, a person's other four senses are so highly developed that the area of the brain devoted to the function of smell is considerably smaller than in lower animals. However, we in the United States have been socialized to have such an aversion to body odors that we have developed a hypersensitivity to them. No other society can boast of a billion-dollar deodorant industry. Sholokov's hero in *And Quiet Flows the Don* who is "turned on" by the odor of his love's armpits would feel quite out of place here. The gynecologists and sex therapists whom I consulted told me their young women patients, enculturated as they are, complain about vaginal smells. For some men, menstrual odors can be a problem. For others, genital smells are a source of sexual stimulation. It is rare, though, for men to record their enjoyment of them. In his autobiography, *The Coming of (Middle) Age: A Journey,* Arnold J. Mandell did just that. He wrote about the "afterglow" following a date when he was a young man; the reflected pleasures of the evening were intensified by "the excitement of her smell on my fingers."[8]

A *Penthouse* Magazine cartoon suggests the potential for pleasure in sexual odors. A strange little man is raking in money from the sale of little girls' bicycle seats. A goon, his tongue hanging out, is buying one. The "For Sale" sign says:

> *New $1.00*
> *Used $5.00*[9]

These men are characterized as "freaks" however: the idea is that one should feel guilty about the impulse to enjoy sexual smells. The inference is that such pleasure is a form of perversion. We "buy" the notion. There was a brief land-office business in vaginal sprays until it was discovered they caused irritation to the lining of the vagina. This matter of smell is often imagined to be a generational problem. Henry Miller, acutely conscious of such distinctions, wrote in *Tropic of Cancer:*

> Anyway I thought maybe you wouldn't mind taking the mother. . . . She's not so bad . . . if I hadn't seen the daughter I might have considered her myself. The daughter's nice and young, freshlike. . . . There's a clean smell to her. . . . (His friend demurs and the hero, Van Norden, is angry.) I don't know how to get rid of the old hen.[10]

Another literary instance of the fantasy about older women's smells occurs in *Midnight Cowboy,* as the hero walks through a tenement building: "The lower halls stunk so dreadfully one could swear demented old women boiled cat pee behind every closed door."[11] Here is the connection between cats and old women. Why does author James Herlihy pin it on the "old girl," when anyone who knows about the smells in tenement hallways can tell you that in addition to the faulty plumbing, men and small boys duck into these spaces to relieve themselves?

Robert Penn Warren offers a clue to the answer to this question in his Pulitzer Prize-winning novel, *All the King's Men*. After a quarrel about the nature of good and evil, the protagonist, Jack Burden, angrily leaves his friend:

> And with that I slammed his door and was running and stumbling down the dark stairs, for it was that kind of apartment house where the bulb burns out and nobody ever puts a new one in and there is always a kiddie car left on a landing and the carpet is worn to ribbons and the air smells dankly of dogs, diapers, cabbage, *old women*, burnt grease and the *eternal fate of man*. (Italics mine.)[12]

The old woman is related to these symbols: the neglected house, the burnt-out bulb, and the dark stairs. Her lack of fecundity reminds man of his fate. Again, onto the older woman man's fear of dying is projected. The palpable smell is the smell of his own death. Of course, male symbols of death do exist (Father Time, The Grim Reaper), but I refer here to the symbolic link between a woman's loss of fertility and death.

This is a prime example of the dynamic nature of symbols: their constant yet shifting meanings throughout the life cycle. The image of the bad mother persists. The witch who spoils the milk is, symbolically, the mother who weans her child. By withholding food, as the Wicked Witch of the West tried to do from the Cowardly Lion in *The Wizard of Oz*, she can starve you to death. When time causes her to cease her menstrual function, she is viewed as withholding life itself. She is resented for forcing an adult to think, as a child cannot, upon his own mortality. Worst of all, today, she also outlives him. The adaptive function of male fantasy could not be clearer: it is about avoiding anxiety. The formula repeats itself: get rid of her and you are rid of the problem. After all, the joke says the difference between a wife and a cup of tea is that you can throw away a tea bag, but you'd like to throw away the "old bag" as well. And magically avoid her fate.

What *are* the physical facts about the older woman? The sex therapists and gynecologists whom I interviewed concur that normal vaginal smell is stronger in some women than in others; and that, in addition, some men are far more sensitive to odors than others. None of the doctors I consulted could tell me if vaginal smell changes after the menopause, except that menstrual odors, of course, no longer occur. Unpleasant vaginal smells are caused by bacteria from a variety of sources: an infection of the lining of the cervix and uterus, an I.U.D. (Interuterine Device), or from a common minor infection like Trichomoniasis, which is asymptomatic in men, but not in women. It can also be caused by a post-partum infection.

The vagina, of course, is not a sterile place; it is normal for bacteria to be present. But after the menopause the vagina is more quiescent; there is diminished cellular division and bacterial production. There is also less secretion from the glands that produce lubrication, which would suggest that middle-aged women would have less odor. Only when a discharge is present do doctors look for an infection, or a pre-cancerous or cancerous condition. In the face of definite pathology, there is indeed a smell.

Popular fantasy to the contrary, middle-aged men and women who come for sexual counselling do not

usually complain about vaginal odor. The fantasies themselves are contradictory: the post-menopausal vagina is
rotting and smelly, or it is frozen and dried-up. It cannot
be both. In fact, it is neither.

But the middle-aged man stacks the odds against
his wife, or any woman who is his contemporary. Her very
existence reminds him of his own mortality, so he "projects" his fear of decay onto her. While his sexual powers
have passed their peak, he cannot forget she still retains
her potential for multiple orgasms. So he focuses on the
myth of the small vagina, imbuing that mysterious anatomical part with the magical power of regeneration for
him. Not only does it have to be "small and tight," it must
be dewy and lubricious as well. The models in the center-
folds of *Playboy* and *Hustler* appear perpetually aroused,
open, ready—even though this effect is achieved artifi-
cially. In a documentary film about the pornography industry shown at a recent meeting of the American Psychiatric Association, one scene pictured the preparations for
the taking of stills for a girlie magazine in which the
model's vaginal area was painted with a substance like egg
white to make it glisten. The model made a grimace of
displeasure during the procedure.[13] Here Henry Miller's
fantasy is played out. "You take the mother, 'the old hen,' I
want the daughter—she's freshlike. . . ."

At the breakfast table at the artists' and writers'
colony to which I retreated to write, a plain-looking mature
woman sat down at a table where there happened to be a
number of young women. She turned to a graying and
balding man who was well into middle age and said rather
wistfully, "You must feel like you're in a candy store." Ugly
is not edible; older is not appetizing. Our culture indulges
a man's narcissism and conspires with his wish for regeneration. It says it's okay to turn away from older
women.

Yet, in spite of all the protestations about the post-menopausal woman, many men have a profound wish to return to the "Old Bag" and that place of ultimate safety. A cover photograph of *Rolling Stone* Magazine by Annie Liebovitz came as a bit of a shock to me because it was such a plain and open expression of such a desire. In the photo, taken on the day he was shot, John Lennon is naked. His wife, Yoko Ono, is fully clothed and lying on her back. Lennon, twice his wife's size, is curled up and clinging to her body, for all the world like a baby monkey. Yoko Ono was older than Lennon and the manager of their business affairs. At the time of his death, Lennon was the "in house" father of their child.[14] Rarely are men so candid in public about their dependency needs. Usually they deny, mock, or disguise them through the kind of humor we've been discussing.

However, William Steig made this fantasy explicit in two cartoons. In the first a man floats in the sea, basking in the warmth of the sun, thinking, "I am at one with the universe." The cartoon is drawn to look as though the man has regressed to the size and shape of a sperm with an egg floating nearby. His universe is within the womb.[15] In the second there is Steig's drawing of a grown-up man sleeping peacefully in a woman's shoe.[16]

A woman lives without the capacity to bear children for twenty-five or thirty years. This is roughly one-third of her lifetime, and she is not a worn-out hag when her ability to reproduce is past. Barring the bad luck of the early onset of a chronic disease, a possibility for both sexes, a post-menopausal woman is a vital and productive human being. But women have curiously internalized men's attitudes toward menstruation and the menopause. They accept the fact that their ability to menstruate makes men uncomfortable, and they do not tune into the fact that, on a deeper level, it is a function men envy. As a result, they

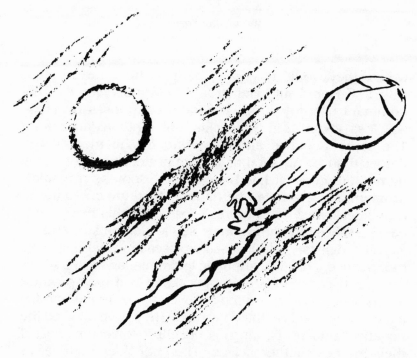

I am at One with the Universe!

From *The Lonely Ones* by William Steig. Copyright © 1942 by William Steig.

have treated the process with shame rather than pride. I have found the onset of menses greeted by men and women with true celebration only in one primitive tribe, the Pygmies of the Congo. To the Pygmies, "menstrual blood means life . . . when a young Pygmy girl begins to flower into maturity and blood comes to her for the first time, it comes to her as a gift, received with gratitude and rejoicing . . . every one is told the good news." The festival that follows, "the Elima," celebrated with rituals, dancing, and special songs, welcomes the girl into the world of adult women and is one of the most joyful occasions in the life of the tribe.[17]

One rarely comes across women who comment on the fact that we "buy" men's feelings toward the menses. Gloria Steinem is an exception. If men had periods, she writes, they would celebrate them. In her satirical piece called "If Men Could Menstruate," she observes that the dominant group justifies the ideas it imposes on those with less power, as in "white skin is better than dark skin."[18] The same negative attitudes cling to the menopause. Rather than being seen as a normal development in the human life cycle, it has been looked upon as a medical problem. For example, the National Institute on Aging, in a booklet called *Our Future Selves*, had this list of "diseases associated with aging": senile dementia, cerebrovascular disease, cardiovascular disease, renal diseases, menopause, chronic lymphatic leukemia, and others.[19]

Of course, it is a biological fact that men produce sperm when women no longer ovulate. So many middle-aged women feel on the defensive. They have allowed the negative fantasies floating in our culture to become part of their images of themselves. They consider themselves inferior—to younger women, and to fertile men.

Part Two

Reality

✥§7§✥

Menopause: The Reality

The real reason men don't want older women is that a man's sex drive doesn't change and a woman's dries up with her loss of estrogen.

Interview with a man of fifty.
December 10, 1983.

Questionnaire about sex after 60:

Do you like sex?

Female, married, 64: *"Yes with all my heart. I don't know how to explain except it is beautiful to me."*

Female, widow, age 72: *". . . I am only 72 and will like it till I die."*

The Starr-Weiner Report

At the seashore, one becomes aware of how different the world looks when a fog lifts and the sun breaks through: houses appear in the distance, small boats become visible, and even the flowers in the garden look up and insist on being seen individually. It is my feeling that a middle-aged woman can emerge just as clearly once she is seen in an undistorted light.

In the mists of history, she was considered old as soon as she was no longer fertile. And although a woman's sexual and emotional needs do not change after the menopause, her feelings about herself and her expectations from others alter in response to the male-created view of her as an undesirable female. Consequently, as she enters her forties and anticipates that symbolic time, the approach of the menopause, her self-doubts accelerate.

One of the more positive results of today's greater openness about sexual matters has been the appearance of advertisements about menstruation on television which show women leading normal lives, using sanitary napkins and tampons. There is a corresponding emergence of frankness about the menopause, which is no longer spoken of euphemistically as "Change of Life." Books and articles are being published and information is coming from the media on menopause as part of everyday health reportage.

It is clear that women want to be more in touch with and in control of their bodies. Middle-class women as a group tend to get more sophisticated information and better medical care. Working-class women and women in smaller communities, however, know less but are eager to learn what to expect as their menses terminate. Just as women used to demand total anesthesia during childbirth because they did not know it was unnecessary to experience intolerable pain, so too many women today, still uninformed, anticipate terrible problems during their passage through the menopause.

Even in our "enlightened" age, old views of the menopause as one of the *medical* problems of middle-aged women still appear, as in the pamphlet put out by

Menopause

The National Institutes of Health cited in the previous chapter.[1] But when the fog has totally lifted, the menopause will be seen as a normal developmental stage in the lives of women.

Menopause is defined simply as the cessation of monthly bleeding, which becomes an established fact of life when periods have been absent for a year. Most women arrive at the menopause between the ages of forty-five and fifty-five. The mean age is fifty-one, and only five percent of women continue to menstruate after their fifty-third birthday.

The act of menstruation follows this cycle: The hormone estrogen causes the buildup of the lining of the uterus, the endometrium, which becomes the "nest" for the fertilized egg. If fertilization has not taken place, the release of a second hormone, progesterone, triggers the sloughing off of the lining of the uterus—or menstruation.

Most women stop ovulating several years before the cessation of their periods. Estrogen is produced primarily by the ovarian follicles, so the decline in estrogen production is linked to the cessation of ovulation. Also, the pool of immature eggs available for ovulation is thought to be exhausted. When ovulation stops, estrogen is no longer secreted from the follicle to build up the endometrium, nor is progesterone produced to stimulate its elimination.

When one speaks to many women as I do, one learns how widely their experiences of the menopause differ. As Avodah Offit, M.D., has pointed out, for about eight percent of women, periods end abruptly.[2] Menstrual flow may be heavy with lengthy periods, or quite the reverse, and they can occur earlier or later than the usual cycle.

Before menopause, a large number of women worry most about whether they will have unpleasant physical and/or emotional symptoms. The reality is that most women go about the business of living and experience minimal discomfort during this phase. Some statistics say that ten percent of women have significant discomfort during the menopause, others report figures as high as thirty-five percent.[3] Such statistics are tricky to evaluate, however. What constitutes "significant discomfort" for one woman might not be so for another, not least because many subjective factors influence individual variations in response: attitudes toward one's body and its functions, the anticipation of difficulty, and the degree of satisfaction with life—to name just a few possibilities.

Some women have headaches, dizziness, or insomnia during the menopause. The most potentially troublesome and surely the most talked-about symptom is the vasomotor changes known as "hot flushes" or "flashes." Again, statistics do not give a clear picture. A woman can report little more than a sudden sensation of warmth, relieved simply by opening a window or removing a jacket, as a "hot flush." Full-blown hot flushes, on the other hand, can be extremely persistent and unpleasant: women wake at night, perspiring profusely; the rapid rise in body temperature, felt mostly in the upper extremities, can be accompanied by an increase in heart rate and followed by a feeling of chill. The experience on the average lasts less than four minutes, but while it's happening, especially during the work day, it can be unpleasant and embarrassing.[4] Women have told me they've had to leave business meetings to put on a fresh blouse because they had perspired so heavily. Lila Nachtigall, M.D., a gynecological endocrinologist, comments that the embarrassment is in itself a reflection of a woman's defensiveness in our culture about the experience of the menopause. When a woman is pregnant and exhibits out-of-the-ordinary behavior such as the food urges—i.e., the wish to eat dill pickles in the middle of the night—it is tolerated as rather quaint and amusing. But not so hot flushes. A woman feels ashamed, wants to hide, and most of all hates the idea that she is revealing her age so concretely.[5] Hot flushes are caused by a complex endocrine process that is only now becoming thoroughly understood. In the normal menstrual cycle hormones from the hypothalmus and the pituitary stimulate the ovarian production of estrogen, which in turn causes the development of a mature follicle containing an egg. When estrogen production drops, the hypothalmus becomes more active and the pituitary responds by producing more than usual amounts of the stimulating hormones in an attempt to increase endocrine output. As a result, the temperature-regulating mechanism is thrown out of balance, and there are "erratic changes in the dilation of the tiny peripheral blood vessels in the skin which are normally responsible for keeping the body temperature constant. A detailed explanation of this process written in readable style is contained in *The Lila Nachtigall Report.*[6]

What can a woman who experiences real discomfort do? Many gynecologists say that a healthy diet and proper exercise have a significant effect on control of hot flushes by keeping up the level of hormone production for as long as possible. Estrogen Replacement Therapy (or ERT) can dramatically control the symptoms, but the use of this hormone is still part of a debate in the medical community: the question that remains unsettled is whether its use significantly increases the risk of developing cancer of the uterus, more particularly of the endometrium. But ERT is potentially very useful to women during and after menopause.

In the early and mid-1960s, ERT was hailed as a fountain of youth. Some doctors predicted that women who used it would avoid most of the normal signs of aging. More conservative practitioners took a "wait and see" attitude until the possible side effects became known. Many menopausal women besieged their gynecologists to put them on estrogen. In the seventies the link between the onset of endometrial cancer and ERT was discovered and women were as afraid to use it as doctors were to suggest it. Epidemiologic studies showing an association of estrogen use and endometrial cancer reported an increase in the incidence of between three to eight times that of the normal population and reflect the high-dose estrogens regimen utilized in the 1960s. This finding declined significantly when women stopped taking the hormone, particularly in the dosages that were being prescribed. There was also some evidence of increase in gall bladder disease and hypertension.[7] The question of the relationship between endometrial and breast cancer has also been raised, but no cause-and-effect association has been established to date.

Many gynecologists now take a middle of the road position about ERT, since the risks of using hormones are more scientifically understood. It is still the most effective therapy for the control of intolerable hot flushes. Doctors now recommend much lower doses over briefer periods of time and advise its use only in conjunction with a second hormone, progesterone, which prevents the buildup of endometrial cells in the uterus.

The negative aspect of this therapy is that for younger women menstrual bleeding can be started again after it is normally stopped. Good practice includes the careful monitoring of estrogen/progesterone use. Many gynecologists advise yearly checkups which include a Pap smear, blood tests, and an in-office biopsy of the endometrium so it can be examined for pre-cancerous cells.

What is the argument in favor of continued low estrogen-plus-progesterone use, even after hot flushes have ceased? Advocates feel that, from a long-range point of view, the *beneficial* effects of estrogen use to avoid some of the more troublesome medical problems of aging outweigh its dangers, particularly if the cancer risk is carefully monitored. ERT is helpful in preventing osteoporosis, which is caused by a progressive, if gradual, loss of calcium. In this disease, bones become thin and brittle and break easily. Easily broken and hard to mend hip joints, for example, occur more frequently in women in their late sixties and seventies. Osteoporosis is observable, too, in the thickening of the upper spine known popularly under the unpleasant label of "widow's hump."

Doctors who favor the use of estrogen to prevent osteoporosis say that broken bones, especially hip joints, which necessitate surgical pinning and long periods of bed rest and convalescence, can cause more medical complications than the carefully-monitored use of estrogen and progesterone.

For women who do not want to use estrogen, gynecologists suggest the taking of calcium tablets, vitamin D, good diet, and exercise as natural precautions against the development of osteoporosis.

The use of estrogen is also recommended by some gynecologists to prevent changes in the genitals of postmenopausal women. A cautionary note is due here, lest we slip back into a description of life after menopause as a deficiency disease or a medical problem. For many, but not all, women, estrogen loss is a slow process. The adrenal gland continues to produce small amounts of the hormone, as do the body's fat cells after menopause.

However, over a long period of time, the drop in the level of this hormone can cause a thinning of the vaginal walls and a decrease in the lubricating secretions from the cervix and vagina; dryness of the vagina can be a cause of painful intercourse. Frequency of sexual arousal and intercourse help prevent the problem. Many women simply use a water-based lubricant like K-Y Jelly, mineral oil, or Nivea oil, or a combination of mineral oil and lanolin to lubricate the vagina. With these lubricants, most women continue to enjoy sex. The use of Vaseline or cosmetic lotions is not recommended.

But estrogen can restore the lining of the vagina to a situation closer to its pre-menopausal state. It can be taken orally or used vaginally in cream form. If the latter method is used, it is important to be aware that estrogen is still absorbed into the blood stream. Again, one must keep a time perspective in view: many of these problems are those of older women and do not occur in the fifties or early sixties. For all women, frequency of sexual activity is a great preventive, whether via intercourse or, if there is no sexual partner, by masturbation.

The women with difficulty are the ones the doctors see. Women I speak to who are aroused by their partners before entry of the penis do not complain about lack of lubrication. Even though there may be some thinning of the vaginal walls, it is a normal process and does not get in the way of sexual pleasure. According to Dr. Saul B. Gusberg, Chairman Emeritus of the Department of Obstetrics and Gynecology at the Mount Sinai School of Medicine of the City University of New York:

> . . . a minority of women have severe hot flushes . . . The same holds true for vaginal atrophy. After all, a great many women have vaginal thinning without complaint . . . The average woman who has had children has . . . no discomfort during sexual relations.[8]

Dr. Gusberg goes on to add that much less estrogen is required to prevent thinning of the vaginal walls than for the production of menses. So even with lowered estrogen production a woman can be without vaginal thinning—and without sexual problems. Statistical information on this subject is provided in the *Starr-Weiner Report* about sex after sixty. Of more than three hundred women between sixty and ninety-one (277 aged 60 to 69, 177 between 70 and 79, and 36 between 80 and 91), only eleven percent reported pain or discomfort during intercourse, with another 5.3% reporting pain "occasionally."[9] Of this number, we are not told how many women used lubricants, or to what degree they were sexually aroused by their partners.

Women who are interested in Estrogen Replacement Therapy should know it must never be taken by anyone who has had breast cancer or a family history of the disease. Nor should it be taken if there is a diagnosis of cancer of the uterus. There are a number of other medical problems that make doctors suggest frequent monitoring of estrogen use: hypertension, diabetes, epilepsy, migraine headaches, obesity, fibroids, a history of heart disease, stroke, or thrombophlebitis.

Women want to know if ERT keeps them "young." It does delay the aging process, in terms of muscle tone, elasticity of the skin, and thickness of the hair. But not forever. And so does good diet and exercise—without any of the risks.

Women approaching the menopause worry a great deal about its physical symptoms, its effect on their bodies, and their sexuality. Many worry even more about what it will mean to them on an emotional level. Menopause and depression were once so inexorably linked in the minds of women, and in medical minds as well, that menopausal depression seemed almost as inevitable as middle age itself. In the past, any woman who had ever felt depressed anticipated that once she had arrived at this period of her life depression and shock therapy lay in wait.

Changing hormonal balance at the time of the menopause does, in fact, have an effect on the emotions. There is a connection between estrogen level and mood; as, for example, in normal post-partum depression (even if transient in women who look forward to their babies), which is caused by the sudden drop in estrogen secretion. During the menopause the rapid decline in estrogen level experienced by *some* women can trigger feelings of depression. But by no means can all the blame for depression at this time be put on biological factors.

Recent research on emotional responses to the menopause reveals that social factors play a large role in depression that occurs during the menopause. Women who have invested heavily in their roles as mothers are more likely to be depressed. There is a natural corollary: women with interests, education, or professions are less apt to become upset after menopause. Research indicates that the reason for this is that they have more options in their lives. By the same token, studies show that women with poor self-esteem and few life satisfactions have more difficulties. It would seem that what a woman does or does not do with herself in this period is a significant source of her mood rather than the old equation that lowered mood is the inevitable response to an exclusively biological process.

Myrna M. Weissman, PhD., Professor of Psychiatry and Epidemiology at the Yale University School of Medicine, reviewed epidemiological and clinical studies and found no increase in the rate of depression in the menopausal years. Depression was found more frequently in women under age thirty-five. No distinct symptom picture was discovered to distinguish menopausal depressions from those that occur before and after this period. Dr. Weissman showed that real-life pressures, not simply the physiology of the menopausal process, are precipitants of depression, as they are before and after this time of life.[10]

As a post-menopausal woman I feel that a personal note is in order. Because of the popular folklore, I recall that my friends and I did indeed worry that we would become depressed during the menopause. Now I would never deny the validity of any statement which says that the arrival of the climacterium is an important psychological event for a woman. It is my experience that, even if she has had as many children as she wants, the end of a woman's menses does remind her of the end of fertility and the passage of time. But the *rite de passage* through the menopause has been, for all the women I have known both personally and professionally, remarkably undramatic. It is true that over time one has to adapt to bodily changes, but there is no dramatic and sudden decline into androgyny heralded by the cessation of the menses. It is *this* myth that is the most destructive to women's self-esteem, that telescopes the physical changes from fifty to eighty. Reaching the menopause does not automatically turn a woman into a hag even though popular culture seems to transmit this message. And never can I repeat too often that hags are disturbed, chronically unhappy women or mythical creatures, not the eighty-year-olds I know!

For centuries people believed that mental illness in a female was caused by disturbances in her uterus, and we are still struggling against the myth that a woman's femininity, ergo, her sexuality, is tied to her reproductive organs. Dr. Helene Deutsch, in the mid-1940s, wrote about the effect of the menopause:

> In this phase a woman loses all she received during puberty . . . the beauty-creating activity of the inner glandular secretions declines and the

secondary sex characteristics are affected by the gradual loss of femininity.[11]

Dr. Deutsch was a brilliant woman psychiatrist whom I heard give a fascinating lecture when she was well into her eighties. According to her theory, the idea of the inevitable connection of glands and femininity is what is destructive to women. It says nothing about a woman's interest in sex, her enjoyment of it, or her capacity for sexual arousal. So we must address the questions: What *is* the effect of the menopause on a woman's sex drive and on her sexual performance? and, Is desire tied inevitably to the level of endocrine secretion and—above all—to a woman's ability to love?

For answers I turn to Dr. Helen Singer Kaplan, who has written extensively about sexuality. In our culture, according to Dr. Kaplan, a graph of women's sexual responses would show that they peak in the late thirties and early forties. This level can be maintained into the sixties. Following the menopause, many women show an increased desire for sex.[12] Patricia Schreiner-Engel, a sex therapist at Mount Sinai Hospital in New York, believes that the increase in sexual desire after menopause is due, on a purely biological level, to the greater effect of the androgens secreted by the adrenal cortex after the decline in estrogen level.[13] But psychological and social factors also play important roles in relation to the sexual interest of the post-menopausal woman. Many women have told me their sex lives have gotten better after the menopause. They say they feel freer when the fear of pregnancy is gone. Women who used an I.U.D. or were on the pill are no longer concerned about the possibility of negative side effects or of physical complications. In my clinical practice women often tell me that with the children out of the house, they're less tired in the evening and feel less inhibited:

they don't have to worry about nudity, or whether the doors are closed for love-making.

It's important for middle-aged women to know there is a wide range of "normal" sexual behavior. The desire for sex fluctuates from day to day in a single individual, related as it is to fatigue, to mood, to the response of a partner. But women remain capable of multiple orgasms; some say they happen more easily as they mature.

Life can be rewarding for many women in middle age. Today they may find a lot of new challenges outside the front door, and that's obviously good for self-esteem. And self-esteem is good for sex.

Of course, we don't know how general the current trend will become with men and women marrying later and delaying parenthood until the late thirties and even into the early forties. These couples are parents of young children in midlife. "Young-middle-aged" friends say that having kids in kindergarden and grade school gives them a different attitude toward middle age. They're perhaps close to fifty and just starting to teach children how to swim and ride bikes, activities their parents were involved in when they were almost twenty years younger. I predict that this change will have a positive effect on women's attitudes about themselves and their sexuality as they reach the menopause.

All the experts agree that if a woman has established a sexual pattern of freedom, pleasure, and frequency of intercourse it tends to be maintained throughout the years. Clearly, a woman's interest in sex does not follow the course of estrogen production!

But, just as clearly, our culture's attitude toward the sexuality of middle-aged women deeply influences a woman's expectations of how her sexual signals will be received by men, and, in turn, her self-confidence and her behavior.

Women alone always say, "But what do you do when you outnumber men and they choose from a very large pool of eligible females, so many of them much younger?" Life is most difficult at times of transition. Past studies show that in cultures where the rules of behavior are set, many women feel safe, and in many instances, more contented, if they look forward to the role of matriarch. But that is changing. Life is more of a challenge in a world like ours, where many events and experiences are in flux, including the image of the asexual older woman.

One way to alter her image is by confronting the myths that persist. One of them is that older men are more interested in sex than older women.[14] In reality, what men are more concerned about is whether their potency remains constant. Because of the differences between the sexuality of men and women, women do not need to express their needs in the number of times they have intercourse. Their sexuality includes the loving, touching, holding, and caressing components of sex. Penetration is the ultimate beauty and pleasure of this joining.

Buck Brown made his reputation in *Playboy* by doing countless cartoons of inappropriate and voracious old hags who chased every man who came down the pike and sent him scurrying in fear and horror. Only once did he draw a cartoon celebrating a woman's pleasure in sex over a lifetime.

In this instance, an usher is approaching the old woman in a movie theater as a scene of sexual intercourse appears, larger than life, on the screen. The usher is saying, "Madam, on behalf of the other patrons, I must ask you to stop cheering."[15]

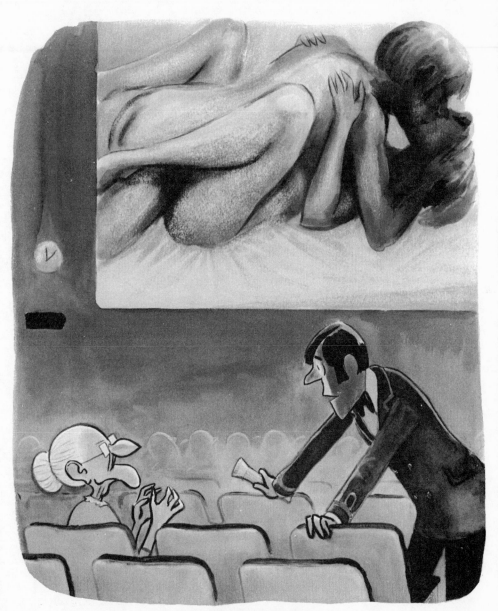

*Madam, on behalf of the other patrons, I must
ask you to stop cheering.*

The Middle-Aged Man: Realities

A forty-eight-year-old man, successful in his private and public life, called me when he heard I was writing this book to say, rather plaintively, "Tell them how hard it is for us, too!" Agreed: It is *not* easy for men, even with the obvious advantages granted by images of power and sustained sexual attractiveness, to become middle-aged in America. I will speak of men who respond to the prospect of aging with denial accompanied by a relentless pursuit of "unchange," personified by exaggerated diet, hyperexercise and the relentless pursuit of young women. They are the Jack Kennedys and the John De Loreans of our culture. But for all the press such men get, for most men, such famous figures are fantasy creatures. Yet many men are acutely affected by midlife awareness of time and transience. Still, some do move through middle age with their sense of masculinity intact. Theirs is usually a quieter and more private experience. There is a growing public awareness of their voices.

Among men over forty artistically examining

midlife crisis, David Rabe's voice is one of the most passionate. His play, "Hurlyburly," for example, used Hollywood as a metaphor for the condition of men at midlife who follow the unexamined life and the external goals of the culture. The men who people this world lead "defoliated" lives, their marriages and careers in shambles, consuming time with drugs, alcohol, and "unrelated" sex.

It is significant, therefore, that *The New York Times* considers the self-examination some men are engaged in newsworthy enough to devote a weekly column in its Sunday Magazine to articles "About Men." John Kenneth Galbraith is among the writers represented by his article on "Corporate Man." David Rabe's men have not made it in the world of power. Galbraith goes beyond Rabe's point of view by commenting on the price men who *do* make it pay. He speaks of how much a man's life is taken over by his job: his very considerable income will be earned at the expense of time spent with family, friends or in recreation; he is never "off duty," is not free to express any public differences with his organization, and even remains relatively anonymous. With few exceptions, we do not, he points out, recognize current captains of industry as once we knew the Rockefellers, Mellons, Carnegies, and Fords. Perhaps the greatest price paid by these men, he writes, is their sacrifice of the internal, the creative dimension of life:

> None, with only the most eccentric exceptions, will ever make any personal contribution in music, painting, the theater, film, writing, serious learning or . . . politics. Once a good income was thought to allow of such diversions; that was its purpose . . . . He wonders if it is worthwhile to give up so much . . . of one's only certain life.[1]

Paul Theroux, unlike Galbraith's corporate man, rejected the conventional route and chose the internal life of a writer. From the perspective of his own middle age, he speaks about how hard it was for him to grow up following this path because becoming a writer was not an ambition that "would make boys into straight arrows." He writes:

> The seal of masculinity was only given to those men who were writers plus lion hunters, heavy drinkers or womanizers, the Ernest Hemingways, James Joneses and Normal Mailers. In America, "to be a man" means to be stupid, be unfeeling, obedient and soldierly and stop thinking . . . the terrible ambition of manliness . . . a hideous and crippling lie . . . (which) connives at superiority . . . (is) emotionally damaging and socially harmful . . . the quest for manliness (is) essentially right wing, puritanical, cowardly, neurotic and fueled largely by a fear of women . . . It is hard to imagine any concept of manliness that does not belittle women . . . (And) there is no book hater like a Little League coach.[2]

I agree that there is a concept of manliness that is puritanical in the sense of the denial required by the Army or the discipline and training for the Olympics. My focus has been on the opposite trend: the public pronouncement of puritanism, as in ritual attendance at church and promotion of school prayer, and men's private pursuit of attractive women as an exercise in power and a reassurance of manhood.

The *Times* essays allowing men to express their feelings about the narrowness of our image of masculinity has even included the public "confession" of Phil Gailey of its Washington Bureau, who acknowledged his guilty secret: that he is a "nonsports fan." He is fighting the assumption that he must be measured by "a jock mentality" and "that . . . any male with an aversion to sports must be seriously flawed."[3]

These are the published voices of men rejecting the

macho view of masculinity, which has been such a significant force in creating a crisis for men at midlife. The crisis
is the greatest among these men when they must find
something to take the place of "a life devoted to the
maintenance of an image."⁴ If one listens to the private
voices of men, as I have, one begins to see that behind the
public clichés which tell men that this machismo attitude
is the only way to be are middle-aged men with a very
different "feel." Many of the men to whom I have spoken
place a very high priority on their sense of themselves as
family men.

Charlie G. is such a man. He is tall, slim, with an
insouciant air and boyish good looks. Now in his late
forties, he works hard, is successful—and attractive to
women. I asked him how he'd feel if he were divorced from
his wife and his houseful of three teenage boys, how he'd
feel if he were single and dating again.

He said he couldn't even contemplate such a
thought. "I've lived through and beyond that stage in my
life. I am a middle-aged man who has just given a birthday
party for my ninety-year-old father; I am *where* I am in life!
What's more, I'd be overcome with horror at the idea my
family could be taken away from me."

I spent several evenings talking to John S. who *has*
lost his family. He has two daughters and two sons at
home and has been separated from them for four years.
He has had several relationships with other women, but, at
fifty-three, feels a tremendous need to return to his wife
and family. He related:

> I want the whole thing back. I want my home, my
> role as husband and father. I feel my identity has
> been shaken. I've lost my neighbors, my com-
> munity. My life was torn apart—like a film that
> breaks in the middle of a movie. I want the rest of
> the experience. I want to be home during the

holidays, and when the kids choose their col-
leges, and when they get engaged and plan their
weddings. Yes, and I want to be there when the
grandchildren come. I don't *want* a new family. I
have one. I want to finish what I started. I feel
sad, rootless, "out of synch" with life.

The experiences of men like John S. are echoed in
the statistics of many long-range studies. Men, whether
divorced or widowed, do not do well on their own. In a
twelve-year survey of more than four thousand widows
and widowers, a Johns Hopkins University study showed
that the loss of a partner had a much more devastating
effect on men than on women. "Widowed men between the
ages of fifty-five and sixty-five, who represented more than
one-fourth of the people in the study, had a mortality rate
sixty percent higher than that of married men of the same
age." The study noted that women seem to be more
adaptable; men have stronger dependency needs which
require that someone look after them.[4] The same findings
apply to men who are divorced and living alone.[5]

Although men may enjoy, and the culture encourages, fantasies about the pleasures of deserting wives
for the pursuit of young women ("What do you do with a
wife of forty? Take her to the bank and trade her for two
twenties."), there are single middle-aged men who express
little excitement about the dating game in general and the
squiring of young women in particular. It is hard for a man
in his fifties to relate in casual conversation what makes
him anxious about a woman twenty years his junior. But in
a clinical situation, he feels free to express his concern
about whether or not he can satisfy a young woman's
sexual needs, whether her appetite will outpace his.

In social situations and in brief interviews one is
more likely to hear superficial complaints, such as a man's

reluctance to get all dressed up and start all over again. "The effort to become acquainted with a stranger can be a real drag," Peter Y. told me. "Silences feel awkward; conversation gets strained." Peter, in his forties, has been divorced for a year now. "After a roll in the hay, I don't have much to say to a kid in her twenties. I know it massages my ego to be seen with a beautiful youngster. But I want to spend time with people with whom I share a past, whose language and associations are closer to mine."

Peter's thoughts are echoed in a cartoon by Jules Feiffer. Two middle-aged men, "Bernard and Huey," talk while they are out jogging.

> *"I can't go out with any more young women. I don't understand them."*
> *"It's like a foreign country, man. You gotta interpret."*
> *"You want to talk hep? You translate into punk."*
> *"You want to talk Coltrane? You talk Talking Heads."*
> *"You want to talk books? Forget it. They don't read. So talk TV. Talk movies."*
> *"Talk nutrition. Talk drugs. Talk exercise."*
> *"Or don't talk. Just make a lot of agreeable sounds. 'Hey!' 'O.K.' 'Right!' 'Man!' "*
> *"It's too lonely for me living like that, Huey. . . ."*[6]

Or, as one man put it, "I get tired of explaining who Herman Goering was!"

This is not to say that there aren't well-informed and interesting women who come into young woman/middle-aged man relationships, but even with love, sex, and a commonality of interests, new problems take the place of old ones. The question of children is one. For men who have raised families of their own, it is hard to start over again some twenty-odd years later. I spoke to Robert S., divorced, fifty-six, the father of three grown children, who has been talking of marriage with Susan G., a never-married woman in her thirties. He said:

> I don't want a new family and I've been honest with Susan about this from the beginning. I don't think it's a rationalization to say I don't even think it would be fair to a child to have it grow up with an aged father at best, or none at all. It's not necessary for me to have children to prove I'm still a virile guy. I doubt that I'd even be a *good* father at my age. It may be very selfish of me in terms of Susan's needs. It's a hard choice for both of us. But if she decides she really must have children, she may have to find a man closer to her own age.

And there is Jerry S., a middle-aged man who *had* a baby in his second marriage at fifty. When he talks about his thirty-year-old wife, his eyes light up. They look quite pleased with each other when I see them together. But when he speaks of his new "life," his expression changes. He is commuting again to a house in the suburbs, and has given up the great pleasure he had in travelling every chance he had. He is beginning to complain about the difference in his wife's and his own scenarios for marriage.

Some of the men I have been quoting, Charlie G., John S., Peter Y., and Robert S., appear to have a conscious feeling about time—that life is lived in stages—in Erik Erikson's sense of the tasks appropriate to a stage of development, which, when completed, are replaced by new ones.[7] These are the men who are most likely to choose mature women when they remarry. Philip J. is such a man. He is living his own definition of middle-aged masculinity. Phil is a bright, highly competitive man who has had considerable financial success. He loves to hunt, to fish, and to ski. His first wife died after a long illness, leaving him with two teenaged children. He is in his mid-forties and has just remarried after six years as a bachelor. He said:

> I was very conscious of age during those years alone. I dated a lot and even lived for a while with a girl in her mid-twenties. I felt self-conscious with her. Then she began to bore me. I got very tired of dating. I knew I wanted to find a woman of my own generation, one who shared my background. My new wife is about five years younger than I am. I got so I began to wonder if *that* was too young! But I needed a person whose mind turned me on too. I hear men my age depreciating mature women, but after that big half hour in bed, I want a woman I feel good talking to, spending an evening with. I see all these couples sitting silently, looking bored at restaurants. That's not for me!
>
> I plan to adopt her four-year-old youngster. We've talked it over and decided not to have more children, so I plan to get a vasectomy. I believe men have equal responsibility for birth control and I don't think it's good for Nina to stay on the pill.
>
> I love the challenge of what I do, but I'm a little ashamed of how easy it is for me to make money. I've put in enough twelve- and fourteen-hour days. I want a new challenge, one that is more socially meaningful. This fall I'm going to start taking a few courses at night. By the time I'm fifty, I hope to have a Ph.D. in history. I like young adults, I get along well with them . . . I'd like to teach. . . .

I do not mean to romanticize this man. I know him well enough to be aware of some of his shortcomings. But he is looking forward to the second half of his life with a positive image of himself as a man of middle age. The basic sense of masculinity he emanates is maintained with appreciation for, and not at the expense of, women of his generation.

There is another widespread belief in our culture that seems close to mythic proportions: that friendships between men and women are hard to come by, and difficult, if not impossible to maintain. We seem to accept the hypothesis that men and women are essentially more comfortable in their own gender groups. The fact that this idea has not been challenged is an important element in the isolation of women. It contributes to the feeling of women alone that they are condemned to live in a single-sex society, that they have indeed become "No Man's Land." The isolation contributes significantly to their loss of self-esteem.

Writers of both sexes reflect this belief in the permanent alienation between the sexes. To quote Letty Cottin Pogrebin, "True friendship is rare between women and men because sex separation is so rigorously ingrained during childhood. Most parents rear male and female children as though preparing them to live in two different worlds. . . ."[8] And Paul Theroux on the upbringing of boys: "The youth who is subverted, as most are, into believing in the masculine ideal is effectively separated from women—it is the most savage tribal logic—spends the rest of his life finding women a riddle and a nuisance."[9]

I once asked a hypermasculine middle-aged man if he had any friendships of a platonic nature with women. "I simply would find it impossible," he replied, "not to go to bed with any woman I got close to." His reply is in contrast to that of a man of the same generation who had been making sexual overtures to a married friend of mine. When she told him she was not interested, he paused, smiled at her, and then said, "Good! Now we can be friends!" Both men were behaving in a manner they had been programmed to believe was required of them. The second man, however, had the grace, the flexibility, and, who knows, perhaps even a sense of relief, that he had been given permission to go beyond "the program."

It's not that women and men do not want to be friends. Until recently, however, most people simply didn't know how to go about it. In a world dominated by a masculine ethos, women have tried to adapt to a man's definition of how to be together by riding on the backs of motorcycles and watching professional football on television. For women to do otherwise was not feminine; for men to consider whether or not women were enjoying themselves was not manly enough.

In the past twenty years or so mores have been changing in ways that are making friendships between the sexes a more natural and normal part of life. Not only are friendships developing between people of the same age, whether over or under forty, but they are growing between men and women of different generations. Friendships grow out of shared experiences, and from the trust that grows from familiarity.

Not only are many parents trying to bring up their children differently, but life itself, whether represented by co-education and the living arrangements on college campuses, or the increased entry of women into professions and the workplace is making trust and familiarity easier to establish. Talking to a number of men who have grown up under these new conditions, men now in their forties, I learned that they enjoyed and valued friendships with women, particularly those they had gotten to know through working associations. They liked having women on a colleague basis and were aware that women brought something new and as yet hard to define to their business and professional experience.

They were fully aware of the sexual tension that existed in many of these relationships, but felt it could be enjoyed, controlled, and sublimated in the challenges and excitement of the work itself. They were aware, too, of setting certain limits for themselves that were often quite arbitrary. Yes, they had to go on trips together, for example, but back in the city they avoided having dinners to discuss business unless it was with a group of people. They were fully aware of office romances, but if their marriage had meaning and they wanted to protect it, then they simply avoided being conquistadors. As one man put it, "My male friends and I really don't even get involved in a lot of salacious talk about women. It really gets boring, seems immature and irrelevant." Sometimes the friendships expand to include spouses, but even when they do, the special history the two share make them feel they have a special bond.

Men in their late fifties, who grew up a generation before the one I have been discussing, have always had important friendships with women. How had they transcended the behavior of many of their peers?

George C., a business man, well-married, and the father of three, speaks for them:

> I always found the "macho" thing limiting. I never wanted to be tyrannized by any stereotyped expectations. I have women friends, some of whom are friends of my wife as well, and some who are not. Their ages vary: older—younger. They are people I find interesting. It's really as simple as that. I know that growing up as the son of an immigrant, made me feel like an outsider. Although I was bright enough to get scholarships to good schools and colleges, I never "belonged" socially. That's kept things fluid and open for me. It's an advantage now. I think I spend a lot of time detaching myself from things other people would have me believe are important.

Life is so chaotic and without essential meaning. If you can create some order and purpose for yourself in the face of all this—and with full awareness of how temporary it is—then you realize how irrevelant gender becomes in making friends. To avoid women is to cut yourself off from half the people in the world.

Since so many of the myths about the sexual undesirability of mature women are based on the projection of men's anxiety about aging and sexual performance onto women, in writing about men it is inevitable that we look at the facts about the sexuality of men after forty. There are normal expectable changes over the life cycle, but men are capable of erection, ejaculation, and impregnation of a woman well into their eighties. Men reach the height of their potential in their late teens, which is followed by a gradual decline. Women, on the other hand, slowly increase their sexuality into their thirties and early forties. The differences between the sex curve in the two sexes are not fully understood on either a hormonal or physiological basis. While these differences are a source of stress in the sexual adaptation of men and women, the facts are such an important antidote to the negative fantasy that the sexual problem of mature men is the lack of sexuality of mature women.

Any discussion of normal sexual changes in men must be prefaced with the statement, that, as with women, there are great differences among men in the strength of their innate sexual drive. Some men (and women) on the lower end of this scale may even give up sex altogether relatively early in life. Others, where the psychological need to maintain an image of virility is great, may need to deny that change is even possible. It is because sexual potential is at its height in adolescence, however, that the latter get stuck in the adolescent model of sexual perform-ance.

It is a model Bernie Zilbergeld describes in his book on *Male Sexuality,* (a book that many sex therapists recommend to their patients):

> In its obsession with sex, the functioning of the penis and the uncontrolled nature of sex, adoles-cent sexuality is the closest most men will ever get to fantasyland sexuality. Our first experience of adult sexuality is therefore similar to the domi-nant model in our culture that is held up as a standard for the rest of our lives. [10]

In one experiment, R. L. Solnick presented a short erotic movie to two groups of men: one group nineteen- to thirty-year-olds; the other forty-eight to sixty-five. He found that the response, measured in rate of arousal to full erection ("maximal penile erection") was six times more rapid in the younger group. The changes, he reports, although gradual, appear to accelerate around age fifty. [11]

Dr. William Masters and Virginia Johnson were among the pioneers who studied normal sexual changes in men. Unlike the immediate response of a young man, who may become erect at the very thought of a woman, an older man may need direct physical stimulation. Erections are not as full and as firm as they were. It takes longer for men to achieve orgasm. Mature men do not feel the same need to have an orgasm every time they have intercourse as they did as young men. By and large, they do not feel the need to have sex as frequently.

Other changes occur over time. There is a reduc-tion in the amount of the ejaculate and increase in the period of intromission, the amount of time required to achieve another erection after experiencing orgasm, and a gradual decrease in sperm count. None of these changes need in any way interfere with sexual pleasure or potency. They do, however, require a secure sense of self on the part of men, because, if normal change appears as decline, the anxiety that ensues can interfere with performance. Sex therapists tell me that *functional* impotence is the chief complaint that brings middle-aged men to their offices. Treatment can include disabusing them of some long-cherished myths. Three of them are:

1. Every sexual contact with a woman must lead to intercourse.
2. Occasional inability to achieve or maintain an erection is the beginning of the end. (There are many reasons why this may occur, none of them having any real significance as a measure of potency. There are possible preoccupations with work problems, fatigue, anger, minor illness or depression, to name but a few potential causes.) One should never underestimate how frightening such occurrences may be to men, however. Some have even abandoned sex altogether after a few such happenings.
3. Many men feel the need to take charge of sex. The need to ask for more activity, more physical stimulation on the part of the partner, can also be experienced as a loss of masculinity.

Some of the sexual changes in men are misunderstood by women. They may feel, for example, that the longer time a man needs to become aroused reflects a decline in their own attractiveness. Couples who cannot tell each other what is going on—and it may be especially hard for some men to recognize, much less acknowledge any change—begin to feel defensive. Unfortunately, women have tended to blame themselves. And men find this is an easy out—as the first half of this book has already shown. Normal changes in sexual responses, then, can lead to crises within a relationship. When a man says, "She just doesn't turn me on anymore," the attempt at rejuvenation with another woman follows.

Above and beyond the emotional responses of men, there are physical problems (and the treatment involved in dealing with them) that can lead to sexual dysfunction. Certain neurological disorders, diabetes, blockages of small arteries to the penis (so-called arterial occlusions) that interfere with penile blood flow, may cause potency disturbances. The prostate gland, which is located just below the bladder, has, as its function, the production of semen, which carries sperm into the ejaculate. After forty, the prostate normally begins a gradual growth. Roughly, after the age of fifty, enlargement of the prostate may begin to interfere with the ease of ejaculation.[12]

Endocrine problems can have sexual consequences. In the past few years research on the chemistry of hormonal abnormalities in men has made a significant contribution to an understanding and reversal of the drop in testosterone levels in some men, with a consequent restoration of potency.

The effects of alcoholism on potency are well known; but the list of drug-related responses that create impotence is a long one, whether the drug taking is self-induced, as with cocaine and heroin, or prescribed for the treatment of high blood pressure, heart disease, or gastrointestinal disturbances, as well as some of the psychoactive drugs which are prescribed for emotional problems. These substances can lead to a decrease in libido (sex drive) in both men and women, an interference with erection and ejaculation in men, or arousal and orgasm in women. Each personal situation is unique, depending on the amount of medication prescribed and the individual's response. Reaction to problems induced by medications should be discussed with physicians, because alterations in dosage or a change of medication often can eliminate the problem.[13]

There are numerous disturbances in potency that may befall the middle-aged man. Moreover, a man's self-image and self-esteem are intimately tied to his sexual performance. It is inevitable, therefore, that actual sexual changes have a strong potential effect on men's lives—and their consequences have a large effect on the lives of the women who share them.

Change is gradual, and although there is a difference between forty and sixty, or fifty and seventy, for healthy men, there is no sudden awareness of change in performance. And individual differences are crucial: one man of seventy may perform like a fifty-year-old and vice versa. The general rule for sexuality over time is that men and women who are highly endowed with libido and have an active sex life when young will continue to be active.

There is another positive note. Just as the menopause does not signal a headlong rush into decrepitude for women, but, on the contrary, can usher in a time of greater freedom and spontaneity, so, too, can life after youth be a time of expanded pleasure for men. *Realistically*, pressures to perform like a youngster should be gone, while the skill and assurance acquired by experience gives self-confidence . . . And this is very attractive to women!

The Narcissistic Middle-Aged Man: Trading in Old Wives for New

I love my wife, but oh you kid!

Song refrain, Jimmy Lucas, 1909

Middle-aged men may seem mature and knowledgeable and all the rest of it, but when they have to have girl-friends of your and Jenny's age, they're not. Deep down they're still frustrated adolescents. Running scared. They're in a panic.

John Fowles, *Daniel Martin*

    I look for good news about middle-aged women wherever I can find it. So I was happy to hear recently that the new generation of stand-up comics is no longer telling anti-wife jokes. My pleasure was short-lived, however. I

turned on a sit-com not long afterwards just as one character was asking another, "That picture in your wallet—Is it
of your wife or your dog?" This is not just low comedy: it is
a reflection of the myths about older women that still
permeate the culture. Such jokes have as noxious an
influence as the toxic emissions we breathe every day.
Their effect on the self-image of mid-life and older women
is obvious. Less clear are the consequences of the myths
on the lives of middle-aged men.

Society sings a siren song to mature men. It impor-
tunes them to get involved in the "action" with young
women. Some men not only *hear* the song, but follow its
call—and strange things sometimes happen to them as a
result.

The Sirens who lured Odysseus and his men with
their seductive singing were sometimes thought to be
souls of the dead who were envious of the living. There
were two of them, we are told. When I think of the sirens
who entice middle-aged men I only think of one of them as
female. This chapter is not about her—the young woman
who envies the social and economic security of mature
wives and wants them for herself. It is not about the young
woman whose emotional needs make her turn to much
older men. But it is about the other siren, a personification
of the culture itself. Its song makes some men feel that the
leap into the sea involved in the avoidance of mature
women and the pursuit of a much younger one is a wholly
enviable piece of business.

Here are some of the words that go with the music:

> *A fiftyish newscaster was reporting the success-*
> *ful surgery on Michael De Bakey for a bleeding*
> *ulcer in November 1984. Dr. De Bakey, the re-*
> *nowned heart specialist, was then seventy-six.*
> *His doctor reported he was doing beautifully.*
> *"He must be doing something right," said the*

*newscaster in a tone of profound admiration.
"He has a seven-year-old son!"*

*Or a TV ad for a diet drink: A middle-aged man is
talking to a colleague at a picnic. A slim young-
looking woman comes up to him. The other
man, with obvious envy and disbelief:"—your
wife?"*

Not only does the culture importune middle-aged
men to emulate models, it *sanctions* such behavior. Men
feel "entitled." From a mature woman's point of view, that
is a strange and unfamiliar idea, but one worth looking
into. Psychiatrist Robert Coles was the person who first got
me thinking about the notion of entitlement. One of his
many interesting books was about the lives of black students who first integrated the schools and universities of

"And they told me it would be lonely at the top!"

the South in the 1960s. He then began to examine differences in the expectations of the blacks from their white middle-class contemporaries. The essential difference in attitude, he discovered, was that the white students felt *entitled* to higher education. This expectation colored their feelings about themselves and profoundly affected their behavior.[2] Many middle-aged men feel this sense of entitlement vis-a-vis women. And they act accordingly. Sally, a fifty-year-old woman recently and painfully divorced after her husband left her for a woman who is younger than their two daughters, said:

> I was at a dinner party at M's house. You know he recently married. His new wife is fifteen years his junior. One of the guests asked him how he had chosen her.
> "I thought it out carefully and deliberately," he said. "First, I decided not to date any of the women who were friends after my wife died. I thought it might be too close."
> You know, I was the only single woman in that room. M. looked at me and said, "Sally, this is going to hurt you—but I also decided not to date a divorced woman, or a woman my own age."

Entitlement. It allows a man to be both judge and jury and foreclose on other human beings. It did not even occur to M., it seems, to spare Sally, who was supposed to be his friend and, at the very least, a guest in his home.

A man's sense of entitlement is rooted in centuries of history. We have but to think of a Turkish caliph and his harem, or a Persian prince giving a hunting companion the gift of a virgin after a successful day in the field. I wonder if this is any different from the attitude H.G. Wells expressed in writing of his love and trust of his wife: "But my other 'love affairs' had much the same place in my life that fly-fishing or golfing has in the life of many busy men."[3] I don't believe Wells considered this attitude a cynical one. A long tradition treats women as objects, so it is not surprising how baffled and frustrated a single middle-aged woman can feel.

Attitudes like these are so deeply entrenched that they evoke a minimum of guilt. So it is not unusual for a married man in his fifties to tell me the success story of a middle-aged mutual acquaintance:

> Jack has given up his business for a job in public administration. Recently, after being appointed to a large state commission, he hired a photographer to follow him around to get his picture in the newspapers and, said my informant with a smile of approbation, found himself a young wife!

Entitlement. Jack's—to the creation of a public image that is complemented by a young companion.

The picture is not that simple, however. With the voice of the culture so insistent, one can suspect that there is more than one reason for the volume of the sound. Germaine Greer offered an additional insight into why the masculine chorus eggs men on like cheerleaders at a football game. She believes that in a society obsessed with sexual performance, the players must constantly be encouraged by the crowd lest their interest flag.[4] Greer is on the right track. I believe we are dealing with a collective fear of loss of masculinity that would be implicit in any acknowledgment of a diminution of sexual interest. Part of the public relations campaign that promotes sex with young women must be to reassure middle-aged men: Not only must they experience no lessening of sexual desire, but no loss of attractiveness to women. This hypothesis is illustrated by a June 1978 *Playboy* interview with George Burns at eighty-two. The interviewer pushed the *Playboy* "party line"—that well-known older men loved to pursue and were highly successful with young women. He insisted that Burns was being chased by young women who found him irresistible—that he must have a lot of "revealing stories" to tell.

> Burns wasn't buying: "Young women like me because I take them out to dinner and let them do their homework."
> The interviewer, not to be put off, asked: "Is it true you have sex four times a week?"
> Burns (now tired of the game) answered: "Four times a night, maybe, but not four times a week! Are you a sex maniac or something? Ask me something else!"

When we switch the camera back to women in the second half of life, we can readily see the consequences for their lives when men get involved with younger women. Here are two vignettes that recently came my way:

> Jean Bishop, mother of three, was widowed at forty-two. Her husband left her with very little money. She was lacking in work skills, but managed to get hired as a teacher's aide. A few years later, she met and fell in love with Charlie, a man her age, whose wife was chronically ill. Although he felt a sense of responsibility for his wife and would not leave her, he declared a passionate commitment to Jean. When his wife died, Jean, at his suggestion, moved to his home town so they could be together. She still maintained a separate apartment where she lived with her teenage daughter. When the girl went off to college, she felt there were no more obstacles. But now, in their fifties, when both were available, Charlie began to hesitate. Jean was confused and frightened. One morning, she called Charlie's house and a woman answered the phone. The woman, she later learned, was thirty-five years old.

Sarah, at forty-six, works in a secretarial pool, a job she has held since her only child started school. Her husband is employed by a moving company. Even though they managed quite well financially, it has been a struggle to put money aside for their son's college education.

Jim hated reaching fifty. Soon after his birthday he began looking in the mirror a lot and complaining that none of the men in his family had ever lost his hair. He seemed bored by all the activities he had once enjoyed with his family and friends. He was clinically depressed, but vehemently denied it. Sarah felt the first wind of trouble when notices for non-payment of rent began arriving in the mail. Then Jim started coming home from work late. Sarah, like Jean Bishop, was confused. It was like writing on water, she told me, to try to talk to him.

Here the story takes a familiar turn. One day when she was putting her husband's shirts away, she discovered a pile of letters from a woman. The postmarks were recent. With them was a large number of unpaid bills.

At the moment, their marriage is at a stand-off. Their adolescent son, normally an ebullient boy, has become very quiet. The woman is twenty-six years old.

The sirens use the words of the myths about older women to entice men to trade in older women for younger ones. As tempting as the songs may sound, they are merely seductive noises, to be listened to or ignored. They are ignored by those men who are able to deal with the changes that confront them in middle age.

In previous chapters I explored the anxiety men feel when faced with the tasks of aging; their concerns about a future that presents them with an inevitable decline in power; their reliance on sexuality as a confirmation of masculinity; and of their fears of passivity and dependency. I analyzed the psychological meaning of the myths attached to older women. Then I proposed that, for men who cannot deal with their anxieties in middle age, the myths once more become emotionally charged and are often used as a rationalization to move away from women who are their peers.

All men, after all, face the same demands in midlife. They must deal with the limits of their creativity, their envy of younger men, and, ultimately, with their transience. Psychiatrist Otto Kernberg believes that this awareness of limits is the basis of what is probably the major task of middle life: of dealing with the challenges to a long-term sexual relationship. What is central to this task is whether a person can resist the impulse to test out the limits of his sexual potential outside the relationship rather than dealing with the inevitable conflicts within it.[5] Dr. Kernberg's statement is addressed to problems generic to both sexes. My evidence, however, is that, in this culture, at this moment in history, women are more conservative about their relationships and lean more heavily on the side of maintaining them than do men.

From my own clinical perspective I would say that the men most likely to fail are those who respond to the passage through middle age with denial, even with revulsion. The latter feel threatened, almost persecuted, by the possibility of changing. They are the men for whom the myths once again become charged with meaning. They are men who have not developed a true capacity for empathy or for intimacy. They are self-involved. Their response is a narcissistic one.

"Narcissism" has become such a buzz word recently that perhaps a definition is in order. We are not speaking here of what, for lack of a better term, we call "normal" narcissism, which is the quality of self-regard necessary for the establishment of self-esteem. We tend to think of the latter in a quantitative sense: that we need "enough" self-love to maintain good feelings about ourselves, and to maintain a stable self-image. I would say that my most troubled patients are those who are so lacking in this internal sense that they rely entirely on the outside world for confirmation. Good feelings about oneself are crucial for successful relationships, for without adequate self-love, one is incapable of loving others.

Joseph Lichtenberg has a definition of "self" that is perhaps useful when thinking about the essence of what one has to feel about oneself in order to deal successfully with the challenges of middle age. He speaks of the special *quality* of a well-integrated sense of self ". . . its cohesiveness, its continuity over time, and its retaining an essential sense of sameness in the midst of developmental changes."[6] Men who have not achieved this kind of stability are the vulnerable ones in middle age. Their response is that of *pathological* narcissism.

In a period of stress, when doubts about their value appear, such men feel impelled to a greater degree than ever before to get reassurance by extracting admiration and approval from the world around them. They feel compelled to find situations *and* people that offer them what Kernberg calls "narcissistic refueling." Clinically, one often finds these people paint a grandiose picture of themselves, which, on examination proves to be compensatory. It is an attempt to camouflage feelings of inadequacy. Other people are used to help maintain an inflated self-image. This defensive process helps them deny that they are changing. What is viewed in oneself as unacceptable is projected onto others who are then devalued. This mechanism now should have a familiar ring. We have seen how often it is the partner who is the recipient of these projections, the wife who is devalued. (*She* has the grandchildren; *she* is the one who is ugly, asexual, older.)

Venus After Forty

In midlife, many couples must re-adapt to being a twosome once the children are gone. This transition cannot be dealt with by a narcissistic man who not only devalues his wife in order to maintain his own feeling of self-worth, but who cannot deal with his dependency upon her. This too, if acknowledged, makes him feel inadequate. The dependency is also disavowed and replaced by a dislike of the person upon whom one has to lean.

Long-term relationships require care and feeding to remain viable, to feel precious. It requires a degree of sentimentality to keep romantic feelings alive. In the insecure man's struggle to maintain a masculine self-image, sentimentality itself is seen as a sign of getting soft, of weakness—and is disavowed.[7] Fidelity, too, can be downgraded. As a middle-aged patient of mine said in the face of his own faltering self-esteem, "I used to think it was important to be completely faithful to my wife. Now I do not even consider it infidelity if I 'do it' on a business trip— if I 'do it' out of town."

Among the men who are likely candidates for leaving marriages in middle age are those who must remain eternally young, whom Dr. Dan Kiley has labelled as having "the Peter Pan Syndrome." I would consider this a variant of pathological narcissism. The self-image of the men he describes is that of a perpetual adolescent; they feel little ultimate need to take responsibility for their behavior. Kiley feels that they have failed to develop a rich internal life. This lack makes them need to take on ever new challenges, often with diminishing pleasure and satisfaction.[8] This kind of immaturity shows itself in many forms. Some of the new challenges may be essentially harmless in their effects on others, like the competitive responses of men who double the number of miles they jog, or who go from hiking to rock climbing. There are men who respond in quite another way, but whose goal, to nurture faltering self-esteem, is the same. These men stop playing tennis the first time their sons beat them, or begin to avoid people socially who are their own age.

Other responses may be much more destructive. What is generic for men who cannot deal with the challenges of middle age—whether in response to the onset of a physical problem, boredom, and burnout in work, or restlessness within their personal relationships—is that, rather than dealing with the issues, they turn to action. For some, it is to food, alcohol, drugs, fast cars, or gambling. For many, it is young women. The aim is to avoid thinking. The behavior is regressive, using action as an adolescent does, to reestablish feelings of well-being. This is behavior that, from a psychiatric point of view, we call "acting out": it describes the attempt to avoid anxiety by keeping memories, feelings, and conflicts out of consciousness— by acting rather than reflecting.

There are some narcissistic men who have used action all their lives. It is their characteristic mode of reducing tension. Psychoanalyst Joyce McDougall believes such people are unable to tolerate emotional pain. Their behavior is not unlike that of drug or alcohol abusers. She believes that action itself may be an addictive form of avoidance. Some people use work in this way; others use other people. She believes that men who engage in repeated sexual conquests use women to give themselves "a shot" of feelings of power[9]—or, as Otto Kernberg would term it, "narcisstic refueling."

In normal development, one's interest matures from a preoccupation with sexuality to an appreciation of a whole person. Where there is severe pathological narcissism and the shaky self-esteem that goes with it, this does not take place; rather, young women are needed compulsively for reassurance, often regardless of the person with whom one is involved.[10]

Not all men who act out at middle age have been "addictive" womanizers. But the compulsive push toward action takes on an addictive quality for a man in crisis.

A narcissistic man feels that a large part of his identity is on the line. His self-esteem may be threatened by younger men at work; he may no longer be able to compete successfully on the tennis court, but, he believes, he can still outperform a younger man in the bedroom. When he takes on a young woman, the threat he has experienced passively is turned into action. Then envy of the competitor is reduced, assuaged, even reversed. Other men, even young men, now regard him with respect and admiration.

William Attwood, shortly after he published his book, *Making it through Middle Age: Notes While in Transit,* commented on men's response when he takes his daughter out to lunch. He saw them look at him with interest, wondering if he is out with his daughter, a call girl, or his wife. "Men talk so much about making it with young women," he said, "that it takes a mature person to ignore it." Dr. Robert Anderson is convinced that envy plays a primary role in motivating men to sexual acting out. He writes, in an as-yet unpublished manuscript:

> The human sexual capacity is one means available to assuage envy, the most universally available means, the great equalizer. In sexual experience we can all hope to be, at least for a moment, number one.

There is an important psychological clue to be examined when men ask the question, Is the man with his daughter, his wife, or his call girl? She can be one and the same. On an unconscious level there is the incestuous wish to have sex with one's daughter. Part of the stimulation and the gratification of acting out with a woman one's daughter's age is the satisfaction of the forbidden impulse. On an unconscious level, a man is also reversing a situation in which he felt envy but was powerless to assuage it: the time when he was in competition with his father for his mother. Now he can make other men envy him.

A man's impetus to act out in middle age resonates with a universal male fantasy pointed out by Dr. Ethel Spector Person. She speaks of the appeal to men of the sexually available woman who is so close to the dreams of the adolescent boy, epitomized by the *Playboy* centerfold. She is easy to arouse or in a constant state of arousal. She is a woman without sexual inhibition who will excite and stimulate an older man and restore him to the feelings of sexuality he had as a younger man.[11]

Of course, there is intrinsic pleasure in the presence of youth and beauty. We know that men always have been particularly responsive to visual cues for sexual stimulation. But we are speaking here of the psychological meanings of men's fantasy of the young woman.

For example, the Prado Museum in Madrid houses Paul Peter Reubens's painting, "The Garden of Love." Reubens painted it when he was in his fifties. In the picture, looking much younger than his actual age, Reubens walks in a garden with his new wife, who is sixteen. Venus, the Goddess of Love, smiles down upon their union. This picture symbolizes what it means for an older man to "borrow" a woman's youth, and thereby to feel rejuvenated, made young again. The search for a new person is often the search for someone who will fulfill the same functions: those of altering one's sense of oneself, transforming the present, and offering a future. This is at the heart of a man's wish for rejuvenation. It contains the fantasy of finding a young woman who is idealized, is perfect. She will make up for his growing sense of deficiency. She will enable him to push bad feelings about himself out of consciousness. This has echoes of the child's earliest dependency on the mother, on whom he leaned for such experiences. It is particularly true of the narcissistic adult whose search for a new person contains such a crucial need for transformation and repair. On some level he is also postponing and defying death!

All other motivations must pale in the face of such existential ones, but I cannot avoid mentioning a vulnerable man's need for adulation. It is offered to him by a young woman in a way that is impossible for a mature wife. A wife of many years may truly respect the accomplishments of her husband and take great pride in them. But she treats him more like an equal than a young woman will. A wife does not offer him the kind or degree of adulation so necessary to a man whose self-esteem is faltering. The young woman's adulation will be a crucial source of "narcissistic refueling." In this fantasy she becomes a latter-day version of the "all-good mother" who doted on her son and offered him uncritical approval.

The fantasy of the adoring young wife serves other needs, according to psychologist David Guttmann. Dr. Guttmann believes that our so-called masculine and feminine qualities are assigned not only by sex, but by life periods. The middle-aged man discovers that feminine traits are also a feature of his own internal landscape. Men have to repress such "feminine" qualities as passivity, tenderness, the sensual "softer" pleasures of poetry and nature for example, in the name of tough-minded achievement. Guttmann feels that women, playing traditional roles, provide a "projective ecology" for men by being an outward symbol of their own feminine needs. The mature wife, who may become more assertive and independent as the years pass, no longer fulfills this role. She may become less of an outward metaphor of his own softer nature. A man with a strong need to deny these aspects of himself will look for a new outward symbol of reassurance—in a more dependent and worshipful younger woman.[12]

In addition to the need to find an adoring young woman, fantasies of the bad mother of childhood have a special relevance for narcissistic men in middle age. I have said that the anxieties of this phase can reactivate fantasies that arise from each stage of early development. The narcissistic man who acts out and deserts his wife of many years is often expressing his ambivalence toward his mother. Whether he is conscious of such feelings or not, there will be some satisfaction associated with his frustration of his wife. On some level, it is an act of retribution. From a clinical viewpoint, it is clear that many men feel vindicated by what they do. It is as though there is an unstated equation that says: men acquire power and freedom to act from the success they achieve in middle age. In this view, women lose their power as they lose their looks. With such thought processes at work, a man can desert his wife and render her powerless in a reversal of his belief that mother repeatedly belittled, controlled, and deserted him. The hostility expressed in the acting out of the narcissistic man in middle age cannot be underestimated.

Although many mid-life divorces have the kind of sexual and emotional overtones discussed in this chapter, not all divorces in middle age are provoked by narcissistic men who abandon their wives for young women. Obviously there are "middle-aged" marriages so lacking in viability or so chronically embroiled in conflict that their termination is entirely appropriate.

In addition, some older men/younger women relationships work quite well, just as some younger men/older women relationships are successful.

Still, there can be negative consequences for men who act upon their impulses to leave long-standing marriages. There is often a downside. Some consequences are widely discussed: the guilt engendered on leaving a relationship of many years, the unhappiness of children of any age when their parents break up. There is the loss of roots, of a shared history, a common past that can create painful feelings of nostalgia.

The psychological consequences are not reported so openly. These I see in my clinical practice. An older husband often has many mixed feelings about starting a new family, particularly when he already has raised one. Unless he truly adores children (and in my experience narcissistic men rarely do), then he not only dislikes the idea of being disturbed at night, when it is harder to fall back to sleep than it once was, but he dislikes the interference with his freedom of movement that a baby brings. Most of all, a man is upset by the loss of attention he originally sought and was given by his new wife. She was supposed to be exclusively interested in him, but once a child is born, she is preoccupied with the fascinating new business of motherhood.

There are problems even more profound than these. The man who was "turned on" by the sexual freedom, the availability, and the eagerness of the young woman now has two new worries. One, already mentioned, is that he will not be able to keep up with her sexual demands, and—its twin—that she will find a younger man who is more high-powered, more sexually attractive than he is.

These anxieties give considerable power to younger wives. Some appear to treat older husbands in a teasing, ostensibly playful manner. What they are doing is publicly humiliating them, exposing their crotchets and idiosyncrasies. Or some young women complain, in their husband's presence, about having to give up tennis for golf, or down-hill for cross-country skiing—or simply that their husbands come home tired every night and fall asleep right after dinner.

And there is the downside for Sam, whom I knew when he was married to his first wife. They had been together for many years and had four children. The two seemed to share a lot—their family, friends, their home, and an interest in music and politics. They had been through a lot, having escaped from political persecution in Eastern Europe and having heroically rescued a number of people along the way.

Sam was successful in his business, but, in middle age, found himself feeling bored and restless. He retired at fifty-eight with the hope of doing something creative. He became involved in the work of a foundation that offered grants to young musicians and ran a music school in a resort area. Caught up in this new interest, Sam spent more and more time with it, much of it away from home. When he fell in love with a young pianist some thirty years his junior, he divorced his wife, married the younger woman, and moved to the West Coast. I lost track of him.

I reconnected with Sam some twelve years later when he came back East with his second wife and two young children and invited me to dinner. He had aged a great deal. His second wife is a vibrant and dynamic woman. Their friends appeared to be young musicians. At dinner Sam turned to me, gave me a long look, leaned over and whispered, hiding his mouth behind his hand, "Do you know how old I am? . . . I'm seventy!" He didn't seem either pleased or proud. I began to see why. He was not being treated like a respected elder by this tribe. Sam has experienced some hearing loss. During dinner he kept asking people to repeat themselves. Finally, in exasperation, he burst out, "Why is everyone mumbling?" His wife, expressing evident exasperation of her own, announced, "I keep telling Sam to get a hearing aid but he's just too vain!" Their marriage, Sam later told me, is in serious trouble.

Since most of the men I have mentioned in this chapter have tended to represent the culture and mores of large Eastern cities, I was pleased to come upon William A. Nolen, M.D.'s book, *Crisis Time! Love, Marriage and the Male at Midlife.* Dr. Nolen writes about his own personal crisis at fifty, and those of his friends and acquaintances. He lives in a town of five thousand people: Litchfield, Minnesota. Dr. Nolen has practiced surgery in this community for twenty-five years. He describes the boredom, burn-out, and fear of aging among the men who are his peers. He talks about their drug abuse, alcoholism, depression, and acting out. And, incidentally, the book reaffirms my own view, that, by and large in our culture, it is the women who want to wait out the crisis and the men who leave the marriage.

Dr. Nolen's crisis led him to drug and alcohol abuse. With professional help and a very supportive wife, he was able to surmount his problems and keep a basically good marriage together. Some other examples of men undergoing midlife problems he presents have no such happy endings.

Jerry, for example, whose story begins when he was forty-four, is typical of a number of men whose acting out began when he first experienced impotence with his wife. They had had an active and satisfying sex life during their twenty years of marriage. But in response to his occasional inability to perform, he turned to a woman in his office, Sheila, who was twenty-five. He found sex with her tremendously exciting. He felt ten years younger. Jerry tells Nolen how he began to relive his youth, how he bought a toupée, a sports car, and began going to singles bars. When his wife "blew the whistle on him," he left her. They were divorced.

Now, at fifty-three, Jerry is not sure if it wasn't a mistake to break up his marriage. He's much less interested in the night club scene than his young wife. He's ambivalent about having any more children. And he's sad about his estrangement from his own three children. His feelings about his former wife are not recorded.[13]

Scattered throughout this chapter and this book are references to the consequences for women of life in a world where so much of their value is gauged in terms of youthful good looks. It takes a very secure sense of self-esteem for a woman in our culture to permit herself to look her age. If a woman follows the dictates of the media and the magazines, she will inevitably be filled with narcissistic preoccupations. A glance through Helen Gurley Brown's bestseller tells her about the possibility of *Having It All:* success, money, husband, career, sex, power, all and forever. Thousands of *Cosmopolitan* readers have been encouraged to follow Brown's prescription, which involves an endless preoccupation with "image." Diet and exercise are to be engaged in with grim compulsiveness. Youthfulness is to be maintained with ruthless determination. I do not think Brown is speaking of the pleasures of being female, the fun and creativity that go with establishing one's own "look," a cachet, an ambience. Her female is a nervous and ambitious one; she lives in the world as though it is a treacherous place. If she follows Brown's advice, she hangs onto a man by playing little games, like dropping golf cuff links into his grapefruit or giving him a silver-handled magnifying glass inscribed with a secret code: IHTHFY ("I have the hots for you.")[14]

The importance of spontaneity and imagination in keeping humor, playfulness, and even mystery in a relationship, especially in a sexual one, should not be devalued. But it seems to me that many women feel that they are put on the defensive when they marry. They feel, and society seems to concur, that it is always their fault if a man "strays."

Popular jokes are replete with references to the dullness of marital sex—and, of course, it is the wife who is to blame. For instance, this terribly tasteless joke, was told to me by a middle-aged man as if it were really funny:

> *A woman was driving in the country. She happened to see a farmer leading a cow out to a field to be serviced by a bull. After the bull had dismounted, the farmer gave him a drink of water and brought out another cow, which the bull proceeded to service. The ritual with the water and a new cow was repeated several more times.*
>
> *The wife watched with interest and growing excitement. That evening, when her husband came home from work, she met him at the door with a drink of water. Every twenty minutes she brought him a fresh drink. Nothing happened. Finally, he asked, "What's going on here?" His wife explained what she had seen that afternoon and asked her husband, "If it worked for the bull, why doesn't it work for you?"*
>
> *"He didn't have to face the same old cow every time," her husband replied.*

Clearly, a man whose self-esteem is at risk at middle age often finds the need to rationalize and blame his problems on sex with his wife. Of course, this complaint may be but a symptom of his conflicts about growing older. The argument could also be advanced that a man who would tell a joke such as this one is a sadistic man whose self-esteem is maintained by his ability to prove his superiority and power in relation to another who is perceived as inferior. David Shapiro believes that "certain rigid men" believe that women must be made to feel inferior and that men's sense of control is provided by sexual conquest—indeed, this is their definition of manliness. In her book, *Reflections on Gender and Science,* Evelyn Fox Keller comments that Shapiro

> . . . understates, however, prevalence of those attitudes and that conception. *Overt sadism merely exhibits in pure form a phenomenon that is pandemic in human psychology; the appetite for domination, whether sexual or nonsexual. Analysis of the psycho-dynamics of domination, starting from the sadistic personality as an extreme case, reveals that domination is a response not simply to difference or conflict, or even to inequality per se, but to inequality* made threatening by the specter of difference dissolving. (Italics mine.)[15]

Keller emphasizes the culture's equation of domination and power. In middle age, whether through the threat of loss of power, or his perception that his wife no longer is willing to fulfill the role of inferior or victim, a vulnerable man, living in a society that promotes and condones his behavior, will act to restore his feelings of power by the domination of a younger woman.

Antidotes for such unfortunate treatment of middle-aged women are long overdue. Because crises in middle age can be terribly destructive for both men and women. People get badly hurt. Changing partners is not a magical solution.

❧§10§❧

The Narcissistic Woman: Women Who Buy the Myths

. . . Ted Turner got on the phone . . . "You're an interesting woman, how old are you . . . forties?" "A little older," I said. "Well, how old?" he said. Knowing even then I was out of my mind, I said, "Fifty-nine." I could feel the telephone ice over.

Helen Gurley Brown, *Having It All*

It takes a very secure sense of self-esteem for a female in our culture to allow herself to "age gracefully." But if the particular life history of an individual makes her vulnerable, she will listen to the dictates of the men, the media, and the magazines and will inevitably be filled with narcissistic preoccupations. A glance through Helen Gurley Brown's bestseller, quoted above, tells such a woman about the possibility of *Having It All:* success, money, husband, career, sex, power, now and forever. Thousands of *Cosmopolitan* readers have been encouraged to follow her prescription, described in the previous chapter.[1]

I don't think Brown is putting down the pleasures of being female, the satisfaction of being creative about one's personal "look," style, and ambience. No one can fault a woman for having a concern about her looks when both her sex appeal and her job may depend on them. But if a woman follows Brown's battle plan, she must become both opportunistic and calculating. Such behavior often leads to self-demeaning relationships. Now it is wonderful, in fact it is essential, to be imaginative and creative in keeping fun and pleasure in a relationship. But it is not so great to have to play little tricks such as those described in the previous chapter to make a man happy. The danger of following such advice is that one feels foolish at best and resentful at worst. Much more crucial is the fact that when so much time and energy go into such one-track preoccupations, the rest of one's self either atrophies or fails to develop. It's too big a price. Moreover, it's bound to fail.

Nobody needs to be reminded that we live in a world dominated by images: images that have been created to sell products. Not only is an older woman constantly told what she should *want* to look like, but everywhere she goes she sees herself reflected in mirrors. In discussing this phenomenon in their book, *Women & Self-Esteem,* Linda T. Sanford and Mary Ellen Donovan point out how many women are displeased with what they see.[2] While I have not come across a study that gives statistics about the numbers of middle-aged women who are unhappy about the image they project, I can safely say that very few feel like Helen Hayes, beautiful at eighty-six, who is content with her wrinkles, and calls them her "battle stripes." Many women, as they get older, are faced with the impossibility of defeating change, and in their inevitable defeat they begin to hate themselves.

The limits to which the beauty industry will go to sell products might appear insane to a visitor from another planet, but for millions of American women the message works. William E. Geist, in a *New York Times* column, wrote about Miss Livia Sylva, "self-proclaimed 'World Famous Skin Care Expert,' " whose clinic favors the application of Rumanian bee pollen for facials, while Madame Ilona of Hungary offers treatments using "whipped quail eggs and bull-blood wine." Princess Marcella Borghese, Geist wrote, is "partial to Italian mud." He also listed a few of the magazine ads for "do-it-yourself" facials: "Age Response System Gelée (2 ounces for $35), Cellular Recovery Complex . . . Activating Serum with Trace Elements, Line Preventor, Wrinkle Eradication, Lift Serum, and Embryo Cell Extract. . . . ."[3]

I have been a "woman watcher" for a long time now, in my personal life, in my practice, and in observations of women I meet when I lecture and attend conferences, and I've noted what happens to women who are obsessed with their images, with themselves. I am not speaking of women who feel more comfortable, more self-confident, when they do what they can to keep looking good; I am speaking of those women who are ruled by an unchanging image of youthful perfection.

Janet T. is a beautiful woman. She has always been courted by men. Artists have asked her to pose for them. She became a dress designer and had a series of great successes and failures, which often left her totally broke. She always manages to look smashing, however, dressing in highly dramatic style, whether her bank account is up or down. Janet has been extremely careful about protecting her complexion from the ravages of both winter and summer. Her skin really is quite marvelous, requiring little or

"Now, don't get panicky. I'll have you looking ten years younger in no time.

no makeup. But around the age of forty-four, she began to talk about a facelift. She had read that women are well advised to have the operation done early, while the skin is still resilient, rather than late. The notion of plastic surgery became an *idée fixe,* and, although it was one of those times in her life when she was in debt, she began to shop for a surgeon. Several of them convinced her that a facelift was premature, but that it would help her appearance to have her eyes "done."

Janet borrowed money to have the procedure. In the weeks that followed she became hysterical. She was convinced that her eyes did not "match," that she had become permanently changed and disfigured by the surgery. Not only did she look at herself constantly, but required her friends to scrutinize her closely and reassure her that she was indeed all right. All of Janet's anxiety about aging, about loss and change, had become focused on her eyes. It took her some months to quiet down. Her eyes do match, but she is not quite sure whether or not she looked better before the surgery.

Terry C. is in her late forties. She is a bright, appealing redhead who has never been overweight. One cannot spend any time with her before her calorie consciousness intrudes on the relationship. At a restaurant or at a dinner party, what she is so self-consciously, so publicly, *not* eating manages to become obtrusive. I once made the mistake of going into a supermarket with her. It took a very long time. Terry had to read the fine print on every package to determine the food value she would not be getting. She's not by any means an anorexic, but in truth, she has become rather scrawny and she takes great pride in this achievement.

When Madeline and Susan began to approach middle age, they began to hate their hair. Madeline decided hers was too thin; Susan decided hers had become dry and brittle. These women do not know each other, but I know them. I can recall the moments they both began to wear wigs constantly. The wigs haven't seemed to help them feel better about themselves, nor have they helped their appearances.

Perhaps the saddest result of our obsession with appearance is the realization of how few women escape this fixation. It even gets to well-integrated, "whole" women. It's like the effect of sitting in the smoking section of an airplane on a person who's trying to stop smoking. For example, I ran into a woman in her forties I hadn't seen in several years. Every since I've known her, she has always managed to look very good, although she never spent much time on her appearance. That day, however, she looked wonderful. Her skin was translucent, her eyes wonderfully alive; she had a glow. I was struck by her totally new hair style which made her much prettier than I ever remembered her. She had developed some gray hair. I told her she looked splendid and that I loved her hair. Her response was a doubtful, "But shall I dye it?"

The obsession with looks can be extended to clothing as well. It's not a rarity in my practice to come across women—not necessarily women with money—with closets full of clothes who tell me they change skirts, blouses, and sweaters endlessly before leaving the house. Nothing they put on looks right because they are convinced they are unattractive, are "over the hill." It is particularly hard for them when their daughters get to be teenagers and start dating. Elizabeth B., for example, is a very youthful-looking woman. She is full of energy, enthusiasm, and ready to go. She has two daughters, one fifteen, the other seventeen. On weekends, she's taken to wearing clothes that look like theirs: tattered blue jeans and oversized sweaters that slide off one shoulder. Recently she got a punk rock haircut. Elizabeth is coy and flirtatious with her daughters' boyfriends. She takes over and dominates the conversation in open competition with them. At office parties she appears in plunging necklines, and gets evasive when asked how old her daughters are.

Betty L., at forty-one, is, to me, perhaps the quintessential example of a woman governed by her fear of aging. She is married and has two children under ten. Every day she exercises non-stop for two hours. Her children may be fighting and tearing up the house, but she does her exercises. Betty has a standing Friday-morning appointment at her hairdresser's and has facials and body massages at least twice a week. She had plastic surgery on her eyes about three years ago. Her dressing table is piled with creams and lotions. She shops for clothing carefully and persistently; her wardrobe is impeccably coordinated. Betty is late for every appointment because it takes her so much time to create herself. She is a takeover person in social situations; she has to be noticed. She does *look* good. However, I sometimes wonder if she feels it's worth the tremendous effort or if she wishes she had found more substantial and fulfilling interests.

It is not enough simply to describe narcissistic women. Their behavior has its own psychological history. For purposes of discussion, I have grouped women like those I have been describing into roughly four types, or categories. Their stories start early. They do not get hooked on being self-involved *de novo* in middle age. The problems get worse, however, as they become convinced that options for the future are closing down.

Helen Gurley Brown tuned into the source of one group of women's preoccupation with appearance. She spoke of her own mother's distress at being compared unfavorably with a gorgeous younger sister. Brown got the message that beauty was what she herself needed. She also knew that her mother did not find her pretty enough.[4] From a clinical perspective, a woman who grows up with a mother who needs her to compensate for her own feelings of inadequacy—of not getting enough love, beauty, or power—more often than not will develop narcissistic problems of her own, although I do not mean to imply that I am drawing such a conclusion about Helen Gurley Brown. People's problems are too complex in their etiology to blame any simple or single causality. When a woman escapes such an outcome, it is often because there is another person in her life, often a father or a close grandparent, who loves her for herself without dictating what she must become. But women who do not get "rescued" take mother's needs seriously. They make them part of themselves: the part of their personality that represents all they idealize—all they strive to be.

The examples in this chapter are composites. In the interest of privacy, I have chosen to select details from a number of women in my practice and from among my acquaintances rather than to describe single individuals. Also, in these, as in any, vignettes, I do not want to give the impression that all human problems are caused by mothers! Children have two parents, siblings, grandparents, and a variety of caretakers. Troubles arise within the family; they can also occur at different stages of a child's life. One cannot discount, however, the importance of the earliest relationships the child encounters.

With that precaution in mind, here is a clinical example of *Type One*. Marjorie B. was nearing forty when we first met. She was a woman with style, although she did not have much to spend on clothes. She came to see me after she had broken her engagement to the second man she had planned to marry. Her mother's earliest years had been chaotic: the family moved about a great deal, as her grandfather kept changing jobs, and he deserted the family when her mother was six. Her mother then spent several years in foster homes while her grandmother struggled to find ways to support them both.

Marjorie's mother married late. She had trouble conceiving, then gave birth to a stillborn baby. She became pregnant with Marjorie a year later. From the moment of conception, Marjorie was an overvalued child. Mother did not like her to crawl because the floor was dirty and full of germs. She disconnected the telephone during her mealtimes so there would be no interference with her feeding. Marjorie became a good, conforming child. She recalls helping the teacher set up finger paints for the other children on the first day of kindergarten, for example. She was a pretty, pleasant youngster, who never got dirty or into trouble. Her teachers loved her; she did well in school.

Mother still insisted on washing and ironing for her and bringing home beautiful clothes when she was sixteen, more than old enough to do these things for herself. Her father was very much shut out of this relationship. Although a man of considerable charm, he was not financially successful. His wife did not forgive him for making them live on the wrong side of the tracks.

Marjorie was depressed when she first came to see me, not only because of her broken engagements, but because she had gone through a whole series of relationships. The men had all seemed desirable to her at first, but would end up, she believed, not being good enough. One man was not educated (enough), another was too short, a third dressed badly. Whenever someone she dated began to evince real interest, she would go into a panic. The fear was always that if she said "Yes" to him, she'd miss out on a better candidate, but she was getting older and was afraid that she'd never get married.

Unwittingly, Marjorie was dedicating her life to her own internal version of what mother had wanted for her— to achieve a kind of perfection that would bring the world to her feet. As an adult, she knew what she expected, but did not know *herself*. She hid behind a facade of sweetness and conformity. Marjorie's focus when she first came to see me was on her search for a man. It soon turned into a search for herself.

Alice Miller, the Swiss psychoanalyst, has written quite sensitively about men and women who have problems like Marjorie's. In her book, *Prisoners of Childhood*, she summarizes her findings about their early lives: "Such a child has an amazing ability to perceive and respond intuitively, that is unconsciously, to the need of the mother (or father, grandparent or caretaker, i.e., to the person closest to the child) to take on the role that had unconsciously been assigned to him . . . He could sense that he was needed and this, he felt, gave him a measure of existential security."[5]

The consequences for these children, she continues, are threefold. First, as a result of this adaptation, they become incapable of experiencing feelings such as anger, envy, even loneliness. Second, in relationships they reveal only those aspects of themselves that they feel the other person would approve. Third, such children are always giving what they believe is *expected* of them; they never get to find out what they want or like.[6] For a lifetime, the Marjories of this world look to others for completion, for approval, for affirmation.

A clinical example of *Type Two*, Eleanor S. first came for therapy in her mid-forties. Two events had put her in a state of crisis. Her husband, thirteen years her senior, had just had surgery for colon cancer, and a few months before she had placed her mother in a nursing home. It was a terrible task for Eleanor to visit her mother. She couldn't bear to look at old people. In addition, she was furious at mother for her decline, their mutual need for one another, and for making her think about death. Mother's placement and her husband's illness were significantly tied to one another in Eleanor's mental life. They were the two people to whom she had been most closely connected—but always in a highly charged love/hate relationship.

Eleanor was a beautiful baby, a beautiful child, and a beautiful young adult. As an only child, she spent a great deal of time with her mother: her father was a quiet man who left the child's upbringing to his wife. When she was growing up, Eleanor recalled, although she and her mother did a lot of shopping together, they did not enjoy one another; they were not friends. Her mother was always highly critical of her. When Eleanor reached her mid-twenties and was still unmarried, her mother began to tell her she had very little time left to find a man. Eleanor chose her husband because "He was there," not because he fulfilled her fantasy of a rich, successful "catch."

I had the opportunity of learning how Eleanor had dealt with her passage through middle age, as she had come to see me again some fifteen years later on in her life. Her more recent crisis was precipitated by her sixtieth birthday. Eleanor had always paid a great deal of attention to her appearance. She had become much more preoccupied and dissatisfied with her looks. She complained that her hair was thinning, her wrinkles were more noticeable. When I first saw her, she was terrified that her husband would die and abandon her; fifteen years later, although his health was stable, she still lived in terror of his having a recurrence of his illness. She was childless, never having been interested in children. At forty-five, Eleanor had been doing some work selling blouses she had designed. At sixty, she had given up all interest in this talent of hers. She slept late. When she went out, she shopped incessantly, although fully aware that she was spending too much money and bringing home things she did not need or did not even particularly like.

At forty-five, Eleanor had nagged her husband constantly because of his lack of financial success. When I saw her the second time around, her husband had retired with a decent pension and adequate savings. He was content to read the newspaper, watch TV, and play cards with his friends several times a week. Eleanor, for her part, complained about her health, her husband's health, and her boredom. Characteristically, she refused to invite people into her house because everyone she knew was richer and had better homes than she did. Both times she came to treatment wanting me to "fix" things, to remake her life. She consistently refused to take responsibility, having fault to find with any and every possible line of action.

In the years between my contact with her, Eleanor had shopped for therapists. She asked and got a variety of medications for her malaise and depression. She had managed to alienate the people who wanted to be of help to her because she was coercive, manipulative, and uninterested in change. With her imperious demands, Eleanor reminded me of Mae West, who used to do a caricature of a woman with airs, a "grande dame," who dressed "rich"—in sequins, feathers, and diamonds—who would turn to her personal maid and say in a bored tone, "Beulah, peel me a grape!" But Mae West never played defeated women like Eleanor; she remained in charge of her own life.

Now Eleanor, as a *Type Two* example of a narcissistic woman, shares some of Marjorie's characteristics, since clinical distinctions are not so tidy. Both are trying to satisfy an ideal absorbed via their mother's definition of success, status, and happiness. Women like this have not mastered the crucial early double task that faces girls. It is normal and necessary for a girl to identify with her mother and take on some of the characteristics of her gender, as well as identifying with particular aspects of her personality. But girls must also learn how to become separate and distinct from the person on whom they have been so dependent. They must feel permission from mother to move out, to become different, to create a special "being" of their own. Where the permission is not forthcoming, girls like Eleanor and Marjorie acquiesce out of fear of mother's displeasure or of loss of her love. Such women live in a state of chronic and angry dependency that is transferred onto other people who come into their lives, most especially onto spouses.

However, there is a significant difference between the two women. Marjorie was adored and cherished by her mother. She felt a responsibility to create a life for her vicariously through her performance as an ideal child. Eleanor, on the other hand, never felt warmth from her mother; she felt perpetually unsure of the degree to which she was lovable. Her coercive behavior began in her childhood in an attempt to get concrete evidence of being wanted, of being cared for. Furthermore, Eleanor was unique in the degree to which she was consumed by envy, an envy in which everything was quantified and measured in these terms: What you possess that is greater than mine, whether it is love or material things, takes away from me and my value to myself.[7] Eleanor was left in a chronic stage of helpless rage. She had never developed the capacity to generate "strokes" for herself.

Charlotte is a *Type Three* example. She is now in her late fifties, had a long and stable marriage. She has a daughter and three grandchildren. When her husband died several years ago, Charlotte was living in the suburbs. She stayed in her house and kept her job, a highly responsible one. When one walks into Charlotte's home, one soon sees that she was a handsome young woman. There are photographs of her everywhere. Unfortunately, Charlotte does not look handsome anymore. The word that best describes her is "blowsy." Her hair is over-bleached, her makeup shrill, her clothes much too tight. It was clear at parties that Charlotte enjoyed being a flirt. Her husband was quite tolerant of her behavior; in fact he seemed proud of her.

The problem for Charlotte now is that while she has

the same need for attention and admiration from men, she is stuck with an adolescent's view of sexual behavior. At social occasions she hovers over a man or sits on his lap. She drinks a great deal and with every drink she becomes more "girlish."

Charlotte talks a lot about going to singles' bars. She refuses to be seen in a restaurant in the company of women. As a result of placing ads in personal columns, she has found plenty of men for occasional sex. None of them turned out to be appropriate, she says. Last winter, however, when she met a man on a cruise, she felt she was at last "onto something." A few months later, she found out that he was married. Charlotte became depressed. It was a terrible blow to her self-esteem. Even though she had not really liked this man, she desperately wants a partner. Without one she feels like a failure, because Charlotte is dictated to by the voice of a sixteen-year-old. Girls must be pretty and popular, it says. The dance card must be filled. In her pursuit of men, she cannot even stop to think about other ways of becoming interesting to men or, given the odds, to face the possibility that she may have to create a satisfying life for herself alone.

Charlotte is left with anger and cynicism. Men are no good; she trusts none of them. In reality, she is angry at herself for growing older, for losing the formula that made her pleased with herself. The anger, however, is being projected onto men. In this, Charlotte resembles narcissistic men; the men who say, "I'm not changed; it's just the 'little woman' who's dragging me down; it's her fault."

Charlotte reminds me of Patsy, who is some fifteen years her junior. She is a younger version of Charlotte. Patsy is married to a very decent man. Patsy, however, is also worried about getting older. She dresses like a much younger woman. In the past few years, she has been having affairs with men at least ten years her junior. Invariably, they are involved in relationships of their own. This is all right with Patsy, since she has no intention of breaking up her marriage. But she is miserably unhappy. She is obsessed by her young lovers: When will they call? Will they remember her birthday? Unfortunately, they do not help her feel young and sexy. They hold up a mirror that constantly reminds her how she looks vis-á-vis them, how she is aging.

The last category is *Type Four* women. All of the women I have described are unprepared for the second half of life. Many of them respond to the crisis of divorce, of widowhood, or simply to the "crisis" of middle age itself, with alcoholism, hypochondriasis, and depression. There is Isabel T., a widow in her fifties, who has joined their numbers. She had a long and symbiotic marriage that made her feel special. She cannot stop mourning the loss of her husband, because although she has friends and a job most people would find challenging, Isabel let her life revolve completely around his. She borrowed her feelings of self-regard from being "the wife of" an interesting man. Her husband was a reporter. Without children, they managed to travel together quite often. Their home, their friends, their whole way of life was created in response to his interests. Without him, without the status she felt as his wife, Isabel is lost.

Dan, her husband, seemed happy to meet many of Isabel's narcissistic needs. He constantly told her she was beautiful, constantly brought her gifts and flowers. Isabel entertained his friends a lot; it pleased her to have interesting and important guests. At these gatherings, Isabel held court. Men were expected to tell her she looked wonderful; women to admire her clothes. Her behavior was queenly. In Isabel's presence you felt you might be expected to curtsey. Everything in her home bespoke her regal attitude: the furniture, the china and cutlery, the art all looked like they were there to create a proper setting for her. And you were expected to admire it, as you were expected to admire Isabel.

All of this added up to a sense that Isabel really was a *grande dame.* She was both elegant and *au courant.* Maybe *soignée* is the best word to describe her. She made you feel she came by the adulation she received by right of birth. There are flaws, however. Isabel is a very vulnerable woman. She cannot handle even minor blows to her self-esteem. She is one of those women who get very upset when they encounter someone wearing the same dress. Even when her husband was still alive to help her, she could go into a real tailspin. It happened once when she was told that the woman who had bought a former apartment of theirs had remodelled it in an extremely creative manner that made it much more attractive than it had ever been.

Behind her grandiosity was a feeling of emptiness. Without her husband offering tribute to feed her narcissism, to fill her with a sense of importance, to lend her an identity, she became depressed. As time went on Isabel began to alienate her friends. She lost her charm, her tact, her light touch and got to be hypercritical. Now when you came into her "presence," you could anticipate she'd find your weakest link: you'd put on a little weight; she didn't like your current haircut—it made you look old; you hadn't fully understood the book she'd lent you; you'd missed the only good movie worth seeing.

Isabel was borrowing a page from Charlotte's and Patsy's book. Charlotte, especially, was critical of men. Isabel was critical of everyone who peopled her world. Women who have no internal reservoir of good feelings depend entirely on the outside to make them whole.

Charlotte relied upon her adolescent view of sexual behavior to attract men; Isabel relied upon her husband, her friends, and her possessions to give her a sense of value. Without the old sources of "narcissistic refueling" (Otto Kernberg's term), there comes a sense of anger and emptiness. These women feel devalued. Their anger is projected onto people who are devalued in turn.[8]

The women encountered in this chapter may seem quite familiar. Some of them you have known personally. Others may be as familiar as such well-known literary figures as Scarlet O'Hara in Margaret Mitchell's *Gone With The Wind*, who may be one of the ultimate female narcissists. We are not permitted to see her in middle age, but at sixteen, when the book opens, she is already totally self-involved, ruthless, and conniving. A few years later, with the South in ruins after defeat in the Civil War, after personal tragedy, the loss of parents, husband, and child, she remains untouched and unchanged. She makes the same demands of life and must face it alone.[9]

Other heroines come readily to mind. Edith Wharton's Lily Bart in *The House of Mirth* is a beautiful, helpless, thoroughly parasitic woman who kills herself at twenty-eight. Her life is over, she believes, because she is now too old to land a rich and powerful husband who (like Isabel's husband) will give her a name, a place, and an identity.[10] There is Flaubert's Madame Bovary, Martha, the vicious wife of Edward Albee's *Who's Afraid Of Virginia Woolf?* and Tennessee Williams' Blanche Du Bois in *A Streetcar Named Desire*, who is alcoholic and delusional in her thirties, a victim of her own grandiosity and inability to compromise.[11]

The movies have given birth to their own breed of narcissistic women, whether on or off the screen. In the 1950 movie, *All About Eve*, Bette Davis played the middle-aged star, Margo Channing, whose public and private life are threatened by an ambitious younger woman. The film is, in some respects, the flip side of the story of Elizabeth B., described above, who is so openly competitive with her teenage daughters. Bette Davis is portrayed as fighting viciously to maintain her position and her image, in spite of her age. Both the real and the fictional women face the same challenge: If they are so self-involved, they can only see daughters, or any member of the next generation, as competition (read also fathers and sons); then their only response is one of envy. Envy leads to denigration and reprisal.

The documentary film that Maximilian Schell produced in 1986 about Marlene Dietrich, called simply "Marlene," offers another portrait of narcissism, a portrait with similar themes. In fairness to Dietrich, I would make one disclaimer, however. She was eighty-two when the film was made; some of her behavior, therefore, may be a factor of her age, or of the state of either her physical or emotional health. In spite of these unknowns, or perhaps because of them, a portrait of a narcissistic woman emerges. In the first place, Dietrich does not allow herself to be seen on camera. No pictures can be shown that are not clips from her public life, taken before her retirement. Of course, she has a right to privacy, but she agreed to be part of a documentary of her life.

Her voice is querulous, her behavior argumentative, cantankerous. Her narcissism is revealed through her self-referential behavior, her hypercritical opinions, and her self-inflating denials. When Maximilian Schell, for example, tries to get some factual material about her life, Dietrich asks, with increasing irritation, why he should want her to tell him such things when everyone knows who has read any one of the numerous books about her life. And she knows precisely how many have been written.

Dietrich appears to be chronically irritated by the outside world, its culture, its dress. She dismisses it all, repeatedly and summarily, as *kitsch*. She is down on most men, on or off the screen. For instance, she thinks Emil Jannings's acting in the role of the professor in "The Blue Angel" was simply dreadful. Marlene claims she never was interested in men sexually. That she loved Ernest Hemingway, but in a "platonic" way; that she admired Spencer Tracy and Maximilian Schell in "Judgment In Nuremberg"—but her overall tone is critical and negative. In fact, the one person in her life, interestingly enough, who is exempt from her criticism, for whom she expresses love, is her daughter.

Dietrich dismisses as preposterous the idea that she felt rootless because she had to flee from her native home in Berlin. She claims to have been an only child, although one of the film editors displays a photograph taken with her sister and makes the comment that she only does that to make herself seem more important.

The portrait of Marlene Dietrich in old age that comes through in the documentary of her life is of a woman who resembles Charlotte, Patsy, and Isabel. What they can no longer conquer and control, they denigrate and blame.

A number of women deal with the passage into middle age by desperately fighting the aging process in an effort to remain unchanged or give up and withdraw in depression and defeat. In previous chapters, I described men's responses, including those who have narcissistic problems of their own. It would be fair to ask in what ways egocentric men are the same as women, and how they are different. Today, more and more men are being persuaded by the cosmetic industry to get involved with lotions, perfumes, deodorants, and facials. They are having plastic surgery, dying their hair, and getting implants. Even so, it is still clear that women depend more on and work harder to maintain their physical attractiveness; the scales are not balanced in this area.

Narcissistic men and women share a rigidity of character and tend to look with abhorrence on anything that is seen as "ordinary" or "average." Compromise comes hard. Living to a stage of life that is labelled "older" is not seen as a part of normal development, but as a loss, as regression. Men and women like this share an almost phobic fear of dying and can only view age in Joseph Heller's term, as "a headlong race toward decrepitude."[12]

There is one significant difference in the responses of narcissistic men and women to the onset of middle age. Although both sexes may try to *do* something such as diet, exercise, or plastic surgery to stop time, it is easier for men to turn to action. Men are accustomed to solving problems by taking charge, by being instrumental. Women have not been conditioned the same way. Most important of all, in this area men have an option that is not open to most women—even if "most women" would choose it: the option to turn to a young person for rejuvenation. "Rejuvenation," after all, is defined thus: "to make young again."

Even though finding a partner to restore feelings of well being may not be a ready solution for many women at middle age, a narcissistic response is clearly not the answer. What should women do? When some of them face this dilemma, they ask me, "Why do you include facts about the sexuality of older women in your lectures, if there aren't any men? And what good is life, anyway, without one?"

It is for these women that I've written the following chapters. It's about women who have found options for themselves, options they could create *because* they were middle-aged.

Part Three

OPTIONS

11

Couples Who Make It

Jean and I, as close to each other as Jennifer and Sigurd were, occasionally had similar conflicts. To an outsider they would seem trivial, perhaps an indulgence in a world that knows as much about cruelty and terror as ours did; but to the partners of a long marriage who are still gladdened, at the end of each day, to be returned to each other and who always were aware, if but on some barely conscious level, that one of them inevitably is to be made desolate by the death of the other, the smallest of quarrels is violent and strange.

James McConkey, *Court of Memory*

We grow up yearning for love, love that finds physical expression. But there is a popular notion that love and sex are equated with love and sex *before* middle age. Our culture's fantasies about the lack of sexuality of older women contribute to society's aversion to the idea of mature love. But, whether society likes it or not, mature love is, today, a vital part of the second half of life. It should be worthwhile to try to discover what it takes for some men and women to develop and maintain loving sexual relationships for a lifetime.

Walking on the beach on a French island in the

Caribbean, I see young couples, the women topless, both sexes beautiful. And there are young mothers, topless, lovely, playing in the water with their infants. There are middle-aged men and women, looking their age; the women also topless or wearing bikinis, with an apparent lack of self-consciousness. Then I come upon one old couple, nude, holding each other, walking in the surf. They, too, were lacking in self-consciousness. They were obviously enjoying themselves. We very much need to have "maturity" become an acceptable word and mature love something we can look at without clothes on.

Psychotherapists trying to define the meaning of mature love believe that infants develop tender feelings before the establishment of erotic or sexual ones. They do not dismiss the importance of Freud's early concepts about the pleasure the child derives from successive parts of the body: the mouth (and feeding), the focus on elimination, and then on pleasure originating via the genital organs. But they stress the child's need for gratifying "whole body" experiences: being held, stroked, and rocked. This need never disappears. The person who offers this satisfaction becomes the source of comfort and safety. Mutually given, these "whole body" experiences are the expressions of tenderness. It is the capacity to integrate tender and sexual feelings that makes bonding possible. It is this integration, based on both pleasure and need, that makes love possible.

When couples achieve this, then the sexual changes of the second half of life can be dealt with without hypersensitivity or defensiveness. As the sex therapist Dr. Arlene Kagle said, "Basically, men and women who have had a good personal and sexual adjustment simply 'tune in' to one another."

Most couples are diffident when it comes to talking openly about the details of their sex lives; after all, sex is a very private matter. It seems most difficult when a couple is together. Kate, speaking to me alone, could be quite outspoken about her longstanding marriage to Gene. They are "tuned in" to one another and now, in late middle age (fifty-nine and sixty-three, respectively), still find each other very desirable. Kate says she thinks their good sex life is one part luck.

> We are two very sensual human beings who found each other. We love to touch, to rub, stroke, and massage each other. One of the best parts of being together so long is that we know what pleasures the other person: For instance, I love to be kissed on my eyelids; it's a minor detail, for sure, but I don't have to ask. Even when we're both very tired, touching and strok-ing is not only relaxing, it still feels very erotic. For me, arousal is easy. But if Gene is dead beat and doesn't get an erection, it's no problem; we can have intercourse another time.
>
> I do think a sense of playfulness is all important. And a sense of humor. Time has given us the freedom to be creative and experi-mental. Different positions can be stimulating, but if one of us is awkward or feels ridiculous, we can laugh about it. You communicate with all your senses when you make love. Sometimes we like the lights on so we can see each other's facial expressions. I love to talk in bed. Some-times, after love-making, I say so many things I never speak of otherwise. Being older has noth-ing to do with that kind of pleasure.
>
> Yes, I'd say we are lucky. We don't have to play games (maraschino cherries in the navel) or indulge in kinky fantasies to get turned on. No pornographic movies, no mirrors on the ceiling. There is comfort in the familiarity, but, thank God, there is still passion!

Linda is another woman who has maintained her sexual desire over time. She married her first husband about a year after his wife died in childbirth. Sex was terrible, she told me. "I held back because I felt John was still mourning his wife." He was aware of her diffidence and did not press her. When they were finally able to talk to one another, the relationship began to work. They found great delight in one another and sex became a central part of their lives. In the course of time, they had two children. They saw to it that they still had opportunities for fun like swimming in the nude at night and making love on the beach.

John had a bad heart attack when he was fifty. He told Linda if he died he wanted her to be sure to find another man, one who was a good lover, because he knew how important sex was for her happiness. He had a second heart attack and died in twelve months. Linda missed him terribly and actively mourned her loss. Two years later, at fifty-three, she met and married Charles, sixty, who was also a widower, with four grown children. Linda, now sixty herself, was happy to answer my questions about what is making this marriage work. "John was right, of course," she said. "I do need a very sexual man. I know I picked Charles in part because he is a good lover."

I asked Linda what she thought has sustained the sexual interest she and Charles have in each other. I mentioned Otto Kernberg, who talks about how often middle-aged couples feel the need to try other partners to prove they are still physically attractive. Among the ingredients that make stability possible, he says, "are the capacity for intimacy, the tolerance of conflict, and the maintenance of mystery within the love relationship."[1] Keeping mystery within a relationship is a notion one does not come across very often these days. (Only a few years ago we were reading about playrooms where couples were publicly switching partners.) So I asked Linda if she felt "mystery" was a part of what kept sex interesting for her with both John and Charles. She said:

> I might call it just being romantic, but I agree it's important. I love to try new perfumes. It's wonderful to create a mood for love, you know. It may sound like Hollywood or a soap opera, but it works: to listen to music, to light a fire, eat a great meal in front of it, drink wine, and make love. I often have candlelight in the bedroom. You can see your lover; the shadows do wonderful things.
>
> When I was younger, I had no concern at all about walking around in the nude. Now since my body has changed, I prefer to wear a pretty robe. Black nightgowns are fine, but I never make love with one on or sleep in one. Charles likes to fall asleep with his hand on my tummy. It seems to fit there. He calls my middle-aged bulge "baby fat." I tell him it's "fat from having babies," but it's very sweet. I can be open and he can be romantic, but he loves my sixty-year-old body because he loves me.

Does the sensual love of these two couples add up to fidelity? What do the statistics say? Philip Blumstein and Pepper Schwartz, in their analysis of twelve thousand American couples, found that couples enter relationships with a desire for monogamy, and that infidelity is almost invariably a source of anxiety and pain for the person "betrayed." Still, some couples claim they have been able to establish guidelines that isolate their feelings about infidelity from their feelings toward one another.[2] According to this study—and it comes as no surprise—more women are monogamous than men, although only by nine percent (husbands, seventy-five percent; wives, eighty-four percent). Wives have extramarital sex with fewer partners, we are told. Infidelity increases after ten years of marriage, but the figures apply to only thirty percent of husbands and twenty-two percent of wives.[3]

Edward M. Brecher's study of *Love, Sex and Aging*, samples roughly three thousand people, all over age fifty. Eight percent of wives and twenty-three percent of husbands (nearly three times as many) report extra-marital sex.[4] Brecher does not tell us how many couples remain faithful because of religious beliefs, family or social pressures, timidity, or inertia.

Beyond the statistics that tell us how many marriages are monogamous is the *quality* of a couple's life together. June and Ben have achieved what I would call a highly creative and monogamous marriage. They are in their late fifties and can look back on the past two decades to reflect on their passage through middle age. June, at fifty-six, has graying hair and a well-groomed look. She is a vibrant person, with a warm, related manner, and one does not think about her age. I know that she is a hardworking, determined, and successful woman. I find her to be very feminine, in the best sense of the word. Her voice is well-modulated. She is responsive, interested, empathic.

She and Ben married young and had two children. She is a landscape architect, a skill that was partly self-taught, partly acquired as an apprentice, and partly learned in graduate study. June has worked throughout her marriage, except for four years when her children were young.

> June: I'm not an activist. I know I am a woman of my time and know what I feel and what I need for myself. Maybe this will explain what I mean: I've had a guiding fantasy about men and women that uses ballet as a metaphor. I started ballet lessons when I was a little kid and went on studying in high school and college. For a while,

Couples Who Make It

I had some thoughts of trying to be a performer, but I am not really built like a dancer—too much bosom and hip, I'm afraid.

When you dance with a partner, you must trust him entirely, because you can be seriously injured if he doesn't catch you after a leap, for example. When he carries you around the stage, you remain dependent on him, since you're still dancing—with your body, your arms, your legs. But then he sets you down, lets you go. You are free and you both dance with space between you. He leaves the stage. You have the limelight for your solo. You do the same for him. So it must be for a man and a woman. There must be timing; there must be reciprocity. I need space; I like to be alone. I love my work. But sometimes I need to be carried, and, God knows, I've needed to feel safe—and I have!

I asked June and Ben if there was anything they cared to tell me about their sex life. I wondered, since they had two children, if their experience conformed to the statistics that indicate that sexual satisfaction declines with the birth of each child and improves dramatically when the children leave home.[5] They both agreed that any parent would say it can be exhausting when a baby cries for a two o'clock feeding, that, of course, it gets in the way of sex when young children have trouble falling asleep or have any one of a variety of illnesses. But they feel that the increased sexual pleasure they have had as the children got older comes from another source.

Ben: I think that when we were young we were so focused on performance. I was concerned about whether I had enough staying power, for instance, to bring June to multiple orgasms; June responded by trying to "give them to me." It got in the way of our total, what shall I say, *sensuality*. With experience, we have become much more relaxed, so that we really get greater pleasure from sex. We can take our time; we enjoy the foreplay; arousal seems more spontaneous and genuine. From "fucking," it has become "loving." Intercourse is just what it should be: the climax of lovemaking.

June: Ours has really turned out to be an easy relationship. We had no particular crisis at middle age. We live in a stable neighborhood; among our friends there was only one separation I can recall and that couple is back together again. I would say we had the most trouble when our son was in high school. He dropped out of school and spent all of his time playing drums with a rock group. He stayed out all night; we never knew where he was. I think on some level Ben identified with him; I had a hunch he was reliving his own adolescence. We had a hard time over that!

We both came from families that fought a lot. We were determined this wouldn't be repeated! Ben is a quiet man. He gets impatient with too much talk. That was something for me to get used to.

Ben: I made a good choice when I married June. In many ways, she's a perfect woman for me. As for my professional life, it was shaped by chance. I planned to go to medical school, but took a degree in biochemistry first. I got a very good job offer in an area that fascinated me, and there I was. It's a profession that suits my style. It has given me time for my family and for my interests. June never was opposed to any of them.

June: Quite the contrary. Ben had much broader interests than I ever had and he introduced me to so many things—painting, sculpture, tennis, foreign films.

At home, I found there was nothing grudging in the way he gave. He stayed with the children if I took courses at night; he added a greenhouse onto the house for me.

Ben: Well, you see, I *like* June. I feel loyal to her

and the family; I wouldn't ever want to do anything to hurt her. So that speaks to your question
abut fidelity! I believe the only way to make a
relationship special is to take care of it, to preserve it. . . . This is an inelegant and inadequate
metaphor for marriage, but let me try it out: I
love wood-working and I've become quite skilled
at it. I've discovered certain tools over the years
that function very well; they have balance, feel
right in your hand. I take care of them. They
mean something. But you can always change
them. You can't do that with people. I don't want
to "trade her in." June is a comfortable presence;
it would be horrendous to try to get used to a
new one. Love is partly familiarity.

June: I have a burning need to know I matter to
someone. I couldn't jeopardize that by being
disloyal. We are close in so many ways, ways that
include and go beyond the sexual ones.

We had the children around for twenty
years. I was sad for a while when the second one
left for college, but now I welcome the change.

Ben: You ask about a sense of aging. When I play
tennis, I'm aware of losing physical dexterity and
stamina. I hate to lose the healthy things you can
do with your body. Some limitations are hard to
take. At forty, you feel less threatened by loss;
I'm much more aware of time now and treasure
what I have.

June: Ben has always had grace in taking what
comes along in life.

Ben: I have great respect for June. We enjoy
living with each other.

June and Ben may have achieved the best of what
marriage has to offer. There is the dynamic interaction of
two separate people who, responding with both intuition
and deliberate care, form a whole. The story of June and
Ben sounds too good, too like a Valentine, to be real. We
are skeptical because good relationships like this are so

rare. Out of fear of failure, we become permanently on guard.

Fidelity suits June and Ben. They seem to fit Kernberg's description of a couple's development: From the original chemistry of physical attraction, he writes, there is "a normal maturation of sexual interests [that do not dissipate, but become] linked to *an interest in the total person*" (italics mine).[6] June and Ben have achieved this. Sexual interests that become linked to a response to a whole person explain the enduring charm of a Lou Andreas-Salomé, a Jane Digby, or a Colette at sixty or seventy, who appear in the last chapter. When men and women in our culture are secure enough to look for this development in one another, they can abandon the notion of young, slim, and adolescent as the ideal.

The capacity to love the totality of what another person has become necessitates going beyond the narcissistic self-involvement of young adulthood. "Gradually, throughout adult life," Kernberg adds, "the pleasure in self-fulfillment and creativity becomes fused with the pleasure of giving and dedicating oneself to those one loves and to the ideals for which one stands."[7]

What of Dr. Kernberg's mention of "the ideals for which one stands?" Is one of those ideals fidelity? This question is one of the thorniest possible about a relationship in a culture that has always given lip service to monogamy and tacit approval to infidelity, especially on the part of men, and, with the new sexual permissiveness, for women as well. The question is particularly difficult, since we use sex to express so many needs, including the need for reassurance, for comfort, to ease the fear of being alone—and even for revenge.

It would take at least an entire chapter to mention all the reasons for infidelity. In her book, *In Praise of*

Marriage, Edith Atkin has a list that includes boredom, curiosity, retaliation, depression, and aging.[8] Some couples do not find infidelity a moral issue at all, but either tacitly or openly accept it as a way of keeping the marriage together. Sometimes one of the partners has a disabling illness. In another situation, one is avowedly disinterested in sex, but the couple are affectionate, enjoy each other, and are committed to keeping the marriage together. A friend has told me about her married lover who is a regular part of her life. She is convinced that their relationship of many years' standing has been instrumental in keeping his marriage together. They are excellent lovers, but there is much more in their friendship. She gets a lot of professional advice from him; they go to a lot of cultural events together and enjoy each other's company.

Men and women have often claimed that after an affair their marital relationship improves because of the renewed interest in sex one of them has attained.

Couples deal with the question of infidelity in a number of ways. Some discuss it openly at the outset of their relationship. Francine Klagsbrun writes of one couple who made a verbal contract. The wife said, "If you are unfaithful I will feel that gives me the license to be unfaithful also." She felt it would be intolerable. Her husband agreed because he could not tolerate the notion of her infidelity either.[9]

How many contracts, written, spoken or unspoken, are honored or honored in the breach, remains to be seen. When one of the partners learns of another's infidelity, however, the pain—and the reactions—can be inordinate. Psychiatrist Roger L. Gould describes in his book a middle-aged couple who came to see him on an emergency basis because of the husband's violence to his wife and threats of suicide when he learned of her infidelity.[10]

The wife, on the other hand, spoke of the pain, the

injured pride, and the terrible disillusionment she felt on learning of her husband's middle-aged extra-marital affairs. She adored him, and believed in monogamy. She knew he liked to flirt with women, but it took her some time to learn that he had been unfaithful on numerous occasions. She felt rejected and ugly and began to hate her own body. In the course of the next few years she had two brief affairs of her own that helped restore her sense of self-esteem. When, after a second crisis, he had promised to end his promiscuity, she decided to stay with the marriage. But the loss of trust affected her sexual response to him. She felt she had a lot of scar tissue; the hurt had not gone away. When she learned of his next infidelity, she ended the marriage.

What about this common phenomenon—the "norm"—the troubled marriage, a marriage like the one above? What can be done for those middle-aged couples who find themselves caught in such a relationship?

There was a time when it was believed that middle-aged men and women were too rigid for psychotherapy to be helpful. There's been a complete turnaround. Roger L. Gould, for example, speaks of the forties as a time when men and women demand "coherency" in their lives. Success in a career or business may strengthen the wish to achieve it in one's personal life before it's too late.[11]

Wayne A. Myers describes in his book, *Dynamic Therapy of an Older Patient,* the successful outcome of therapy of a man with two failed marriages and a lifelong problem with potency. He began treatment at the age of fifty-nine.[12]

Otto Kernberg focuses on the psychotherapy of narcissistic men and women such as those in Chapters Nine and Ten. He believes that the prognosis for these patients is better in their late forties and fifties than it was when they still believed that "the next success will solve all their problems." When that fails to happen, they become much more motivated for change.[13]

The British analyst Pearl King writes of the particular pressures and conflicts of this phase of life which people must face, regardless of their overall problems. It is these phase-specific concerns that bring persons of early or late middle age into therapy, she believes. She reports the case of a man in his early sixties, whose problems have a familiar ring: he was in a panic about growing old. He projected his own aging onto his wife and saw her as an old hag, while he indulged in fantasies of affairs with younger women. He was depressed because of his fear that, if he carried out his fantasies, he would be impotent.[14]

Pearl King's case offers evidence in support of my belief that Oedipal problems can reappear in middle age. In this man's fantasy, his wife, the "old hag," represented his aging, bad, withholding mother, while the young woman represented the good and beautiful mother of his childhood and adolescence. For this man, sexual potency was equated with life, and the idea that he might sublimate any of his sexual impulses seemed unmanly. Therapy helped him avoid acting out his sexual fantasies and gave him an ability to enjoy some pleasures other than sex. In his emotional life, King writes, he was "forming a bridge between childhood and adulthood."[15] The focus of the therapy, as in any therapy in middle age, was to stop the futile waste of time in this our one and only life.

In many longstanding marriages, sex is all there is. In many, sex is the least of the couple's concerns. Many couples who made it can have a sustained and physically gratifying sex life which extends over many years without having a good marriage or even a relationship that is particularly friendly, not to speak of intimate. Clearly, sex is not the only variant in distinguishing what it takes to achieve mature love. On the other hand, in a world eternally preoccupied with sex and sexual performance I would be doing a disservice to the whole idea of the varieties of mature love if I failed to speak of intimate couples who have never had a highly charged and passionate love life. Clara and Tom come to mind. They have been married forty years; thirty-five of them have been spent in one house. He stopped working at sixty, was restless, and found a post-retirement job. They married right after college and soon had five children. Clara is outspoken, feisty; Tom a bit lower-keyed, more conservative. They tell me there was a lot of stress when they were first married, had no money, and had to live with Clara's parents. They had plenty of fights over the years, especially if Tom had a couple of drinks after work. But they agree on one fundamental thing. "We've always been committed to each other. Our kids tease us. We hold hands in church!" Theirs has been a relationship that can be characterized as more affectionate then passionate. "With five kids around," says Clara, "well, you find that an awful lot of your energy goes into them. I guess that is the way we wanted it; it suits our needs, to choose the role of mother and father. Our sex life has been warm and friendly, not innovative, not an urge that is so powerful it must constantly be met."

What is most striking about Clara and Tom is how thoroughly they are *wedded* to each other. It's not that they are symbiotic: they have strong, independent interests, but that they are so *attuned.* Tom says, "When I speak to Clara over the phone, I can tell in a second, by the sound of her voice, if something is bothering her." Clara says, "It's like living in this house: I can walk through the rooms at night without a light and never bump into a piece of furniture. I recognize all the sounds it makes—the stair that creaks, the shutter that bangs." Mature love is firmly bonded. Clara and Tom have developed the kind of attunement to one another that has its roots in the best interactions between parents and small children. This kind of responsiveness, which promotes security and trust, is of crucial importance.

Of course, there can be mature love well before forty. I think Clara and Tom are in this category. They appear to have been pretty grown up and knew what they wanted when they got married. There can also be many stable relationships one would not label as "mature," even though they have lasted a long time and the couples would describe themselves as happy. Such persons develop a "fit" that is based on needs, often of a childlike nature, of dominance and submission, of giver and taker.

The subject of love and intimacy has become a popular one in the field of psychotherapy. Practitioners of various theoretical persuasions have become interested in understanding what love is, and what it is not. Psychiatrist Theodore J. Rubin, speaking at a recent all-day conference on "Love, Intimacy, and the Fear of Commitment" from which several hundred people, all of them professionals, had been turned away, offered a larger canvas on which to paint a picture of mature love.[16] He asks how two people ever become genuine "helpmates," since he does not believe love is ever purely altruistic. A couple that is capable of altruism, however, can surmount the self-promoting impulses so encouraged by our society. It is relatively rare, Rubin finds, for a couple to relate in a truly cooperative manner, with a style that is natural and spontaneous, and who do not attach a lot of conditions in order to make it work. The latter Rubin calls "Adversarial Relating," and advises watching soap operas to see it in action. There, the mutual contract is: I'll make you look good and promote your ideal of what you want to be: strong, brave, vigorous, as long as, and only as long as, you do the same for me: make me appear generous, funny, sexy.[17]

Jane and Mark qualify as one of Rubin's "cooperative" couples. In addition, they add several other special attributes to a definition of mature love: not only have they developed a cooperative relationship that got them through a big challenge in middle age, but they have nurtured their capacity for fun, or play, which has enhanced their mutual pleasure in and out of bed. Above all, they have maintained a flexibility of attitude and style that has made the changes in their lives possible. Rather than maintaining a vested interest in the position that "what I am, what I believe is better," they have been able to identify with and enjoy their differences. Furthermore, Jane and Mark have been able to make peace with uncompromisable differences between them, so that they do not remain a constant irritant within the marriage. In sum, they don't act like sibling rivals.

From one perspective, Jane and Mark sound like a traditional couple. Jane worked to help put Mark through law school. They have four children and a house in the suburbs in a moderate-sized city in the Midwest. But when Jane was forty-three, she entered politics and got elected to the city council. In the process, the whole family had to go to work to support her.

At the time of this writing, he is fifty-two, she has just turned fifty. He is a tall, thin, energetic, and verbal man with an off-beat and maverick soul. She is quieter, more considered, and controlled. When he is not practicing law, he is an avid hiker, gardener, and botanizer. She, who tends to love books and travel, has become more interested in the outdoors and in hiking in the past few years. Both of them are very expressive about their marriage:

> Mark: I would say that frustrations in our public lives—our careers—put the most pressure on our marriage. I'm aware of my own personal frustration, not being able to fit my iconoclastic style into an academic costume. I've made a success of public law. But I always loved to teach. I even wanted to become the dean of a law school. But institutional politics always makes me angry and depressed. I'm not good at it. So I've been having to come to terms with the limits to my own horizons. I've had some bitter struggles with myself, because I am ambitious. In the middle of all this, Jane's life took a dramatic turn.
>
> Jane: I taught history while Mark was in law school. This was not a problem. My generation was programmed. Wives helped husbands get started in their careers. I do not say this in a cynical way. Mark could have made it without my help; he did as an undergraduate. But we also wanted to save some money so we could have children. We had them each two years apart. I continued to work part-time. I only had a bachelor's degree, so along the way I got a master's.
>
> I always enjoyed my home, but I think we lived in it more like graduate students than as a middle-class couple. We didn't care that much about how it looked or how neat it was. We'd rather read, listen to music, talk to friends.
>
> When the children were all in school, I became very active in The League of Women Voters. I began to get involved in local issues, gave a lot of speeches. Mark was working "super" full-time, then. But when I became middle-aged, I found myself feeling irritable, restless. I no longer enjoyed teaching. I began to think of getting a doctorate in history, but suddenly I realized what I really wanted to do was to go into

politics. My mood had created tension between Mark and me. I was trying to make a career out of something I no longer valued. What's more, because of my attitude, Mark didn't value it either. Up until the time I entered politics, I'd come to feel I'd been making too many compromises. You could say the balance of power in our relationship was heavily weighted in Mark's favor.

I asked Mark if he felt he had to make a lot of compromises of his own in order for Jane to enter politics.

Mark: No. It was an exciting thing for me. I felt I was "in on" something terrific. That was the spirit of it. She took over the spotlight, but I felt like the impressario. It was good because it created a parity between us. The impresario part, in retrospect, was a bit of low comedy. All four kids were still living at home. When we took over, the household was in chaos. Jane is a competent woman; she's much more efficient than I am. And she's a fantastic cook! We did pitch in. The kids and I worked so mother was free to raise money, go to meetings, campaign. We pushed her. But it was arduous. I have long hours. Shopping and cooking weren't well handled. At times, we were all on edge.

Our sex life was what suffered most of all. Jane was out giving speeches, going to conferences. I had evening commitments of my own. She was often terribly tired when she got home. It turned out to be quite a serious problem for us, because sex has always been an important part of our lives. I've always loved being innovative and playful; Jane is responsive to that. It's kept sex interesting and alive. Happily, now that she has been elected and re-elected to office, her public life is under control—and so is our private one.

So what has been the biggest on-going problem between us? In my view, it's been one of communication. We're the reverse of most couples. I want her to talk about subjective things, but *she* can't! It's a character difference between us. By now, we've adapted to this. We still don't talk much about critical things; the talk is more elliptical. We know each other so well; we can check each other out without a lot of words. We *are* different in our interests. She lives more in the pleasure of the "here and now"—politics, social issues. She's not involved in the meanings of things. For instance, I worry about death; she doesn't. It's not that she denies it, but she's too engaged in living to think about it much.

Part of our tension came from external problems, but part of it came from my inability to engage her, to excite her about philosophical matters. I used to try so hard, I'd work myself up so, I was like a dragon breathing fire. It didn't even touch her, because she'd withdraw. She'd turn to stone and I'd end up just burning my own nostrils. She'd win those battles, because I'd wear myself out. We were bad at negotiating these temperamental differences and would both be hurt and shaken by them. But we'd get back to reality. This difference couldn't be compromised. We're okay at handling it now. Retrospectively, I can see how Jane's steadiness, my inability to get her so charged up, became a source of safety, a sea anchor for me.

I enjoy deferring to her, because it gives her pleasure. I enjoy giving her the bigger piece of the pie. The world isn't fair: Why did my father have to die so young? It's all so haphazard. I like to beat the system when I can. Who said it should all be equal? I go on vacation to places she likes because it pleasures me to be in her presence when she's happy.

Jane: My kids would say we're not ideal parents. We both wanted them to be independent because there was so much we had to do in our own lives. They'd say Mark was impatient and that I was a bit cool and unresponsive.

>Mark: Looking back, I'd say there is something
>else, a bottom line for long-lived marriages.
>Some people have a commitment to sticking
>things out, wanting to finish a job that's started.
>We'd be very reluctant to give up on what we've
>undertaken. I don't find that irrelevant to mar-
>riage. Do you?

It should be fairly clear that the strength of this marriage derives from the cooperation which the partners freely give to one another. But it goes further than that. In Mark's satisfaction in what he has gotten from furthering Jane's pleasure in areas of interest quite different from his, the marriage begins to approximate what Dr. Rubin considers the rarest form of intimacy: "creative" relating, in which each partner really takes pleasure in and is enhanced by supporting what the other wishes to be-come.[18] Such behavior offers the affirmation human be-ings need over a lifetime. In this best of all possible marriages, couples like Jane and Mark, June and Ben achieve a complementarity. ("Complement": defined as "either of two parts that complete the whole or mutually complete each other." "Complementary," adj. From genet-ics: "Producing effects in concert different from those produced separately."[19])

When I began to wonder about what other ingredi-ents from the endless possible variations of loving could be put into a definition of mature love, I found concepts borrowed from child psychiatry surprisingly useful: they turn out to be responses to basic human needs that persist over a lifetime and thus become integral aspects of what can be defined as *mature love.*

First: psychotherapists who have observed the be-havior of parents and children have noted the importance of the creation of what they call "optimal space" or "optimal distance." They see this as a parent's ability to give a child enough leeway to explore without letting him go so far as to feel unsafe or abandoned.[20] In an adult relationship, it is what the psychiatrist Leopold Bellak calls "The Porcupine Syndrome," which he defines as the ability of two people to live close enough for warmth but not too close for comfort. And in Kahlil Gibran's *The Prophet* is this metaphor for marriage (paraphrased): Two trees cannot thrive in each other's shade.[21]

Second: It is within this space that a child begins to differentiate from his parents in order to develop the qualities that will be uniquely his or hers.

Third: Fred Pine, Ph.D., a sensitive observer of children, speaks of the growth that takes place that is, in fact, *facilitated* by disequilibrium.[22] He refers to changes, large or small, that constitute challenges for a child: the development of speech bringing about the need to be understood in a different mode, the birth of a sibling, or the beginning of school.

Carol Gilligan, borrowing on the work of Gerald Piaget and Erik Erikson with children, takes this concept farther. She speaks of the opportunities for development that take place at times of major disequilibrium—of crisis—whether in childhood or later life. Gilligan believes we can use the "heightened vulnerability" felt at such a time to create opportunities for change that will break through repetitive patterns of behavior.[23]

These concepts, translated and applied to the particular challenges of middle age are relevant to the story of Ann and Jim. Ann H. first came to consult me after her mother had been diagnosed as having a highly treatable form of cancer. Ann was preoccupied and agitated. This behavior puzzled her, however, because, although very close to her mother, rarely in the past had she been so thoroughly thrown by a problem.

At forty-three, she was a well-established member of a firm of industrial designers. She worked hard, made a good living, and enjoyed her career. Ann had been divorced for about six years; for four of them she had been involved with Jim O., an attractive, driving man of forty-eight. He worked in the marketing division of a medium-sized corporation. He, too, was divorced, and the father of two teenagers. Jim's office was located some distance away from the city. He found it convenient to maintain an apartment close to his job, so Ann and Jim were not living together "full-time." About six months before I first saw Ann, Jim had bought an old rundown farmhouse in New England which he had just begun to remodel. The two spent weekends there.

It soon became apparent that what had really brought Ann in to see me was a developing crisis in her relationship with Jim that she had been desperately trying to ignore. She could not put her finger on what was happening. They did not argue; their sex life was good. It seemed like nothing had changed. They had two or three long telephone conversations every day. In addition to weekends, they managed to see each other several nights a week. But when she let herself examine the relationship, Ann became aware of growing discomfort. She was becoming self-conscious when they were together. There were moments when she caught herself being silent or overcompensating, becoming manic and over-talkative. Not long after she had begun therapy, Ann got a long, painful letter from Jim speaking of his dissatisfaction with the relationship and his wish to end it.

When Ann and Jim had first met, Jim was having a crisis of his own. His marriage was in such disarray that he had moved out of his house. He was working many hours overtime; his business had just been bought out by a conglomerate. He had developed a stomach ulcer. When they first got together, Jim was more aware than he had ever been of his vulnerability. He loved Ann's spirit, her sense of humor, her unusual competence, kindliness, and concern for him. Because he felt uprooted and needy, he wanted to marry her as soon as his divorce was final. There was plenty of physical space in their relationship, but Jim wanted to "move in" emotionally.

Ann was wary. From the kind of men she had always dated, and above all, from her choice of a partner in her first marriage, she had the idea that she had always needed dynamic men who were sought after by other women to confirm her feelings of attractiveness and self-worth. Jim was such a man. She knew she loved him, but was afraid to commit herself.

The two worked out a *modus vivendi*. With Ann a dependable figure in his life, Jim settled down. He got his job under control, paid more attention to his health, and found time to be with his children. The equilibrium between them began to shift, however, when he bought the farmhouse. It was very much *his* project. He became so enamored of his plans to remodel it that he arranged his life to spend an additional night there every week. Although Ann liked the place, she was quite passive about it, doing nothing that was of particular interest to her. The house became a symbol that Jim no longer needed her in the same way. She began to feel there was too much emotional distance between them. Jim had, in fact, stopped talking about their future. Now she was feeling dependent on him.

Until she began psychotherapy, Ann was not aware of her response to the marked alteration in the balance between the two of them. She realized that she had begun to think obsessively about marriage. She was horrified by the arrival of the "Dear Jane" letter from Jim. He listed a number of concrete criticisms of her which he summed up by saying that he felt she had become a much less interesting person.

Jim was unaware of the change in his own scenario. But the purchase of the farmhouse had been symbolic for him as well. Now that he was feeling healthy again, feeling more in charge of his life, some of his old ambivalence toward women had reasserted itself. He began to resent the mature, competent qualities he had initially admired in Ann. From being a much-needed person who would always be there for him, Ann's increasing availability began to seem intrusive and demanding.

Jim resurrected his adolescent dream: He would find a beautiful and exciting woman who would make him feel great. For a time he could avoid having to work out a relationship which contained a mixture of closeness and distance, of dependence and self-sufficiency. All Jim was fully aware of when he wrote Ann the letter was his restlessness and the fact that his forty-ninth birthday was approaching. He began dating younger, less successful women who were rather classically beautiful.

Ann's response to his leave-taking is instructive. After several weeks of depression, fits of weeping, and terrible insomnia, she stopped blaming Jim and began to think about her own behavior. In her growing wish to please him and bind him closely to her, she had begun to cling, to lose her individuality. She no longer saw her former friends, who were writers and poets. In fact, Ann had written short stories all of her life and had published in several magazines. But in the past year, in the evenings she did not spend with Jim, she was content to watch television and read bestsellers. No time for writing, she had said to herself, no time for projects intended to complete her apartment. Now she turned to the unfinished business of her own life; she began to pay attention to her writing, to her home, and to her personal appearance. She was amazed at what she had allowed to happen to herself and determined never to repeat it.

The story of Ann and Jim does not end here. The two had never been entirely out of touch with one another. Jim discovered that he really missed her. He began to move back in her direction. They had both changed. Jim felt chagrined by his own superficiality in thinking he could recreate his past with other women. He realized how much he valued Ann's ability to listen, how good they could be together, how close they could feel.

He was delighted with her renewed creativity—and with her sense of independence. Their crisis made them reconsider their own priorities; it helped them define the degree of emotional closeness and separateness they needed to make the relationship work. Not long ago Ann called me to say that she and Jim have been back together for two years. They feel no pressure to get married; but they plan their future together.

We can make few predictions about the future of marriage. Phyllis Rose in her elegant book, *Parallel Lives: Five Victorian Marriages,* expresses her own feeling "that marriage still displaces too many other possibilities in our culture."[24] Marriage, in spite of its enormous difficulties, is probably still the most satisfactory arrangement we have yet devised that creates—if that is what you want from life—the possibility of security, a measure of long-term stability, and intimacy. For the many women who find themselves alone in the second half of life, however, there are challenging models of women who are single, female, and over forty.

◄§12§►

Single, Female, and Over Forty

. . . once you fully apprehend the futility of a life without strug-gle you are equipped with a basic means of salvation.

Tennessee Williams, "On A Streetcar Named Success."
The New York Times, November 30, 1947.

Colette on Mae West:

She alone out of an enormous and dull catalogue of heroines, does not get married at the end of the film, does not gaze sadly at her declining youth in a silver-framed mirror in the worst possible taste, and she alone does not experience the bitterness of the abandoned older woman.

From a newspaper clipping sent to me by a friend.
(Colette source unidentified.)

Watching old movies from a 1980s perspective is a striking lesson in sociology. So often husbands in pictures of the 1930s, 1940s, and 1950s tend to be engaging egocentric boys, their wives long-suffering, martyred mother figures. Bob Hope's 1955 "Seven Little Foys" is a good case in point. Colette, in her observation quoted above, comments on the stereotype of the older woman of this era, on her "progress" from saintly self-denying wife or mistress to woman abandoned. In this scenario, if she is without a man at middle age, she is fated to be passive and helpless. The popular novel, *Back Street,* by Fannie Hurst that deals with such a fantasy was made into a movie three times: in 1932, 1941, and 1961. Unfortunately, some women still respond this way, a point already made. But happily, women have rewritten the script. We have a new model: the single middle-aged woman who is in charge of her life.

Whether she comes from a working- or middle-class background, is or is not well educated, whether she's struggled financially all of her life or had it relatively easy, whether divorced, widowed, or never married, she shares a lot of characteristics with her peers. Many words come to mind to describe her: She can sort out priorities at middle age; she doesn't shrink from risk-taking. She has developed a sense of pride and independence. She knows when she's reached a road block, when she has to make a decision, has to make a move.

There's a heroine of mine who's a lot like her. I've talked about her to some women patients when they were feeling helpless and sorry for themselves. She is Sadie Thompson, heroine of W. Somerset Maugham's melodramatic story, "Rain."[1] Joan Crawford played her with Walter Huston in one film version of the tale. The action takes place in the tropics during the rainy season. Sadie Thompson is a prostitute who works the bar of a hotel frequented by sailors. She dresses flamboyantly in a black and white striped satin dress, a feather boa, and lace stockings. Walter Huston plays the role of a preacher who takes it upon himself to save Sadie's soul. He transforms her. She becomes devout, gives up makeup and jewelry. She takes to wearing plain, dark, nun-like clothes. Sadie and the preacher spend hours together in prayer while the rain beats down incessantly, forcing them into an intense symbiotic relationship. Sadie has given herself over completely to this man. She has become innocent and trusting. One night, however, the preacher becomes aware that the fervor with which he wants to possess Sadie is not a spiritual one: he wants her sexually. He loses control and rapes her. Overcome by shame and guilt, the preacher commits suicide. Initially, Sadie feels betrayed, lost, abandoned. She had tried to become everything this man wanted her to be, and even *he* treated her like a whore. The next day Sadie reappears in the bar. The camera first catches her wonderful legs, the lace stockings, the high-heeled shoes, then moves up to the striped satin dress, the feather boa. Above all, what the camera captures is the posture, the walk of a woman who has reclaimed her self.[2]

There have always been women like Sadie Thompson, who was active rather than passive, who responded to crises by taking charge. Among them were the wives of plantation owners, often pampered and protected women, who took over the management of large estates when their husbands were fighting in the Civil War; pioneer women who learned how to defend their homes from attacks by Indians; countless single women who went as nurses, teachers, and missionaries to strange and unknown parts of the world. For a good account of these women, see Chapter Four in Nina Auerbach's *Woman and the Demon*.[3]

The rise of the middle class in the nineteenth century changed the aspirations of women. With money came the opportunity to emulate the aristocracy. The position of a successful man was strengthened if his wife stayed at home and became living proof of the fact that he did not *need* to have her work. In my own lifetime, in the Midwest where I grew up, with the rarest exceptions only unmarried women had careers, worked for pay. In my family I was the first female in three generations to go to work. The ideal, the woman who stayed at home, had children, and had time for golf and volunteer work, fostered by Hollywood, the soap operas, and "True Romance"-type magazines, became the model to which millions of American women aspired. When I became a therapist I was surprised at the number of women in their forties and fifties today who, although they knew they would go to work, were still brought up with the same expectations. But they have been touched by the Women's Movement; many have been divorced; have had to establish themselves in a "single" life. What has fallen away is the dream of being realized by a man.

There are some interesting models among the women who became single again in middle age, who have had to learn how to make a life on their own. Nina S. is one. Mother of two, grandmother of four, and on her own for over fifteen years, she recently became a neighbor of mine. She relates:

> I grew up knowing I'd marry and have kids; I did—right after college. In four years' time I had two children. And although I knew the marriage wasn't right, it took me twenty years to leave. My husband loved the children; I felt it would be wrong to deprive them of a parent; I knew it would be awfully hard to raise the children alone.
>
> It wasn't a bad life. My husband was do-ing well; we had friends, the family. There was nothing really wrong with him. But I felt we did not *enhance* each other. He never made me feel wonderful; I never made him feel wonderful. He wasn't happy in his work. I knew he had the potential to develop in ways that would be more satisfying, but he always felt stuck. I supported his wish to change jobs and really meant it when

I said we could do with less money. But some-how he couldn't move. I felt his unhappiness; it cast a pall over the marriage.

Meanwhile, I had gotten a part-time job. I loved to cook so I began to edit some cookbooks at home. Then I wrote one of my own. I had a modest success with this. But at the same time, I knew I was changing. I think this altered the balance in our marriage. My husband needed me to "think" dependent, while I began to think of separating. We talked about it from time to time, but he was violently against it.

Initially, I think I wanted a man to solve all my problems; I found out he couldn't. Grow-ing up—as a kid—I always felt I had a "destiny" to do something with my life. I was very vague about what form this "doing" would take. At forty-three I decided I couldn't rescue him, but had to rescue myself. So I initiated the separa-tion and, ultimately, the divorce. I felt I had to live alone, had to work things out, had to *deal* with myself.

I guess I always felt a mixture of security and insecurity. I did well in school, got a lot of recognition there. Typically, my parents ex-pected more of my brother than they did of me and paid much more attention to his failures than to my successes. That made me wonder just how important I was meant to be to any-one—or to myself. Boy, when I left my marriage, I was much more in the "Lost" column than the "Found." And, God knows, I couldn't tell which way I was heading or how I'd recognize it if I found it.

I moved to a town fairly close by. I came back for half of every week for a year until my second child finished high school. I started a cooking school in my new home; it went well. After the kids were in college and my divorce was final, I moved again. By this time, I felt a bit more self-assured. I found a partner, a couple of backers, and we opened up a shop that specializes in cookware. I think I still need challenges to prove to myself that I am competent. So we recently started to make a surprising "go" of a mail order business in interesting household equipment.

How has Nina managed to become so independent and successful? One means is the way she tackles problems. I've watched her in action. She refuses to dwell on past mistakes. "It's finished; I don't want to talk about it," she'll say. When she's confronted with a new challenge she struggles for awhile. She listens to what both her feelings and her judgment tell her. Then she makes a decision, moves on, refuses to second-guess herself.

Speaking of her personal life, Nina says, "I had to learn to be alone; I've done that. There are times when I come home and feel sad, but I start a telephone 'blitz,' call some friends and talk, or make a date to go to a movie. It works." Nina did not leave her marriage looking for a partner. She says, however, that she has never had trouble finding men to date. In the years she has been on her own she has developed close friendships with men and has had several extended relationships. She does not rule out the possibility of remarriage, but, she says, not if it means a repetition of the compromises she lived with for twenty years.

Nina is a person who has resolved significant doubts about herself. She did not have a genuine sense of self-esteem until well after forty. We all have the potential to grow, to develop over a lifetime. If, like Nina, we're going to try to feel better about our middle-aged selves, we'd do well to find out how a sense of self and self-esteem gets established in the first place.

Psychiatrist Joseph Lichtenberg has a definition of "self" that addresses the question of identity over time. He believes a person must have "the ability to maintain a sense of *cohesiveness*, of *continuity*, an essential sense of *sameness* in the midst of developmental change."[4] I would also include in a definition of self such aspects as an image of one's physical, intellectual, and moral self. This is an ideal that can be worked toward. If I were to make a linear chart and place on it each woman over forty I quote in this chapter, I'd find they are at significantly different places in terms of their psychological growth. What is important, however, is the progress they are making.

To go back to the beginning, where it all starts: I believe that from the earliest years, a process occurs in which a child takes in positive responses from parents and other people of importance to him or her. Children respond to what has been popularly called "The gleam in mother's eye," or the "Watch me!" phenomenon. An excellent illustration of this can be found at a community swimming pool which is usually populated by a lot of youngsters—and a lot of mothers. The mothers of children competent enough to be in the water by themselves sit around the edge of the pool and socialize. Whenever a child wants to try something new—say jump off the diving board—he first says, "Watch me, Mommy!" He repeats the request with growing urgency until he gets the eye contact he wants. Then he jumps. Before his head is even fully out of the water, he looks at his mother for her encouragement and approval. Her positive response gives him pleasure and the impulse to try again. When this process is successful, mothers usually have to drag children out of the pool, even though they're shivering and their lips are blue.

When children get enough positive feedback, their feelings of self-worth become less dependent on the outside world. They develop an internal function that regulates self-esteem. I liken it to a built-in thermostat. When it's working, a disappointment or rejection does not hit them so hard that they feel frozen. They know their own value, and simply call for more heat.

In spite of such internal resources, everyone needs affirmation over a lifetime for the maintenance of self-esteem. As adults, we have the advantage of seeking it from people or activities of our own choosing, of setting our own standards of value. We get a special boost from what psychiatrist Christopher Bollas calls "transformational experiences."[5] The event can be of major or minor importance: climbing a mountain, learning to drive a car, baking a good loaf of bread. Its significance lies in the enhancement or consolidation of one's sense of confidence, of *belief* in oneself.

Sally Field received an Oscar for Best Actress of the year in 1984 for her role in "Places In the Heart." After the award ceremony, she told the assembled newsmen and women how good it felt to have doubts about her ability assuaged; how much it had hurt whenever she felt she had not gained the respect of an audience. What was most impressive, however, was what she said when she was awarded the trophy for the second time (Her first Oscar was for her role as a labor organizer in "Norma Rae"), her name up in lights on marquees all over the country. She had made it in one of the toughest, most competitive industries in the world. And in her acceptance speech she said, with a mixture of rapture and wonder, "People like me! They really like me!"

In order to like yourself, you have to have and to acquire a pretty good picture of who and what you are, and what you are capable of doing. Eleanor C. is a dramatic example of a woman in the process of becoming, who, in her mid-forties, is still consolidating her sense of self. She seems so quiet and self-effacing that one is quite unprepared for her story.

She is forty-five and has been divorced for seven years. She is slim, well-groomed: her clothes are conservative in style. This is what she says:

Mother never worked and Dad didn't make much money. My parents were not educated people, so school was never emphasized in our home. I didn't get good marks; I didn't think I was smart enough. Mother only knew how to encourage me in one area: my social life. So I'd bring home hordes of kids and made it my "thing" to be popular. Both my parents got a lot of vicarious pleasure out of that.

I went off to the University of Illinois at Champaign/Urbana. I was afraid to crack a book there, because I was convinced that I was below average in intelligence—that I couldn't learn. So I flunked out by the end of the first year. I came home and worked as a clerk and hated it. At twenty I was convinced that it was time to get married. I met the man who was to be my husband. We were engaged in three weeks, married in three months, and had three children.

I was controlled by him; he was so thoroughly in charge that I even had to tell him exactly how I spent my household money. It's not surprising that our marriage was not a good one. We were in and out of marital counselling for years, trying to make it work. At one point we happened onto a group whose aim was to teach parenting skills. I was so intrigued by the books that were mentioned to us that I began to read a lot of them. The leader used to make us take turns being in charge of the group meetings. I found it a challenge. I started to take classes. It was the one activity of mine my husband approved. Then I began to lead parents' groups myself. I went on studying for almost ten years, taking courses in self-development and self-awareness.

Venus After Forty

At one point there was a member of one of my parenting groups who was an officer in a bank. He asked me if I thought I could work with his staff and teach them communication skills. Then I was invited by a pharmaceutical house to train their sales force in ways to approach a customer. I tried it, following an outline they gave me, thinking of the self-awareness classes I'd taken—and improvising.

After two years of this, I began to gain some confidence. I decided to go out on my own, to start a business—and to get a divorce. I'd wanted out for a long time, but the marital counsellors were always against it. Once I made this decision, although it was painful, I never looked back. I've gone on to open my own consulting firm and am now very successful. I'm doing work people with Ph.D.s do, and competing with men and women who have been in this field for twenty years. It's not been easy. I got a rotten financial settlement in my divorce so I've worked terribly hard for my children. My women friends were very uncomfortable with what I was doing. They called me a radical and a "Women's Libber" for divorcing my husband. My parents agreed, even though they disliked him. But I've given my children a good education. Now that I can afford it, I'm planning to take them away on a lovely holiday. My oldest child is starting graduate school and the youngest is about to finish high school. Next year, I'll be totally alone. This will be a whole new chapter for me.

I talked to a psychologist briefly when I was getting my divorce. I was thirty-eight. He said, "You'll be too old for the men you want to date and the young ones will be inappropriate." My husband, incidentally, married a woman twenty years his junior. Well, the psychologist frightened me a lot; I began to date a lot of men indiscriminately. It was pretty awful. Then I met a younger man whom I've been seeing for five years. We get along well. He's a very good person. I've helped him get started professionally. But now he wants a family, so it's time to separate. I'm able to take care of myself, still I'm scared. I don't quite trust myself, though, because of some of the men I've chosen. I need to learn about intimacy. Sometimes, I feel I'll never remarry. I hope to. But I have a lot of pride in what I've done; I can never let myself be so controlled again.

I told Eleanor I thought she was fantastic. She looked at me and self-doubts flickered in her eyes. "Do you really think so?" she asked.

Nina and Eleanor are two women who, after trying to make their marriages work, left them because of their conviction that their relationship with their husbands was a serious constraint on their own growth and development. Their initiative made me wonder if women who become single against their will, whether through divorce or widowhood, have a qualitatively different experience.

It is apparent that a woman who is left, whether by divorce or through the death of a spouse, feels abandoned. In contrast to the woman who is widowed, the woman whose marriage breaks up against her will has a sense of failure. Often, she feels ashamed and vulnerable. One of Martha A.'s male friends, for example, responded to the news of her separation with the comment, "But you'll suffer such a loss of status!" Maxine and Ruth, who went to the same divorce lawyer feeling anxious about the future, were each told in pontifical tones, "I may be able to get you a good settlement, but I can't get you what you really want—*him!*" Society shakes its head, clucks its tongue, and takes a dim view of the lives of the women who are left, as though they are permanently disadvantaged—without a future.

Widowed women, on the other hand, get more

Venus After Forty

sympathy and support. Our culture has rituals to deal with death that it lacks in dealing with divorce. Yet widows are not protected from humiliation, either.

But there is a special hurt for women who are left via the breakup of their marriage. Betty P., who is forty-five and has been divorced for twelve years, says she will never get over feeling sad about the fact that she had only one child, especially when her former husband subsequently had two children with his second wife.

Initially, when women are left or widowed, their lives feel out of control. Three or four years later, however, one is often amazed at what they have accomplished. Many say they fought self-pity, were determined to make a good life for themselves, worked terribly hard at it, and, in the process became very creative. They have not only regained but increased their feelings of self-esteem. However, there *is* a difference between women who leave marriages on their own and those who are left. There is trauma in being left against one's will. It leaves residual pain, although the wound may heal normally and no longer actively interfere with the person's life.

Phyllis S. is one such woman. Her husband had an affair for several years and had left the marriage. He wanted to return, but before their differences could be worked out he died of a stroke. Phyllis is forty-nine and has been widowed for less than a year. She was in a state of shock when she learned of his death. It was not until she began to try to take charge of her finances that she learned what she was facing. Her only child was finishing high school and had plans to go on to college. During her marriage, the three of them had gotten along well. They owned an apartment in a good middle-income housing development, had a car which they enjoyed, and paid their son's tuition at a private parochial high school. But it wasn't until she got in touch with her husband's employer that Phyllis learned how heavily he had borrowed on his pension and life insurance. She was unaware of how much he had been gambling—betting on the horses and on basketball games.

Phyllis, a black woman, comes from a large family. She had to start work at sixteen and could not finish her education; her jobs, therefore, have not been highly-paid ones. The period of confusion she felt after her husband's death did not last long. She knew she had to organize her life. She found additional work; her son unearthed a higher-paying after-school job. The two of them began a campaign for college scholarships and tuition subsidies. They got back on course.

Phyllis's boy is now away at college. For her part, she has been surprised by the degree to which the rest of her life has improved. Her husband was a nay-sayer; he had become socially withdrawn. She has felt freer to pursue her own interests. First, she began taking courses in English and math, then went on to taking courses in computer science. She has become very active on committees in her apartment complex. She has a lot of friends, is an excellent hostess, loves to entertain, and loves to dance. "I have to think of my own future now," she says. "I depended too much on my husband. I have to save some money. Maybe there'll be another man, someday, if he seems dependable—and full of life."

Phyllis shares many of the reactions of other women on their own. Gladys, widowed, got a great boost out of taking over her husband's business. Sylvia, an elementary school teacher, also widowed, knew she had shared an interest in athletics with her husband. But she knew she had also watched football games endlessly on TV out of a sense of obligation while her husband was alive. Now, on her own, three children grown, she has the opportunity to redefine herself. She did not go back to teaching, but has allowed her passionate long-time interest in horticulture to develop. She is now working at a nursery, learning a great deal more about plants and gardening. She is very enthusiastic about this new development in her life.

Why could these women not have changed directions in the ways they have while they were within a relationship? Why did they feel they had to be single in order to do so? To try to find out, I distributed a questionnaire at a conference at which I gave a talk addressed to single women.[6] It asked how the lives of formerly married women seemed different. This was a self-selected group to be sure, because married women in their forties or fifties did not attend, nor did single women who had made significant new connections. Yet it was striking how, in spite of all the consciousness-raising of the Women's Movement, all the talk of equality, these women felt they had had to cater to their husbands, to become satellites around a more powerful star. In reviewing the answers I was struck by a recurring theme that had to do with freedom and independence. A woman of fifty who has been widowed for two years, although she is dating again, wrote about how free she feels, "because now I do not have to and never will let myself be in a position where I have to explain my actions, my whereabouts, my spending, my work, my time, to anyone." A woman of forty, divorced for two and one half years, wrote, "I can come and go as I please, much more than before, because I felt I had to answer to my husband's needs and wishes. I can give my children much more of me—that's greater than money can buy."

Women who are divorced or widowed at middle age have mixed feelings. They are often lonely and would prefer to be sharing their lives with a man. They know that adjustments and concessions are part of living with a

Single, Female, and Over Forty

partner. But they are no longer willing to make compromises that stand in the way of their own growth—including their relationships with their children or their friends. The divorced women in this sample do not want to be married to their former husbands. A number of them reported experiences like this one: "When I meet a person I haven't seen for some time, a friend who doesn't know about my separation, he or she will invariably murmur, 'Oh, I'm *so* sorry!' This response comes as something of a shock. I don't feel sorry; in fact, the opposite is true."

In this book I have quoted some terrible jokes about old maids and spinsters that are still making the rounds of out-of-the-way night clubs and are included in joke books. One of the more encouraging trends I've discovered, however, is the decline of the image of the prune-faced, sexually starved, never-married older woman. (One day we must find a better term than "never married" woman. The psychiatrist Carol Nadelson refers to the state of being unmarried as "singlehood." Maybe it will take!) Yet if we take as a given that almost every woman grows up with the idea of getting married, and since society still gives its seal of approval to married women, then one could wonder how never-married women establish and maintain their sense of self-esteem. Three examples come to mind. The first, Edna C., is a single woman in her late forties who has never been particularly career-minded; the satisfactions of her life have come from her well-developed interests. Bonnie P. has a successful career. The focus of her life in her forties has been on her adopted son. Beverly W. is a former patient of mine who had to struggle to change her negative opinion of herself in order to gain self-esteem in middle age.

I met Edna C. on a trip I once took to the Far East. She is a quiet and somewhat reserved woman, a wonderful traveller and interesting to be with. She, too, reached maturity without getting caught up in the Women's Movement. Coming from a small college town in Pennsylvania, she felt comfortable accepting the goals set by her family and her social milieu—to follow the conventional wife and mother path. She says:

> I had no career ambitions to speak of. I did not go to graduate school. Instead, I came to New York and worked as a junior editor for a big publishing house. I managed to save enough money to take a six-month trip on a freighter. That hooked me on travelling. As for men, I did have a long relationship with a fellow from my home town. We'd see each other when he came to the city. Once we took a long vacation to-gether—a marvellous trip to India. I knew, as time went on, that we weren't getting closer, but it did throw me when he told me he was en-gaged. I went through a period of what I call 'continental drift.' I was upset, cried a lot, mourned him, quit my job. Then I decided it was time to put my life together. I went to work for a travel agency that organizes special-interest tours, with a focus on such things as art, gar-dens, or wilderness travel. I've had a chance to lead some groups and to go on my own.
>
> In addition to my passion for travel, I adore films and ballet. I have many good friends, but if there's no one free and there's something I want to do, I'm quite content to do it alone. I spend a lot of time with men—in my work and when I travel. I date, but have no grand passion at the moment. It's clear to me that I'm disap-pointed about not having a family. At this moment of my life, however, it would be a tough decision to start to live with a man. I suffer fools badly and wouldn't be able to make compromises.
>
> I think I'm lucky to have lived to a time when there is no stigma attached to being single.

There are some awfully good models. Do you know about Gertrude Bell, an English woman who lived from 1868 to 1926? She went to Oxford when women were first admitted there. Bell was a mountain climber and world traveller. When she arrived in the Near East, she got caught up in archaeology. She became involved in important digs in Iraq and helped found the wonderful archaeological museum in Baghdad. Gertrude Bell had a fascinating time of it. She never married; I'm quite sure that I never will—I have a good life.

Edna and Bonnie P. are close in age. They are both single women. Other than these two facts, they have little else in common. Their characters, their lifestyles, and the worlds they have created for themselves are totally different. Bonnie has always been academically ambitious. As soon as she got her bachelor's degree, she went on to get her doctorate. In twelve years' time, she has become a tenured professor of history in a college in New Jersey. I wanted to interview Bonnie because she is a participant in a group called "Mothers By Choice." All of the women are single parents who have adopted babies or had them by artificial insemination.

In truth, although I sincerely empathize with a woman's wish to have a child, I went to meet Bonnie with some prejudices of my own. I thought it selfish for women to have babies as single parents. Every child needs a father. Besides, it is difficult enough growing up adopted with *two* parents—let alone one.

I entered Bonnie's house through the kitchen. (She had, she said, had a terrible struggle getting this place. Ten years ago single women had to fight to get banks to give them a mortgage.) Smells of baking filled the room. Bonnie was making a cake for her son to take to a school party the next day. The house was old and roomy. A lot of work had gone into its restoration. It looked like the kind of well-loved home that could have been created by any academic couple. Two rooms were rented out to students who helped pay the taxes and who filled in as babysitters.

I had a chance to see Bonnie interact with her lively six-year-old son, Lee. After he went to bed, we talked.

This is what Bonnie had to say about herself:

I like my life. It didn't just happen, though. I've shaped it, chosen it. Twenty years ago when all my peers were busy getting married, I just wasn't seriously interested. I was fascinated and totally challenged by modern history and political science. I knew I wanted to study, to write, to teach.

As for my personal life all these years, I like men and I love sex. I've always had loving relationships with men. One of the persons I cared for the most was killed quite suddenly in an automobile accident. He helped me restore this house. My closest friends are men. As for marriage, maybe you could say no one ever measured up to my father, who was a generous, warm, and committed human being. I don't see much of that in my generation. My present lover is an interesting man. But he is neither affectionate nor generous. I know I will end it.

I'm still looking for a partner. But I share the feelings of other women who are single mothers. The biological clock told us we could not wait any longer. So we have a child. It doesn't mean we don't want to marry. Especially now that I'm in my forties, I'm thinking about getting older, and I don't want to be alone.

Now let me tell you about my little boy. He was a lovely baby. I was delighted with him and so were my parents. They were very supportive of what I was doing. We discovered when he was less than a year old that he had a congenital heart defect that required major corrective surgery. I took him to a number of doctors, but I could not avoid the operation. He has done beautifully; he's perfectly fine physically.

With that big one out of the way, I turned to the question of creating a support system for the two of us. Luckily, as a professor, I have some leeway in my schedule. For instance, now I am always at home from the time he gets out of school until bedtime.

There is a network of single mothers; we have a publication. We've gotten to know each other. That's a help. I have my neighbors; they're very important. There's a father who lives down the block who works at home. His wife works in town. We help each other. I'll cook something for them or take care of their kids some afternoons—and he'll come help if my furnace goes out or he'll come use his snowblower on my driveway—and he'll play with Lee.

All of us without husbands think a lot about how to get father people into our children's lives. My dad died two years ago, and I was so upset, partly because he loved Lee so much. After that, Jerry, my dearest friend, an older man, because he knew how important it was to me, came and stayed here two nights a week until just recently, when he moved out of town. I know this is an important area. Lee asks about daddies all the time. I feel I can be ingenious about working on this one. Meanwhile, Lee's doing wonderfully in school. We have great times together, and I'm so happy to have him.

I came away from my interview with Bonnie gaining great respect for what she and other women like her are doing. As if I needed any more evidence, on my way out, I stopped to look at pictures that were taken at the airport when Lee first arrived from a Third World country. Bonnie was holding him; the tears were streaming down her face. "I still can't look at those pictures without crying," Bonnie said.

I don't want to romanticize Bonnie's life, or the lives of those of any of the other people—men or women— about whom I write. I realize I am telling success stories. And even these will not have fairy-tale endings. For example, for an account of the struggles of a single woman, the conflict between her love of her child and her passion for the man who first awakens her sexuality, see Sue Miller's novel, *The Good Mother.*[7] But just as I was beginning to feel like I might be making life seem too rosy, I came across a story that made me optimistic again about the task called "development in the second half of life." I called a never-married women in her fifties, Amy B., who had filled out one of my questionnaires. A few words she had written about the discovery of new options in middle age had caught my eye. They were, "I now have a family by adoption." In a brief telephone conversation, she told me she was a former nun who has adopted three hard-to-place children. One is learning-disabled, one was physically and sexually abused, and the third has behavior problems. Two boys are teenagers and the girl is only seven. When Amy got her first child, she asked him what he wanted to do most in the world. "Go to Disneyland," he replied. "So we took off," Amy said. This is what she told me about her life with the children:

> I have a lot of resources to help me. There are other families in my area, mostly couples, who have adopted older children. Several of the new parents are divorced women. We each pair up with another family in a "buddy" system, so there's always someone to call, someone to talk to. I like having these children. I feel much more alive. The idea came to me when I was on a hike just about three years ago. I love the outdoors; it was a particularly fine day. But a relationship that didn't work out had just ended. I was feeling down. Then the thought came to me, "I don't have to be married to adopt a child."

Single, Female, and Over Forty

Am I totally absorbed in being a mother? Yes and no. The children are older so they can be in after-school programs. Their teachers are very helpful, too. When I was a nun I worked in an administrative capacity for many years. Recently, I started graduate work in government and political science; I plan to teach on an undergraduate level. I am studying part-time, however. As for the rest of my life, I'd still like to get married and have a complete family. My desire to love and be loved includes but extends beyond the children.

Bonnie, Edna, and Amy are good examples of the process of individual growth at middle age. Beverly, a patient of mine, by contrast, was stuck. She had moved to New York from a much smaller town in the West, after giving up both the person she had been living with and her job as a laboratory technician. She came to New York to find a new man and a new career. When she found neither, she managed to find a therapist. She had been in town for about five years and hated her life here. Beverly supported herself by running a small office for a man who worked as a consultant. He was away most of the time. She was essentially alone every day with very little to do.

Beverly had a dependent, waif-like, uncared-for quality. For example, she'd be totally unprepared when it rained and would come in to see me with wet feet and dripping hair. She had a terrible time taking care of money, whether balancing her checkbook or paying her bills. She spent a great deal of her time in a neighborhood bar and restaurant where she got to know the owners. Occasionally, she would meet a man who would befriend her. I saw Beverly for several years. She worked hard in therapy. Today she is a bright, independent, well-educated woman. She had passed her fortieth birthday when I last saw her. Beverly had pulled herself together, both mentally and physically. She had embarked on a job in hospital administration in a competitive, full-of-people world. She even liked being in New York!

The women I've been describing share three qualities that give further meaning to the idea of change and growth in middle age. First, they have developed a realistic sense of time; time now works for them. Because of the biological clock and the approach of the menopause, these women, in contrast to middle-aged men, have to abandon the fantasy that they can relive their youth. Eleanor, at forty-eight, for example, knew she would have to separate from the young man she lived with and begin to deal with a period of being alone, when he announced he was ready to have a family. By the same token, Bonnie knew she had to have her child, even if she had not found a partner, since time would not let her wait. The onset of menopause itself forces women to think about life and time in a way that men cannot.

Since women have the chief responsibility for childrearing, the maturation and departure of children during these years confronts them with the task of planning the next stage of life. One can say that the same holds true for married women. I would add that one reason that women who are divorced or widowed at middle age do better on their own than men is that they have been forced to begin preparation for the second half of their lives.

I was impressed with the number of years the once-married women who answered my questionnaire had already been on their own by their mid-forties. Part of this phenomenon, of course, is the increase in the number of divorces that occur among people of middle age and of their ultimate prospects of widowhood. These women have learned a second necessity: the capacity to be alone. Edna, my never-married friend, was especially good at this. Bonnie and Amy, on the other hand, had developed a third talent, one that many single women talk about: the ability to create a community for themselves. These two women found other single people who were parents of adopted children and in so doing created a situation of greater security. To borrow a term from child development, these women were building a "holding environment" for themselves within which they could feel safer. I was impressed with how often single women told me about close groups they had formed. Sylvia started a small business with five single women. They got to be friends; she introduced them to me as "my family." Patsy bought a ramshackle house in the country. Some of her friends, couples and single men and women, helped her restore it. They live in it together now in the summer. She calls it "my commune." Paulette loves family gatherings. Her teenagers are still living at home. She's been having the same friends, her "mob," over every Thanksgiving for years. "I'm not worried about being alone when I get older," she says. "The 'mob' and I will take a place together when we're retired, and I'll be the housemother." These women have become, in fact are still in the process of becoming, well-integrated human beings, solid at the core, who know what they value, what they believe, and the image of themselves they wish to project.

Finally, I would say these are not angry women consumed by feelings that life is unfair. They use the energy that could be turned upon themselves in self-defeat and depression to become active, to solve problems. I know from a clinical perspective how important it is for women to be able to deal with their anger (if she hasn't had the baby she wanted, if her former husband has most of the money, if he's remarried and she's not . . .). Free women can use their energy for work and for pleasure, for play, for fun.

The last person I interviewed, Sara, told me "I felt

so guilty when my marriage broke up I had to see a therapist. I was so angry, shaken, and nervous when my next relationship ended that I found myself adding locks to my front door, thinking the enemy was outside. But now I've got it together. My kids and I are fine. My work goes well; so does the rest of my life. I wake up every morning just feeling grateful!"

The stories of these women make me think of Jim, the slave who was freed at the end of Mark Twain's *Huckleberry Finn*. "I'm rich now, come to think of it," he said. "I own myself!"[8]

The question still remains: how do single women deal with their sexuality? Their behaviors cover a very wide range, from the belief in recreational sex to the firm conviction that sex without a caring love relationship is totally unthinkable.

Most single women, I have found, are going about their lives as though they may remain alone. But they do not shut the door to the possibility of finding a partner. "After all," as Bonnie P. said, "I've made a lot of good things happen in my life. If the Census Bureau reports there are fifty-four men to every hundred women between the ages of forty-five to sixty-five, why shouldn't I be among the fifty-four women who find a person who is right for them?"

One thing these women share: their self-esteem is in place. A sense of themselves as sexual beings is part of their self-images. They share with the women who are the subjects of the next chapter the ability, regardless of age, to send out sexual signals, to be sensual human beings all of their lives.

❦§13§❦

The Sensual Older Woman

For I have never ceased to be young, if being young is always loving.

George Sand at 67
Letter to Gustave Flaubert,
September 14, 1871

. . . . I can neither live up to ideals nor serve as a model for anyone else. But I can most certainly live my own life and I shall do it come what may. By doing that I am not representing any principle but something much more wonderful, something that lives in me, something that is quite warm with life, rejoices and wants to break out.

Lou Andreas-Salomé
Letter to Hendrik Gillot
Rome, 1882

Istanbul, the city of Byzantine rulers, Crusaders and Ottoman Turks, is like a fine, aristocratic woman of advancing years, who rewards the persistent by slowly revealing her secrets and treasures.

Joseph B. Treaster. *Istanbul.*

In spite of some men's fantasies that have created powerful myths about the sexual undesirability of older women, there have always been women whose lives belied them. There are—and have been—a lot of them: Isadora Duncan, Jennie Churchill, mother of Sir Winston, George Sand, Misia Sert, Colette, Aline Bernstein, Lou Andreas-Salomé, Marcia Davenport—women famous and not so famous—and all the anonymous and unheralded ones, who come forward when one's interest in this subject becomes known. Do they possess any special qualities that make them eternally attractive, so that they are not subject to the taboos? After all, most little boys found their mothers charming and delightful creatures. Even if they were more comfortable growing up believing mothers were asexual, every man remembers a sexy lady visitor who came to the house—relative or family friend—or a movie star or pop singer about whom he spun sexual daydreams. And he recalls the special excitement of his date with an older girl.

In our culture as well as others, it has been acceptable for a young man to be initiated into sex by an older woman, but traditionally she has been a degraded object, often a prostitute. And of course, it has been all right for a man to acknowledge his interest in an older woman if she had a special aura, a star rating that added to his own lustre—an Elizabeth Taylor, a Dietrich, a Loren.

The women who defy the cultural imperatives share some special qualities. They may or may not be physically beautiful or overtly seductive: they do not have to be "femmes fatales." But they appear to be women who are sure of their own sexuality; they take it for granted that men will treat them accordingly. Some women generate excitement because of their intense involvement in life. They are not static; they continue to grow and develop with age, their sexuality maturing along with the rest of their being. At fifty, they have no interest in emulating a girl of twenty-five either in or out of bed: they are far more knowledgeable and too sophisticated to play that game. And for all the propaganda that men are attracted to passive women, these women are very active. They are in charge of themselves and their lives—not in an aggressive sense, but because it is natural for them to be.

Yet the taboos are powerful. Open acknowledgments of the sexual appeal of older women are not a part of everyday reading and reportage. Even in Stephen Vizingzey's book, *In Praise of Older Women,* the oldest one found praiseworthy is a woman in her early forties.[1]

Women who have been sensual all of their lives speak for themselves. Jane Digby el Mezrab, for example, is both a creature out of the Arabian Nights and an eloquent example of a woman whose sexuality, femininity, and intellect continued to flourish as long as she lived.[2]

Her story begins in 1807, her birth seemingly attended by all the same fairies who bestowed special gifts on the princess in *The Sleeping Beauty.* She had beauty, wealth, and brains. Jane grew up in an ancestral British country house, attended by servants, governesses, and nurses. She became one of those wonderful British horsewomen who ride faultlessly and fearlessly. She was a romantic, an adventurer (not an adventuress—an exploiter of men), and an Amazon, able to shoot a pheasant while riding at full gallop.

Very little of significance is known about her early life. Her mother was young when she lost her first husband. She then married Admiral Digby, an adventurous seafaring man. No information on her seems to predict the kind of woman Jane became. One nanny in particular, Margaret Steele, spent her life trying to turn Jane into a conventional woman. We are told she had one brother to whom she was devoted. He became a minister. Jane grew up to be one of the freest-living, most-talked-about women of her time.

It's easier to speak of social than psychological influences on Jane Digby's life. She grew up in Regency England, before the mores of the Victorian era took hold, when even widows who dared to remarry were not admitted to Court. During the Regency, however, the aristocracy was remarkably casual in its moral behavior. Still, there was a double standard: women could not initiate divorce proceedings and were forever getting pregnant whether or not they wanted to.

Jane's early life coincided with the great burst of romanticism in England and on the continent. It conjures up pictures of Lord Byron in Greece, or Delacroix painting his brilliant pictures of Turkish harem women. Moorish gazebos began to sprout in country gardens. In Paris, George Sand was to be seen wearing Turkish trousers, while Merimée favored a mandarin's robe. One of Jane's cousins, Henry Anson, set off in 1827 in Arab clothes to try to reach Mecca and enter its forbidden sanctuary.

Whatever the complex reasons, Jane Digby grew up believing in the power of love. In every romantic attachment, she was convinced it would be loving and sexual forever. Her sense of freedom gave her a kind of fearless appetite for life and an ability to ignore the conventions and the inhibitions under which so many women, then and since, have labored. She cared a great deal about the people with whom she became involved, their families, their lives, and their cultures. And they, men, women, and children alike, adored her.

She was not the prototype of a Hollywood beauty. She was described as having natural and careless English good looks, a vital "morning" appearance, combined with a sensuality and a sense of style. She was not a narcissist, preoccupied with her image. What is special about Jane

Digby is that she never seems to have missed a beat as she moved on in life. She had a wonderful ability to adapt to new situations, both to enrich and enjoy herself, no matter how strange the milieu. It was her ability to take charge of her life, I believe, that makes her a model for other women. I can guess her secret: she never lost the wonder of early childhood, when the world seems to exist to be explored, and everything is possible.

Jane's parents were ambitious to make a good match for her. Before she was seventeen she was married to Lord Ellenborough, a widower more than twice her age, who looked prematurely old, an unpopular man and an indifferent husband. They had one child.

Felix Schwartzenberg, an Austrian prince, was her first great love. He was secretary to his embassy in London. He was Catholic and married, yet Jane had a child by him. He was posted to Paris to get him away from some of the scandal in London. Jane followed impetuously, totally indifferent to the furor her behavior created in both capitals. Lord Ellenborough sued for divorce, which, at the time, was a slow and laborious process. During this period, approximately two years, Jane lived with Schwartzenberg, and had a second child.

There were rumors that she had a brief liaison with Balzac. Clearly, during her stay in Paris she overcame the disadvantages of an indifferent education. She became known as a well-read, sophisticated, and witty woman, an intimate of both artists and writers.

In 1831, when she was twenty-four, the affair with the prince ended. Lady Ellenborough decided to move on, this time to Munich, where her lover was King Ludwig, a charming and educated man who had been a protegé of Napoleon. Jane soon shared the king's fascination with Greek culture. She studied classical Greek and took lessons in sculpting and painting. Her passion for archaeology developed at this time. The king was deeply involved in designing Greek buildings for Munich. Soon the two of them were exchanging "blueprints with the same fervor as billets-deux." By the end of 1832, however, the affair had cooled, although she and Ludwig always remained friends.

Jane married Baron Carl-Theodore von Venningen, a young Bavarian nobleman. A month after the marriage she delivered the baron's son. For two years they enjoyed a good life in Sicily; when they returned to Germany, Jane grew restless. She was not one to settle into matrimony; she required the stimulus of new challenge and adventure. She fell in love again, this time with a Greek nobleman, Count Spyridon Theotoky. The baron challenged the count to a duel: Jane was the prize. The baron nearly won. After Jane had nursed her lover, the count, back to health, they travelled to Athens, leaving Baron von Venningen and their two children. They continued to correspond affectionately for the rest of their lives.

What is most marvelous to ponder is the nature of this woman's special hold on men. Every one of her lovers remained loyal to her. Was she some kind of an innocent, without guile or guilt? Women like Jane do make their own rules, and somehow, although organized society rails against them, they experience little guilt or remorse. Rather, they go on loving and flourishing. They live outside the morality of a culture. It is a privilege normally *extended* to men in general and *taken* by some women.

Jane managed a divorce from the baron by being baptized into the Greek Orthodox faith, then she married Count Theotoky. In Athens she was welcomed by his family as "Lady Ellenborough"; it was as if the Baroness von Venningen had never existed. Her husband was appointed the aide-de-camp of King Otho of Greece, who was the son of her former lover, King Ludwig of Bavaria. Otho, too, fell in love with her. All of Athens seems to have followed suit. They called her "the Queen of Love and Beauty." She had had a sixth baby, a son, the first of her children to whom she became deeply attached.

Jane's adventures continued through her middle age. At forty-six, she had a passionate romance with an Albanian, Hadji-Petros, the Chief of the Pallikars, a man in his late sixties, a fantastic horseman, who appeared in Athens in native garb. The man's allure was too much for Jane: she galloped off with him to Albania and lived with him as a chieftain's wife. But Hadji-Petros was polygamous by background and tradition. When she found out he had solicited the favors of her personal maid, she decided to move on, heading for the Near East.

Jane never looked back for long; her pleasure in exploring the world was too great. She wanted to visit Palmyra, Baalbek, and Jerusalem. Her passion for different cultures, archaeology, music, sculpture, and literature was as much a part of her as her love of the wilderness, of horses, of people, and of men.

A month after she left Greece, she had an interim lover—a young Arab with whom she led the life of a Bedouin in the desert for a while. Soon she determined to set out with her own party across the desert to visit Palmyra, in spite of the fact that the area was full of brigands. She travelled like most of the British of her day, with her own damask, fine linens, and silver. It was when she was arranging for a camel caravan to take her on the nine-day journey across the desert that she met the man who would become her fourth husband and her love for the rest of her life: Sheik Abdul Medjuel El Mezrab. He was intense, well bred, and intelligent, and a few years younger than Jane, who was now forty-seven. We are not told how she managed to divorce the count, but the sheik, realizing that Jane would never accept the polygamous culture of the Moslems, divorced his wife.

Half of their time was spent in the desert "a la Bedouin"—living in the black tents, riding, hunting, and exploring ruins. Fortunately, she remained a tireless horsewoman. The other half they lived in European style in a beautiful house Jane had built in Damascus. Visitors have recorded the warm summer nights spent on the rooftop open to the breeze, with Jane, her eyes painted with kohl in the fashion of Eastern women, smoking the *narghile* (the water pipe), and speaking in any of nine languages, including, of course, Arabic. She was described at sixty-one by Isabel Burton, who met her in Damascus:

> She was a most beautiful woman . . . tall, commanding and queenlike . . . refined in manner and voice. . . . her beautiful hair in two long plaits down to the ground. . . . She looked splendid in Oriental dress and if you saw her in the bazaar you would have said she was not more than thirty-four years of age.[3]

A year later Jane wrote in her diary, "Sixty-two years of age, and an impetuous romantic girl of seventeen cannot excel me in ardent passionate feelings."

By then, she seemed equally at home sitting in Parisian clothes in her octagonal drawing room doing needlepoint and discussing Syrian ruins with visiting archaeologists or riding into battle, like an Amazon, with her husband at times of intertribal war. Jane Digby found the most fulfilling love of her life in her late forties. Although she maintained her good looks, she was nonetheless a middle-aged woman who had had six children. Her attraction to men went far beyond the question of age. Women like Jane put men in touch with the riches mature women have to share.

She died at seventy-four in a cholera epidemic in Damascus. Her funeral was as romantic as any other moment in her life. Her husband could not bear the sombre funeral procession. He burst out of the carriage and disappeared.

> The service was conducted to its close; the last majestic words of the burial service were being read by the parson when there was the sound of horses' hooves thundering nearer. Medjuel had returned. On Jane's favorite black mare he galloped up to the open grave. . . . Her Bedouin husband and her Arab horse were there beside her to the last. For Jane Digby, life's poetry had never sunk to prose.

Romantic and passionate to the end. Is Jane Digby so unique that her life has never been parallelled by other women? No. There have been women like her in every age. They are often found in the arts, like Isadora Duncan and Sarah Bernhardt, where the line is thinner between romantic fantasy and reality. They remain special human beings at a time of life when other women settle for so much less.

Lily Harmon, the American artist, is, in her own way, a twentieth-century reflection of Jane. Born in 1912, as a young woman she lived a Bohemian life, was an offbeat kind of *wunderkind* who refused to become the staid and virtuous middle-class lady her family wanted her to be. She seemed to enjoy being outrageous. Lily Harmon had Jane Digby's free spirit in good measure. She loved painting, travelling, good food, fun, and above all—people. She had five husbands; her fifth marriage took place when she was fifty-seven. Joseph Hirshhorn, the art collector and founder of the museum in Washington, D.C. that bears his name, was her fourth husband and the father of her two children. Like Jane Digby, she held onto men's affections long after she'd left them. Well past middle age, three of her former husbands returned to her for periods of varying length. Her *èlan vitale* made her irresistible to them.[4]

I have talked to a number of women from forty to eighty who are on their own—divorced or widowed or remarried—and who have taken charge of their lives and of their own sexuality. They do not think, "Am I still attractive to men?" Rather, knowing that they want men and meaningful sex as part of their lives, they see to it that it happens.

These women come from various backgrounds and places: Poland, Brazil, San Francisco, Baltimore, a farm in Indiana, a small town in upstate New York. They work at various occupations: one cleans business offices, one is a television producer, one is a retired factory worker, one is a divorced housewife who went back to school and got a master's degree at fifty-five and began to write. For the most part, what they share is the same high energy level.

Some have chosen long-term relationships. Others choose freedom and autonomy rather than making a compromise for security. They do not look to men for confirmation. They are out-going social creatures, yet able to be alone. They enjoy their grown children, have friends and are available to them. They are risk-takers, and do not make excuses for themselves. In an age when it has become second nature to blame every failure on one's parents, it's refreshing to hear a woman of seventy describe her terrible childhood—and how she surmounted it!

Perhaps the greatest measure of the sexuality of these women is their refusal to be dominated by the daydreams of their twenties. They know they are different people with different needs—and so are the men they encounter. They are willing to take men as they are: if they're involved in protracted separation and divorce proceedings, if they do not wish to remarry, if they are older or younger. The image of the traditional dependent wife is not relevant; these women take life as it comes.

A few stand out particularly among these self-determined, autonomous women who are finding middle age the best period of their lives.

Susan G. is a divorced woman in her mid-fifties. She left her husband about ten years ago after a marriage that lasted two decades. She has one grown child, a daughter to whom she is close. She worked at minor part-time jobs during her marriage, but essentially played the role of wife and mother and felt dependent on her husband. Her successful career in the television industry did not get launched until after her divorce:

> My marriage wasn't bad in the beginning. My husband was an ambitious, hard-working man. At first I loved staying home with the baby, but when I got involved in any kind of work, my husband resented it. Our sex life was always good. He turned into a driven and emotionally unavailable guy. When things really fell apart between us, I was the one who left.
>
> My sense of freedom has been an astonishment to me; I feel like I've been released from jail. It's like I had been living with daydreams of what I wanted my life to become, and now they're real.
>
> There are interesting new dynamics in my relationships with men now. I know in many ways I've become a demanding and uncompromising person, but demanding in the sense of having standards about the person I care to

spend time with. In addition, in a non-married relationship of your own choosing, when you both have responsibilities and lives to lead, you don't want to nail his feet to the floor. It suits me fine that I have to travel and often will spend some time every month out of town. That leaves a lot of "play" or space in a relationship that is harder to achieve in a marriage, I think.

A few years ago I broke up with a man I'd gotten very used to. We shared a great love of music and of travel. Sex was fine. But one day, for a number of good reasons, I realized that this was not a person I wanted to spend the rest of my life with—and I asked him to go. And it's not only that I have high expectations, I can no longer be a hand-maiden or a placater of men.

I think single women are experimenting with freedom versus attachment in middle age. The rules are different. Women feel less guilty about their sexual needs. It can be joyful and spontaneous, even if it isn't for forever.

I met a geologist out West one summer; the sexual experience is all mixed up with my sudden awareness of colors in the desert, of striated mesas with their tops in the clouds and flying through canyons in his plane.

Where do you meet men? The number of possibilities do shrink as you get older. The first man I slept with after my divorce in my mid-forties was someone I'd known for years. We're still loving friends. Non-sexual friendships with men are very important to me. I guess the answer is you can met men everywhere. A man at the supermarket was behind me at the check-out counter one evening and said, "You look like you're shopping for one." Another time a flight to Chicago was cancelled at the last minute. A man and I began to talk about appointments we couldn't miss, so we took a taxi to another airport and by the time we landed in Chicago we knew we wanted to spend more time together.

There is a downside to all of this. When I'm with my married friends I sometimes feel jealous. Not that I envy their lives, but because our society still makes negative judgments about single women. And when I see an older couple together on the street, I think, it would be nice if there were to be someone to take care of me when I get sick or when I'm old. And if you get to like somebody a lot, if the thing gets intense, it's hard if he lives hundreds of miles away, or if his life can't bring him closer to you. You may end up wanting more than you can get.

Since my divorce there have only been a few months in my life that I've been without a man. I think I have developed sexually; I am much more passionate in a relationship than I was in my marriage. I don't hold back.

You have to learn to live differently as a single person. You can't make a lot of negative rules like "Never have sex until the third date," or "Don't ever telephone a man." When you're upset, you have to be tough with yourself, and think things through. You have to pull up your socks— 'cause no one's going to tell you what to do. One other thing. I enjoy my career, my success, and the independence it's brought me. Because of this I have to be careful not to become selfish and too demanding. I've watched men who, when they get some power, begin to want "subjects" in their lives. Or they become Don Juans or trivialize relationships. Now that women have some power and the same freedom to choose you have to be careful—not to pick a guy just because he's so beautiful or only because he's so good in bed. I try to be honest. I guess it's not easy to be my lover because I don't want an unexamined relationship.

I worry about the way I look, but men do too . . . (a pause) . . . Isn't it ridiculous that a woman of fifty-five is so involved in all this romantic stuff? I don't feel alone. I go out a lot; people come and stay with me. When I'm home by myself, it feels very peaceful. And in all honesty, in the last ten years there's not been anyone I've *wanted* to marry.

By way of contrast, some free-standing women who are enjoying life well into and beyond middle age, have had modest careers, live simply, and do not reflect profoundly on the lives they have chosen. They are aware of the need to have pleasure in their lives, and sex is one of their greatest pleasures. Beth H., who lives in a middle-sized Ohio town, was looking back on her life from the vantage point of seventy:

I married very young, and I had three babies in a hurry. Then I went back to teaching and had responsibilities both at work and at home. My husband and I knew we weren't having much fun, so one night we went to a dance hall with an unmarried couple. We told people we were brother and sister so we could have a good time. My husband eventually met a woman and divorced me; I never remarried and can't tell you exactly why. I've had a very good life. I love going out to dance, to eat at restaurants, to picnics. I knew I didn't want to date men from my church— they're too dull and settled. So I guess I found people I could enjoy. I've been very selective, never promiscuous. The men have been salesmen—or legislators who come here to the state capitol. A man in his thirties wanted to marry me; I knew he was after the money I saved. I told him I was on to him. Since then, he's become my friend. He told my daughter I was a charming woman. I don't know about that, but I have enjoyed my life. Men still call me.

There is another group of women who are as determined to make their own lives as the ones I have already described. These women work out their problems of freedom versus dependence, of autonomy versus the role of hand-maiden through their choice of younger men. Lou Andreas-Salomé was such a woman. Friedrich Nietzsche adored her, as did Rainer Maria Rilke. She was a passionate woman but remained married for years to an attractive and brilliant man with whom she refused to have sex. She was an intimate of Freud's when he was introducing psychoanalysis to Vienna.

Like Jane Digby, Lou Salomé was unconcerned with the bourgeois morality of her time. Anaïs Nin called her an intensely feminine woman; men were attracted to her like moths to the proverbial flame until she was long past middle age. But Nin points out she lived her life "like a man," meaning that she was pushing back the boundaries of what was permitted to a woman and experimenting with new ways of living that would allow for self-determination. Because of her single-mindedness, she was able to develop as a writer and a psychoanalyst. Unlike most women, Lou felt little responsibility to the men she left. She chose powerful men, but never let them interfere with her sense of autonomy.

Lou Salomé was less of a romantic than Jane Digby. She believed in the possibility and the desirability of friendship as well as love between men and women. She wished to care for a man, but never sacrificed her own growth in the process. At first she turned to men because they were teachers and creative thinkers. But when she felt they wanted her to become a disciple, an "inspiratrice," or a caretaker, she left them. Nietzsche, she thought, wished her to be a follower. Even while planning a trip to Russia with Rilke, she was looking into her own future: in her diary she wrote, "Rilke must go." "Loyalty for loyalty's sake was alien to her. She would have called it self-betrayal."[5] It appears that she did not become sexually active until midlife, when she turned from older men to younger ones.

Lou Salomé was born in 1861 in St. Petersburg, the sixth child and first daughter of a rich and aristocratic family of German background. Her mother, a highly conventional woman, was always at a loss in knowing how to deal with her precocious child. But to her father, Gustav von Salomé, a general in the Russian Imperial Army, she was a delight. He welcomed a daughter, especially since, almost sixty years of age, he had waited a long time for her. She was very much her father's child. The general was more lenient with Lou than with his other children. Her independence was encouraged, rather than inhibited, by him—and by her brothers as well. She was raised in the company of men. Like Jane Digby, Lou grew up with the wealth and privilege which give to their owners a sense of power and entitlement. Unlike Jane, however, she did not live a quiet provincial life as a child, but was born in an exciting world capital. She was influenced by the liberal attitudes that were developing among young intellectuals in Russia. Women were getting involved in higher education. Some were going on to Switzerland to study medicine in order to return to Russia to live and work among the impoverished peasants. Others chose platonic marriages so that they would retain their freedom, viewing marriage as an encumbrance. They were models Lou was to emulate.[6]

At seventeen, she reached a critical point in her life; her father was ill and dying; her mother was expecting her to be confirmed in the Lutheran church. Lou not only refused to be confirmed, but threatened to leave the Church as well. It was at this point she acted in a manner already typical of her behavior. She turned to Henrik Gillot, a pastor at the Dutch Embassy. He was in his forties, well-travelled, a charismatic orator, and a highly educated man. Lou sought him out, not for religious instruction and not for romantic reasons, but because she felt he could help her find direction in life. She met secretly with him in his study, since, because she was a girl, it would have been considered a highly unorthodox teacher-pupil relationship. Gillot introduced Lou to comparative religion, anthropology, philosophy, and French and German literature. She was such an extraordinary pupil that soon she was writing sermons for Gillot to deliver. Theirs became a highly charged emotional connection. For Lou it was excitement of an intellectual sort, in spite of the secrecy and the hours spent alone with an attractive male. She denied its obvious sexual implications and was shocked when Gillot announced he was prepared to leave his wife and children if she would marry him. This was a pattern that would repeat itself many times: Lou would become passionately engaged in an intellectual friendship with an older man and insist that it remain an intellectual friendship, while the man fell in love. Gillot's proposal confused her. She decided to leave St. Petersburg. With her mother as chaperone, she left for Zurich to study.

There she became a brilliant student of philosophy, comparative religion, theology, and art history. She soon met another intellectual companion, Paul Rée. He was thirty-two, a philosopher and author of a book on the origins of morals, when he fell in love with her. It was to Rée that Lou proposed her dream of sharing an apartment with two male friends. Rée agreed reluctantly; he too wanted to marry Lou, but accepted her terms. He proposed Friedrich Nietzsche, then thirty-eight, as the third member of the triumvirate. Again, the pattern was repeated: Lou interested in a man's intellectual power; the man in love with her. She travelled with Nietzsche on a vacation to Tautenberg, Germany, and wrote Rée, with no thought of his possible jealousy. Were they not friends? Part of her letter reads:

> Yesterday we spent the whole day together and today we spent a beautiful day in the dark quiet pine woods, alone with sun rays and squirrels . . . Talking with Nietzsche is very exciting . . . our conversations . . . range from the nearest to the most distant realm of thought. . . .[7]

Nietzsche, too, fell in love with Lou. Both men were terribly upset by her refusal to respond. The *menage à trois* was never to be. But Rée continued to accept her terms that they live together as friends. She dedicated her first book, *A Struggle For God,* published when she was twenty-four, to him. The two shared an apartment in Berlin. Lou was soon an accepted member of a group of men most representative of the vigorously-challenging intellectual and scientific atmosphere of the day. Friedrich Carl Andreas appeared on Lou's doorstep, attracted there by her reputation. He was born in Java, some fifteen years before Lou, of German, Malaysian, and Persian descent. He was a linguistics scholar, a specialist in Persian dialects, a world traveller, steeped in archaeology, history, and science. Andreas had a Near-Easterner's view of the role of men and women in marriage. On the eve of their engagement, Andreas gave himself a serious stab wound. A suicide attempt? A form of blackmail? If it was the latter, it was successful—to a degree. They married. Their relationship was a bitter struggle for several years. Lou refused to consummate the marriage. She insisted on her right to see other men and suggested that Andreas take a wife substitute. He gave in and began a long relationship with their housekeeper. Lou and Andreas remained married in a strange yet bonded relationship for the rest of their lives. Despite her marriage, Lou was essentially free. She used her freedom. She managed to live in all the great capitals of Europe and in a ten-year period produced eight books and fifty essays, articles, and book reviews.

Lou consistently fought conventions; she refused to be chaperoned as a young girl, wouldn't wear stays or corsets, travelled and lived openly with men. But as far as we know, she did not become sexually involved with a man until she was in her mid-thirties. It is not certain but it appears that the person she chose for a sexual partner was seven years her junior, a man who was more emotionally centered than the others she had known. He was Friedrich Pineles, a well-to-do Viennese physician, and, like all the men she was interested in, a learned and cultivated person. Lou became quite attached to him. His family was charmed and accepted her. She kept her connection to Pineles as his "unofficial wife" for about twelve years, coming and going according to her own design. She feared she could never remain faithful to one man and, in this, she was correct. Two years after her involvement with Pineles began, Lou met Rainer Marie Rilke, the poet. She was thirty-six; he was twenty-two. He loved her from the moment of their first meeting; three years of "love and poetry" followed.

In her memoirs, she recorded the heady feelings aroused in her by Rilke:

> I was your wife for years because you were the first reality; body and man undistinguishably one, the unmistakable fact of life itself. I could have said . . . "you alone are real."[8]

She was both a passionate and maternal wife/mistress to Rilke, helping him develop his work and having a great influence on it—as she had on Nietzsche and would have on Freud. Lou and Rilke were observed on one of their trips to Russia when she was thirty-nine. She was described as "a woman of tall stature . . . probably his mother or older sister."⁹ Rilke remained in love with her till his death in 1926.

In her forties, Lou was a radiant woman with a contagious sense of humor. Her hair was silver blonde, her breasts full, her waist and hips were narrow. She walked with grace; and often wore furs and boas. Lou grew as a woman in her middle years. She was able to overcome her sexual inhibitions. Her personal appearance became much more feminine. She began to develop close friendships with women as well as men. And in her forties she became pregnant and earnestly wished to have the child. There is considerable mystery about the fate of this pregnancy. Reports indicate that Pineles was the father. It is possible Lou miscarried. It is also said that she so feared Andreas' temper that when Pineles was about to ask him to give her a divorce she proceeded to have an abortion.

A lover, Poul Bjerre, who was a Swedish psychotherapist and fifteen years her junior, introduced Lou to Sigmund Freud. Lou met Freud in 1911, when she was fifty. Freud, too, was impressed by her brilliance, her quickness of mind, and, above all, by her optimism. They became close friends. A year later she was in Vienna, spending six months studying with Freud and his group. She became a psychoanalyst, and practiced this profession for the rest of her life. And, there was a passionate new lover, Victor Tausk, a brilliant if unstable follower of Freud's, some sixteen years her junior.

Age seems not to have diminished Lou's appeal. Viktor von Weizsäcker, the founder of medical anthropology, came across her book, *My Gratitude to Freud*, and was so impressed with its sympathetic tone that, in 1931, he began a lengthy correspondence with her. At a time of personal crisis in his life, von Weizsäcker paid Lou a visit. She was seventy. He wrote, "I was very much moved by her femininity and her natural warmth. . . . The extraordinary woman was still blonde and she moved with the supple movements of a young tree. . . . She was endowed with a graceful searching or groping empathy. . . ."[10]

The richness and intensity of Lou Salomè's involvement in the intellectual life of her day cannot be conveyed by citing her exciting personal involvements with men. Her brilliance and good looks were hers by inheritance; her passionate nature was activated by her experiences—especially in midlife; her accomplishments were the product of her own determination.

Her sexual liberation is of special interest, because while men were eternally attracted to her, she was finally free, in midlife, to love in return.

As a therapist, I have found that patients have to work out problems with their parents before they are free to love. It would be presumptuous of me to try to be definitive about the nature of Lou's conflicts based on a small amount of biographical information. However, her life story raises interesting questions—especially now, as more older women and younger men are getting together. It is interesting to speculate whether some of Lou's behavior was based on her refusal or inability to identify with her mother, who played a culturally symbolic role as wife and mother. Was her early refusal to have sex with the men with whom she had intellectual relationships based in part on the fact that they were all twelve or more years older than she? She needed to see them positively as effective teachers, but her personal feelings toward them were ambivalent. She placed herself in situations that were bound to arouse them sexually and then rejected them. Clinically, such behavior indicates an acting out of conflicts with one's father, demonstrating both attraction and taboo. From this perspective we might wonder if her loss of sexual inhibitions occurred only after she herself became a mature woman. At this point her sexual role shifted. Not that sexual feelings representing mother-son attraction is any less taboo than that between father and daughter. However, apparently in Lou's case this was a more tolerable position. She could become a mentor to a man, more mother than daughter. Lou was still avoiding men who would have been the conventional or "normal" choices, men who were either her peers or older. Lou seemed to have found a *modus vivendi* which enabled her to become a sexual woman without real insight into her conflicts. Had she had the insight, she might have been able to have a close relationship over a longer period of time. As it was, her solution worked for her.

Lou always lived outside society's rules. It is not that she was without guilt about the consequences of her actions. But she believed that passion was an elemental force that could not be stayed. This may have been the rationalization that made it possible for her to ignore the fact that her behavior had ruthless aspects. But she was usually a generous and forbearing human being. A Queen Bee, seductress, earth mother, exciting companion—an independent woman.

Colette, born in 1873, was another woman who eventually turned to a younger man for love. In her case, she was able to establish and maintain a long-lasting relationship. The facts of Colette's life are probably more generally known than those of Lou Salomés: her deep attachment to her mother, her unhappy first marriage to an older man, her development as a writer along with a career as a music hall dancer and actress.

If one rereads *Cheri* and *The Last of Cheri,* Colette's two novels on the older woman-younger man theme, one is struck by the fact that it is the young man who is in despair and the older woman who is in charge of the relationship. Colette was not to find this type of relation-

ship personally until, at fifty-two, after her second unhappy marriage, she met Maurice Goudeket, who was then
thirty-six. They remained together until her death at
eighty-one; their marriage took place when Colette was
sixty-two. I would agree with her biographer, Mary
Kathleen Benet, in her book, *Writers In Love*, that:

> Having failed to establish the egalitarian relation
> she sought with Jouvenal, (her second husband)
> who was her counterpart in age and prestige,
> she was ready to look for it with someone whose
> adoration of her made chauvinistic behavior less
> likely.[11]

She remarks further that Colette reveals her feelings about older women in her novels as taking strength
from "the vision of themselves as the givers of love and
therefore the ones who cannot lose their independence."
But Colette, newly in love with Goudeket, does not sound
like a cool and independent woman. In a letter to a friend
she wrote:

> Oh! la, la, and again la, la! And never enough la
> la! She's a proper one, your friend. She's in a
> lovely fix, up to her eyes, up to her lips, and even
> further than that! Oh, the devilishness of quiet
> men—I refer to that lad Maurice. Would you like
> to know what he is, that lad Maurice? He's a
> skunk and a this and that, and a nice guy, and an
> exquisite creature. And that's the state I'm in.[12]

Colette did not believe that love could last in conventional marriages. She perceived them as business
transactions having more to do with sex and money. She
found love to be most pure if it was among outsiders; thus
she considered her life with Goudeket. With him, Colette
continued to write productively. In addition, the two
shared many pleasures. In the summer they lived in a
house on the Mediterranean with friends, gardens, won-

derful food. In Paris, visitors would hear the two of them laughing together as they approached their apartment. When asked why, Goudeket answered: "Because I was with her and she was with me."[13]

Colette's wish for an egalitarian relationship in which she would be the giver of love and maintain her independence is one important key to the pleasure many women are currently finding in relationships with younger men. "I have to tell you," Alice G., a patient of mine, said, "it's absolutely amazing to be treated with respect. By that I mean, respect for what I say, and what I am." She is talking of the fact that she has recently begun to date men up to ten years her junior. Alice is in her mid-forties and was married twice before to men older than she. "I think," she added, "that competitive men compete with their wives. As they get older they need to inflate themselves at our expense. It doesn't feel that way with younger guys."

Women have been so conditioned to think in terms of *favors* bestowed on them by men that often it is with surprise they discover the positive things men discover in them. Young men admire their success, their prestige, and their status. Rather than being threatened by successful women's careers, younger men are often impressed. Living by new rules for relationships, they usually decide to share the economics of living, and he, no longer the sole provider, does not have to lockstep in a career. Men in such relationships are more willing to experiment or take risks—and to enjoy life. As Lou Salomè demonstrated in her role with Rilke, the older women is often a mentor to a younger man, a source of pleasure and growth for both of them.

In my practice, I find that women have to work out their problems with older men before they feel comfortable with those who are their peers or younger. A friend in

The Sensual Older Woman

her forties, who is getting a doctorate in psychology, told me about an affair she had had for many years with a man several years older than her father. He was a fascinating person, a public figure with a crazy and exciting life. She was very caught up in his world. She had had a distant and formal relationship with her own father whose career had taken him off to another country to live. When his mother died, she wrote her father a long emotional letter about loss, separation, grief, and love. She was convinced that he'd never realize what she was trying to say. To her surprise, his answer was not only understanding but the beginning of a real rapprochement between them. She ended the relationship with her lover a few months later. She now is involved with a man who is younger. Due to more self-awareness, she realizes that she no longer needs to give a daughter's adulation to an idealized figure. She no longer needs to live vicariously through another person, as a child must inevitably do.

A client of mine, Ann G., is a professor of anthropology at a Western university. Since her divorce she has chosen relationships with younger men. Currently she has a ten-year-old relationship with a talented man twenty years her junior. This is her story:

> I see now, looking back, that I wanted my husband to take charge of my life. I think I chose him because it was a way out of a small town and of a family that had very conventional expectations for me. John and I started dating when I was in nurses' training; we married as soon as I got my RN. He was a man who made decisions easily. I let him tell me what to do. The marriage didn't go well, however. John was an administrator of a large inner city settlement house; he had very long hours, so essentially, he wasn't at home a lot.
>
> I badly wanted a baby. I had a very hard

Venus After Forty

time conceiving—had to go through a lot of painful tests and procedures. But we finally had a lovely little girl. I'd been feeling the need to finish my bachelor's degree. So while Joanna was little, I went to school part-time. I had a fantastic professor of public health. That turned my life around. I decided that I would go on for a graduate degree and try to have a field work assignment in a Third World country.

John supported me in this; in fact, since we had decided that I would take Joanna along with me, John helped us get to Nigeria, where I would be working for eight months. He planned to take vacations with us. But as soon as he got home, he wrote me a letter saying he wanted to end the marriage.

I was really thrown for a while. But, I decided, I had pinned so many hopes on this experience I would make it work in spite of what faced me when I got home. It turned out to be quite extraordinary. Joanna thrived. We lived half the time in a small village. There were wonderful people. I learned a great deal.

When I got back, not only did I have to face a divorce, but my mother had become ill. Then I got sick, too. I developed terrible headaches and double vision and ended up having surgery. I was in luck: I had a benign tumor and had a complete surgical cure.

Mother died; my financial settlement was pretty bad, and I still had to finish my doctorate!

I won't go into all the details. I managed to work part-time, to be with my daughter (who was now in school a full day), and to work on my dissertation after she went to bed at night. I didn't feel like a superwoman and don't think that I was. I just was very interested in each part of my life.

When I began to teach public health, I found that the male students in my class seemed interested in me. Over a period of years, it seems to me I dated men my own age and men who were older and men who were younger.

As I reached my forties and began to find my own style as a teacher and to gain in poise and self-confidence, I found myself turning more and more to younger men. I'm not exactly sure why. But I know I was observing the relationships of my friends and colleagues, and finding so many women who were in conventional relationships feeling frustrated and impotent. The men they were with, by and large, seemed to need to be in positions of power and dominance; the women responded by becoming subtly manipulative. I didn't like what I saw.

I met Tim when I was forty-six, he was twenty-five. He was just starting out in journalism. He's an imaginative guy, with a lot of spirit and enthusiasm. He is loving, supportive, and admires what I do. He's been great with Joanna. I wouldn't say we haven't had problems. My family and friends had a hard time feeling comfortable with us for quite a while. But there are so many things we enjoy doing together. I'd say we are a good couple. Our relationship works.

These two women I have cited are powerful women who attract men by their reputation or position. Celeste, on the other hand, is a working-class immigrant woman— an example of an average woman seeking new vistas. Celeste is fifty-five. She came to the States about twenty years ago from Colombia, South America. In the mornings she cleans people's homes and in the afternoons she cleans offices until late in the evening. She sleeps all day Saturday and sometimes Sunday, as well.

Despite her labors, Celeste is a woman of great energy; but she also has a *joie de vivre,* an antic sense of humor; she's honest and direct. She has a voluptuous body—and is very appealing to men.

Celeste loves to dance. Friday and Saturday nights

she goes to a ballroom but never goes home with a man. She has a lot of friends of different ethnic backgrounds. She loves to cook, and often gives parties, inviting several dozen people to her home at one time.

She only dates one man at a time. Once she was engaged to a fellow from Colombia, but really doesn't like the way Latin men treat women. Currently she is engaged to an Italian engineer who has settled in this country. He is about fifteen years her junior.

Even though she was born of an impoverished Indian family where only the males were allowed to get any education, Celeste has done incredibly well financially. By her family's standards, she is already a woman of property. Celeste has saved money; a lot for her; she buys good clothes and paintings which she gets "on time." She's bought a home in Colombia and another in a local suburb, both of which she rents out. By her own measure, she is a personal success, who has managed a trip to Europe, is teaching herself about art, and has put a fulfilling life together. She works very hard, plays equally hard. She is a loving, dynamic, sexual human being who happens to be middle-aged.

Is the older woman/younger man relationship a viable alternative to more conventional ones for women over forty? For some couples, it certainly seems to be, particularly at this moment of time when it may be hard for older men to accept what younger ones admire in older women, i.e., their freedom and independence. Is it possible that younger men are growing up to be more open and expressive than their fathers? It would seem so, and this quality, which makes for greater communication, appears to be valued highly by women at midlife.

Arlene Derenski and Sally B. Landsburg, who interviewed more than fifty such couples for their book, *The*

Age Taboo, were able to extract three common qualities that attracted older women and younger men to one another and made their relationships work: 1) an unusual willingness to take risks, 2) assertiveness as acceptable, even necessary, behavior in both sexes, 3) mutual emotional supportiveness. They found that women, past or present, who make these relationships work are willing to live unconforming lives and extend the definitions of a traditional woman's role of what is feminine behavior.[14]

Not all older women who remain in charge of their lives and their sexualiity are cast from the same mold. They by no means possess the same degree of bohemianism or independence as those I have been discussing. Nor are they all so *manifestly* sexual in their appeal to men. Yet most fulfilled middle-aged women choose to make sex an integral part of their lives. Some may find their greatest love well past middle age. They tend to fall into at least three categories: the quiet, agreeable woman, eager to please a man, who is very sensual and in need of gratification; the "sex kitten," whose experience has made her sure of her attractiveness to men; and the intelligent, mature, and womanly person, who is deeply expressive and caring.

Beth I. is typical of the first group of women. Over sixty and the mother of three boys to whom she is devoted, she left her husband ten years ago. Their sex life had been very active and satisfying, but as he grew older he became compulsively unfaithful to her. She was unable to leave him until she met and fell in love with another man.

By nature, Beth is not a free spirit like a Jane Digby or Lou Salomé. For most of her life she conformed to the cultural norms she grew up with—among them, that a girl should let men make decisions, that she should try to be a selfless wife and mother. However, men have always liked her; she was popular as an adolescent and in college. Women like Beth are much more kitten than tiger. Many men like their quiet softness, their apparent need for protection. (Tigers, on the other hand, must be stalked and captured—a totally different challenge.) Beth followed a pattern that is common for many women in middle age. A man whom she knew and loved in her youth turned up and, since they already had a past, a commonality, it was easy to begin a relationship. Beth left her husband for him. Unfortunately, their marriage plans ended with his sudden illness and death from leukemia.

Beth, even though she has not remarried, has never been without an intense sexual relationship. She is a sensual woman, easily aroused and in need of fulfillment. She is also shy and rather modest. Neither paragon nor pioneer, she does not have a famous name or reputation. However quiet the signals she sends out, they are received and responded to by attractive men. Beth would rather be married, give up her job, and spend time caring for a man. She is still looking. But I have seen her turn men away whom she felt were too dull or overprotective. In her desire for a fulfilling relationship, she will not compromise.

Recently, I met a woman of eighty who has been widowed twice. she married for a third time about seven years ago. Her new husband adores her. She has obviously been and still is a sex kitten used to being petted, fussed over, and given a bowl of cream. She is one of those women who seems to know instinctively how to please a man—not in a pandering or self-denying sense, but simply that she is comfortable in this role; it's what women *do*. She is not a bit passive. She runs things—but in the nicest, quietest, most natural way. The colors and the style of her home are feminine. It is a privilege to be admitted to this her private space, because of her giving spirit.

Finally, let us consider two women who found the great loves of their lives in middle age. These women would be first to say that they are not glamour girls in physical appearance nor flamboyant in their character style. They are bright, competent, womanly women.

Marcia Davenport was born in 1903. Her mother was the opera star Alma Gluck. She grew up living with music. After a brief marriage at nineteen, she spent a number of years on the staff of *The New Yorker* magazine. She wrote several books that were widely read, among them a biography of Mozart and the novel, *The Valley of Decision.* Her second husband was Russell Davenport, editor of *Fortune* magazine. Mrs. Davenport worked very hard at her trade and was exacting in the standards of the research she did on her books. Much of this work was, of necessity, done in Europe. After the breakup of her marriage to Davenport, she fell deeply in love with Jan Masaryk, son of T. G. Masaryk, the first president of the Czech Republic. Czechoslovakia, which had established itself as a true democracy in post-World-War-I Europe, was sacrificed to Hitler by Neville Chamberlain in 1938. After World War II, Jan Masaryk, as Foreign Minister of the Czech government in exile, was deeply involved in negotiations, particularly in Moscow and at the newly-formed United Nations, attempting to reestablish the democratic government. Masaryk returned to Czechoslovakia as Foreign Minister and fought heroically against the tide of Stalinism that swept away the Benes government. For two weeks in January 1948 Marcia Davenport was with him in Prague. She had escaped to London where, a few days later, she heard of his death—probably his murder—at the hands of the Communists.

They had their happiest time together when Marcia's friend, writer Marjorie Kinnan Rawlings, lent them her house in Cross Creek, Florida. In her autobiography, *Too Strong for Fantasy*, Marcia Davenport wrote about the relationship with Masaryk:

> He was then sixty years old. I was forty-three . . . .
> He was at ease among people as I had never
> learned to be, he had presence and those amaz-
> ing gifts of language and wit and charm. . . . He
> was a man who preferred people who had lives of
> their own . . . people who would not be depen-
> dent on him emotionally or socially. . . . I liked
> this . . . Independence and self-reliance are es-
> sential to me. . . . He could not have found me
> witty or amusing. . . . I was not young . . . and
> surely I was not beautiful. He said he found me
> intelligent. [15]

Of the weeks spent with Masaryk at Cross Creek, she said:

> . . . Several times I have written her (Marjorie
> Rawlings) what has proved to be permanent
> truth, that in her house, that winter I knew the
> only perfect happiness I have ever had. [16]

So much of what was intellectually and emotionally central to Marcia Davenport's life was made up of elements that could only be added incrementally. While still in her twenties, she had fallen in love with Prague, where she did research on her Mozart biography. Prague was a city that had worshipped Mozart; she saw it through his eyes. Her love of Czechoslovakia and its people became a part of her novel, *The Valley of Decision*.

The intelligence Masaryk found in Marcia Davenport was made up in considerable measure by her empathy for the struggles Masaryk was engaged in to save Czechoslovakia from Soviet domination. Her deep knowledge of and love for that country gave her a sensitivity to the agonies of the man who was fighting for democracy in a world of power politics.

When she left Russell Davenport at forty, she was motivated by the need for achievement, by her wish to create art by dint of hard work. She planned to live her life alone. Looking back after Masaryk's tragic death, she wrote, "The fruitful art is living for the necessities of others."[17] Via the transforming experience of her love at middle age, she was able to integrate *both* human needs: the need to realize her *self* and the need to love.

Women who choose to take charge of their lives at midlife are inspiring. Polly S., a woman in her fifties who is moving to Texas to get remarried is, like you and me, an "Everywoman." She says she knows she is not good looking, has a mature, not a slim figure, is not "a sexy lady."

She was the devoted mother of two children when her husband left her for another woman. She felt devastated. She knew the marriage had become troubled, but like so many women, was dedicated to trying to make it work. She was then in her mid-thirties. There were a number of men in her life, but she would not settle for them. One had four children from a previous marriage in his custody, two of whom were clearly having severe emotional problems. Other men, she found, wanted to move into her life and "play house." She felt that they wanted her to be an earth mother and take over their lives.

The man she is going to marry had been in an unhappy marriage. They both have interesting and demanding jobs. Although it has been a difficult endeavor, she has been able to get a transfer to the town where he will be taking a new assignment.

Polly says, "I know he's not an uncomplicated man, but I'm very excited at the thought of marrying him. Our sex life is wonderful; it's lyrical; it's the best I've ever had." I happen to know Polly well enough to say she's made this happen because she wanted it and was ready for it. Her children are off to college; her job performance has reached a high and independent level. She has reached a place in her own life where she can freely express her individuality. Her lifetime of living, her grace, her deep ability to care, her wit, her fine intellect, and her sexual passion have made her the woman she is today.

I know a widow in her mid-eighties who has always liked men. She is a retired factory worker, the daughter of immigrants. She has always lived very modestly. For years she took care of a sick husband. Since he died, she has spent a lot of time at a club for senior citizens.

Not long ago, she met a man a few years her junior and was very attracted to him. The two began a relationship. On a recent Christmas she asked her daughters for a gift: a sexy nightgown. Recently, a flare-up of phlebitis took her to her doctor. He told her to stay at home, take things easy, and try not to get excited. She looked at him thoughtfully and said, "Then I guess I'd better not have Ralph come to see me."

Few women aspire to lead the lives of Jane Digby or Lou Salomé. Many women, however, are struggling to achieve some of the freedom of spirit, the independence of being, exemplified by them—and the others I have described in this chapter.

The old model of symbiotic dependency between men and women doesn't work either emotionally or economically (I still recall my mother hiding fifty-cent pieces in a pocketbook in the bottom drawer of her bureau, trying to cajole my father into buying a new stove—and voting the way he told her to). Still, many women are held back in their autonomous growth by the fear of being labelled aggressive and unfeminine. Confusion between behavior that expresses normal self-assertion and aggression remains. Yet no healthy child grows up without saying to an adult, "No, let me do it." Women with an inner sense of freedom have never been passive, and do not allow their lives to be taken over. Independence is an important and imperative value for a rich, rewarding life. Despite this, many of my women patients let the men in their lives make decisions that are wrong for them; and then they blame their men. Their only "argument" is a form of withdrawal. It is not enough and women who employ this means of non-expression of their feelings often are frustrated and ornery.

Assertiveness is not the equivalent of aggression. Aggression carries the affect of anger, and sometimes spills over into rage. Women freed from this confusion begin to find they feel more feminine as they become more open in the expression of their needs, including, of course, their sexual ones.

A middle-aged patient described a dream in which she was raped by a man because she had approached him and asked for something. During the session, her associations had to do with her growing ability to be more open and expressive with her lover and her fear that he would punish her as a result. She had always felt that she drove people away when she made her wants known. She carried this to great extremes, trying to be so agreeable she could not even state a preference for a restaurant or a movie. When her partner would say something nice to her, she'd be sardonic and give an off-putting "Oh, sure!" response. She was convinced she would overwhelm him if he knew how badly she needed to hear his words. But in therapy she is learning to trust this man. No longer does she automatically read his bad moods in the old way, thinking,

"He's turned off because of something I've done." She is becoming more feminine in the sense that she is allowing her feelings of empathy to surface. So when he is "down," she can ask, "Is something troubling you?" This change in her has pleased and delighted him. He asked how she could possibly read him so well. But as her dream demonstrates, she is still struggling with the idea that self-assertion is an act of aggression worthy of punishment, but she is beginning to feel and act on the distinction between the two forms of behavior.

Evelyn Nef, who became a psychotherapist in her sixties after a life as a puppeteer, world traveller, and writer, is a model of the change of which some women are capable. We met at a weekly seminar at the Institute of the Study of Psychoanalytic Psychotherapy which we each attended for several years.

Evelyn, now in her seventies, views change in middle-aged women from the vantage point of her own life. She quotes the psychoanalyst Lawrence S. Kubie, who defines mental health as the ability to change when circumstances change. She feels that many middle-aged women fail to do this and set themselves up to become embittered, uninteresting people who let themselves be overlooked.

She hasn't! What is particularly fascinating about Evelyn is that she refuses to use the traumatic experiences of her early life as an excuse or a justification for failure. She was one of four children. Her mother, depressed after the birth of her youngest child, tried to commit suicide when Evelyn was three years old. Her mother had to be hospitalized. Her father, a self-made man who had gone from being a tailor to a designer, died of a heart attack when she was fourteen. Mother was once again severely depressed, became mute, stayed in her room and refused to get dressed.

The Sensual Older Woman

Evelyn, who didn't even finish high school, has become a highly educated, dynamic, and vital woman. Her first husband was Bil Baird, the puppeteer, with whom she worked. Her second was Vilhjalmur Stefansson, the Arctic explorer.

Stefansson died when she was forty-nine. Just over a year later, she met John Nef, who proposed to her after five days. He founded and headed The Committee on Social Thought at the University of Chicago, the first inter-disciplinary graduate department in the United States. The two fell deeply in love. They married when she was fifty. I once saw a photograph of the two of them taken shortly before their wedding. They were walking along the street arm in arm, "a picture of middle-aged love," Evelyn says.

She has a lot to say about women who are passive about their fate:

> So many women of middle age, even today, have been conditioned to put other people ahead of themselves—husbands, children, and parents. They make such a virtue of being nice and un-selfish that it's easy for them to fall into a state of martyrdom. And because they haven't ever learned to consider their own needs, they easily get depressed.
>
> I don't buy the "I can't find any man" attitude. If you put yourself into a place where you can find one, you usually can. A lot of this "I can't" attitude is a screen to hide behind, be-cause of a woman's inhibitions, her fear of being active, her need eternally to be a good girl.
>
> Some older women abdicate their own sexuality, their own autonomy. If someone be-comes really convinced she can't find a partner, she should make a virtue of it. Every nun in a convent is not a desperate human being!
>
> The passivity, the helplessness is too easy, to feel abandoned or trapped and hope-less. It becomes a world view. I believe that if

Venus After Forty

you're really stuck, you should get help. Treat the depression. I tell my women patients they think they're in prison, but they haven't tried the door.

Surely one way middle-aged women can alter the negative image of themselves is to listen to Evelyn Nef, who says, "There is nothing more positive than the way you present yourself to people, when you get to understand the contagion of enthusiasm, of spirit!"

Of course, a woman of fifty is at a different place in life than a woman of twenty. She is experienced and knowing in her sexuality. Above all, she has a different sense of time. She knows that a "forever" love can't be the same at fifty as it was at twenty. So much more readily than she could have as a young woman, she is able to live in and enjoy the present.

As for middle-aged men and women, existing in a time of anxiety about the future of the planet, it can only diminish us to live in a subjective world of terror about aging. Insights lead to understanding. With understanding, perhaps we can begin to see each other as we really are.

Notes

Introduction

1. Robert N. Butler, M.D., *The New York Times*, May 22, 1984.

2. Susan Sontag, "The Double Standard of Aging," *Saturday Review of Literature* (September 23, 1972).

3. Nelson S. Davis, *The New York Times*, July 22, 1984.

4. Peter Collier and David Horowitz, *The Kennedys. An American Dream* (New York: Simon and Schuster, 1984), p. 235.

5. *The New York Times*, September 16, 1984.

6. William Geist, "About New York," *The New York Times*, October 26, 1984.

7. Philip Blumstein and Pepper Schwartz, *American Couples. Money, Work, Sex* (New York: William Morrow & Co., 1983), pp. 32–34.

8. Ingrid Waldron, "Why Do Women Live Longer Than Men?" *Social Science and Medicine*, 10 (1976), p. 349.

9. Robert Darnton, "The Meaning of Mother Goose," *The New York Review of Books*, 31 (February 2, 1984), p. 1.

10. Colette, *Earthly Paradise, An Autobiography* (New York: Farrar, Straus & Giroux, 1966), p. 307.

11. William Attwood, *Making It Through the Middle Age. Notes While In Transit* (New York: Atheneum, 1982), p. 6.

12. Philip Roth, *The Ghost Writer* (New York: Farrar, Straus & Giroux, 1979).

13. "The Graying of America," *Newsweek*, February 28, 1977, pp. 50–65.

Venus After Forty

Chapter One

1. G[ershon] Legman, *Rationale of The Dirty Joke,* First Series (New York: Grove Press, 1969), p. 622.
———, *The Limerick* (New York: Bell Publishers, 1964, 1969).
———, *No Laughing Matter: Rationale of The Dirty Joke: An Analysis of Sexual Humor,* Second Series (New York: Breaking Point, Inc., 1975).

2. Leland J. Davies, "Attitudes Toward Old Age and Aging as Shown by Humor, *The Gerontologist,* 17:3 (June 1977), pp. 220–226.
Erman Palmore, "Attitudes Toward Aging as Shown by Humor," *The Gerontologist,* 11, 3:1 (1971), pp. 181–186.
Joseph Richman, "The Foolishness and Wisdom of Age: Attitudes Toward The Elderly as Reflected in Jokes," *The Gerontologist,* 17:3 (June 1977), pp. 210–219.

3. L. Bryce Boyer, Chairman, Daniel M. A. Freeman, Reporter, Panel on "Psychoanalysis, Folklore and Processes of Socialization," *Journal of the American Psychoanalytic Association,* 25:1 (1977), pp. 235–252.

4. Joseph Campbell, ed., *The Complete Grimm's Fairy Tales,* "Commentary," (New York: Pantheon Books, 1944), p. 862.

5. Marta Weigle, *Spiders and Spinsters, Women and Mythology,* (Albuquerque, New Mexico: University of New Mexico Press, 1982).

6. *The American Heritage Dictionary,* 1969.

7. Robert Graves, *The Greek Myths* (Baltimore, Maryland: Penguin Books, 1955) V. I 53–56.

8. Albert Barrière and Charles G. Leland, eds., *Dictionary of Jargon, Slander and Cant* (London: The Ballantine Press, 1939), p. 6.

9. Robert N. Butler, "Coping with the Midlife Crisis," *Dynamic Maturity,* 12, 2 (March 1977), pp. 11–16.

10. Joseph Heller, *Something Happened,* Scapegoat Productions, 1966 (New York: Ballantine Books, 1975), p. 26.

11. Iona and Peter Opie, *The Classic Fairy Tales* (London: Oxford University Press, 1974), p. 74 ff.

12. Vance Packard, *Unprintable Collections,* quoted in Richard Dorson, *American Folklore* (Chicago: University of Chicago Press, 1959), p. 100.

13. James D. Carrothers, *The Black Cat Club* (New York: Funk & Wagnalls, 1902), p. 84. (Dialect changes: Rita M. Ransohoff)

14. Peter Arno, *Sizzling Platter* (New York: Simon and Schuster, 1949), p. 27.

15. Graves, *op. cit.* 1, 105.

16. Quoted in Philip Mayerson, *Classical Mythology in Literature, Art and Music,* (Lexington, Mass.: Xerox College Publishing, 1971), p. 24.

17. Heinrich Zimmer, *The King and The Corpse,* Joseph Campbell, editor, Bollingen Foundation. II. (New York: Pantheon Books, 1948), p. 90.

18. Carl Carmer, *The Hudson* (New York: Rinehart & Co., 1939), p. 386.

19. Campbell, *op. cit.,* pp. 725–733.

20. Alex L. Finkle, "Emotional Quality and Physical Quantity of Sexual Activity in Aging Men," *Journal of Geriatric Psychiatry,* 1:1 (1973), pp. 70–79.

Chapter Two

1. William Steig, *The Agony in the Kindergarten.* (New York: Duel, Sloan and Pearce, 1950).

2. Edith Jacobson, *The Self and The Object World* (New York: International Universities Press, 1964).

3. Margaret S. Mahler, Fred Pine, and Anni Bergman, *The Psychological Birth of The Human Infant* (New York: Basic Books, Inc., 1975).

4. Daniel N. Stern, M.D., "The Early Development of Schemas of Self, Other, and Self with Other" in J. D. Lichtenberg and

S. Kaplan, eds., *Reflections on Self Psychology* (New York: International Universities Press, 1983).

5. Mahler, *op. cit.* Chapter Six.

6. Carol Gilligan, *In a Different Voice* (Cambridge: Harvard University Press, 1982), p. 42.

7. Dorothy Dinnerstein, *The Mermaid and The Minotaur* (New York: Harper Colophon, Harper & Row, 1976).

8. Ethel Spector Person, M.D., "Sexuality as the Mainstay of Identity: Psychoanalytic Perspectives," *Signs,* 5 (Summer, 1980), p. 4.

9. Peter Blos, *On Adolescence* (New York: The Free Press of Glencoe, 1962).

10. Person, *op. cit.,* p. 626.

11. O. E. Rolvaag, *Giants In The Earth* (New York: Harper & Bros., 1927).

Chapter Three

1. Alex Comfort, *A Good Age,* (New York: Simon and Schuster, 1976).

2. Elliott Jaques, "Death and the Mid-Life Crisis," *International Journal of Psychoanalysis* (1965), pp. 502–14.

3. Ernest Becker, *The Denial of Death* (New York: The Free Press, 1973).

4. Daniel J. Levinson, *The Seasons of a Man's Life* (New York: Alfred A. Knopf, 1973).

5. Arthur Miller, *Death of a Salesman* (New York: The Viking Press, 1949; Compass Books edition, 1963), p. 139.

6. Gregory Rochlin, M.D., *The Masculine Dilemma* (Boston: Little Brown & Co., 1980), p. 258.

7. Arnold J. Mandell, *The Coming of (Middle) Age. A Journey* (New York: Summit Books, 1977), p. 52.

8. Charles Simmons, *Wrinkles* (New York: Farrar, Straus & Giroux, 1978), pp, 77, 79, 178.

9. Norman Mailer, "The Prisoner of Sex," *Harper's* (March 1971), pp. 41–92.

10. Peter Collier and David Horowitz, *The Kennedys. An American Dream* (New York: Simon and Schuster, 1984), p. 222.

11. Philip Bernaum, ed., *The Sabbath Prayer Book* (New York: Hebrew Publishing Co., 1977).

12. Thorkill Vangaard, *Phallos: A Symbol and Its History in The Male World* (New York: Internat'l. University Press, 1969, English Edition, 1972), pp. 80, 89, 183 ff.

13. Peter Blos, Ph.D., "The Split Parental Images in Adolescent Social Relations," *The Psychoanalytic Study of The Child* (New York: Internat'l. Universities Press, 1976), p. 12.

14. Hans W. Loewald, M.D., "The Waning of the Oedipus Complex," *Journal of the American Psychoanalytic Ass'n.*, 27, #4 (1979), pp. 751–76.

Chapter Four

1. *Bedtime Story and Nursery Rhyme Book* (London: W. H. Smith & Sons, 1976).

2. Stephen E. Rich, "Now It's DO-RE-MI-FAT: Diet and Opera Stars," *The New York Times Magazine*, February 12, 1978.

3. Nikos Kazantzakis, *Zorba the Greek* (New York: Simon and Schuster, 1952), p. 244 ff.

4. Isaac Bashevis Singer, "A Party in Miami Beach," *Playboy* (June 1978).

5. William Hamilton, *Husbands, Wives and Live-Togethers* (New York: G. P. Putnam's Sons, 1976).

6. *Peter Arno's Sizzling Platter* (New York: Simon and Schuster, 1959), p. 80.

7. Bernice L. Neugarten, *Middle Age and Aging: A Reader in Social Psychology* (Chicago: University of Chicago Press, 1968), p. 140.

8. B. A. Bodkin, ed., "Uncle Bill's Story" in *Folk-Say, a Regional Miscellany* (1931), quoted in B. A. Bodkin, ed., *A*

Treasury of American Folklore (New York: Crown Publishers, 1944), p. 695.

9. Abby W. Kleinbaum, *The War Against the Amazons* (New York: McGraw Hill, 1983), p. 94.

10. Lela W. Clark, "Women, Women, Women. Quips, Quotes and Commentary," quoted in *The New York Times,* November 26, 1977.

11. Claude, *The New Yorker Album 1955–1965* (New York: Harper and Row, 1965).

12. Stanley H. Cath, "Individual Adaptation in the Middle Years," *Journal of Geriatric Psychiatry,* 9, #1 (1976), pp. 19–36.

13. Luck, Bob Apel, ed., *The American Cartoon Album* (New York: Dodd Mead and Co., 1974).

14. Honoré Daumier, Françoise Parturier, Preface. *Lib Women (Bluestockings & Socialist Women)* (Paris-New York: Leon Amiel, Publishers, Inc., 1974).

15. *The New York Times,* June 23, 1978.

16. Gregory Rochlin, M.D., *The Masculine Dilemma. A Psychology of Masculinity* (Boston: Little, Brown & Co.), p. 264 ff.

Chapter Five

1. Roger Lancelyn Green, "The Girl with the Rose-Red Slippers," in *Tales of Ancient Egypt* (Harmondsworth, England: Puffin Books, Penguin Books Ltd., 1967), pp. 180–4.

2. Iona and Peter Opie, *The Classic Fairy Tales* (London: Oxford University Press, 1974), pp. 27, 117.

3. Sir Arthur Quiller-Couch, *The Sleeping Beauty and Other Fairy Tales* (London: Hodder and Stoughton n.d.), p. 70.

4. Ruth Amdur Tanehaus, Curator, catalogue of exhibit: *The Great American Foot,* p. 7. See also Andrea Dworkin, "Gynocide: Chinese Footbinding," in *Woman Hating* (New York: E. P. Dutton, 1974), Chapter Six.

Notes

5. "Your Feet's Too Big." Words and music by Ada Benson and Fred Fisher. Fisher Music Corp. Copyright renewed 1963. Lines quoted are in part from Waller's improvisations on a tape cassette, "Fats Waller, A Legendary Performer." RCA, 1978, RCA Records.

6. Poster: Property of the Bettman Archive. Museum of Contemporary Crafts of the American Craft Council. New York April 14, June 30, 1978, Sponsored by the Kinney Shoe Corporation.

7. Lewis and Faye Copeland, *10,000 Jokes, Toasts and Stories* (Garden City, New York: Doubleday and Co., 1965), p. 188.

8. Kim Chernin, *The Obsession: Reflections on the Tyranny of Slenderness* (New York: Harper & Row, 1981).

9. Ella Freeman Sharpe, *Dream Analysis* (New York: Bruner/ Mazel Publishers, 1937), p. 26.

10. Henry Miller, *Tropic of Cancer* (New York: Grove Press, 1961), p. 6.

11. Ernest Hemingway, *A Moveable Feast* (New York: Charles Scribners & Sons, 1964), p. 190.

12. Leonard Kriegel, *On Men and Manhood* (New York: Hawthorn Books, Inc., 1979).

13. *Playboy* (January 1983).

14. Abby W. Kleinbaum, *The War Against the Amazons* (New York: McGraw Hill, 1983, p. 113.

15. Mario Puzo, *The Godfather* (Greenwich, Connecticut: Fawcett Crest Books, 1969), p. 27.

16. Myron Brenton, *The American Male* (New York: Coward-McCann, 1966), p. 165.

17. Carl Sandburg, "My Pretty Little Girl," in *The American Song Bag* (New York: Harcourt Brace and Co., 1927), p. 313.

18. *Playboy* (June 1978).

19. David Franklin, "*Myth of the Tight Pussy,*" in *Screw* (June 1978), p. 9 ff.

20. Harold Robbins, *The Betsy* (New York: Simon and Schuster, 1971; Pocket Books, 1972).

21. Harold Speert, M.D., George Kleiner, M.D., Maj-Britt Rosenbaum, M.D., Arlene Kagle, Ph.D., John O'Conner, M.D. and Beth Lieberman, M.D.

22. Tom Robbins, *Even Cowgirls Get the Blues* (New York: Houghton Mifflin Co., 1976; Bantam Books, 1977), pp. 112, 137.

23. September 8, 1983.

24. Anthony Pietropinto and Jacqueline Simenauer, *Beyond the Male Myth* (New York: New York Times Books, 1977), pp. 190–7.

25. David Reuben, *Everything You Always Wanted To Know About Sex* (New York: Bantam Books, 1971), p. 414 ff.

Chapter Six

1. John S. Farmer and W.E. Henley, *Dictionary of Slang and Its Analogues*, Revised Edition (New Hyde Park, New York: University Books, 1966), I.

2. Cartoon by Erkki Flanen, *Penthouse* (October 1978), p. 90.

3. Bruno Bettelheim, *Symbolic Wounds: Puberty Rites and the Envious Male* (Glencoe, Illinois: The Free Press, 1954). Otto Kernberg, "Barriers to Falling and Remaining in Love," *The Journal of the American Psychoanalytic Association*, 22, #3 (1974), pp. 486–511, 494. Edith Jacobson, "The Development of a Wish for a Child in Boys," *The Psychoanalytic Study of the Child*, 5 (1950), pp. 139–52.

4. John Steinbeck, *The Grapes of Wrath* (New York: Viking Press, 1939), p. 618 ff.

5. Simone de Beauvoir, *The Second Sex* (New York: Alfred A. Knopf, Inc., 1952; Bantam Books, 1965).

6. *Hustler* (December 1977).

7. Wolfgang Lederer, M.D., *The Fear of Women* (New York: Harcourt Brace Jovanovich, Inc., 1968), p. 37.

8. Arnold J. Mandell, M.D., *The Coming of (Middle) Age: A Journey* (New York: Summit Books, 1977).

9. Cartoon by Revilo in *Penthouse* (October 1978), p. 94.

10. Henry Miller, *Tropic of Cancer* (New York: Grove Press, 1961), p. 91.

11. James Leo Herlihy, *Midnight Cowboy* (New York: Simon and Schuster, 1965; Dell Publishing, 1969), p. 109.

12. Quoted in Gene Lyons' review of Robert Penn Warren, "A Place to Come To." *The New York Times Book Review* (March 13, 1977).

13. "Not A Love Story: A Film About Pornography," Bonnie Sherkline, Director. Produced by the National Film Board of Canada, Toronto, Canada, May 18, 1982.

14. *Rolling Stone* (January 22, 1981).

15. William Steig, *The Lonely Ones* (New York: Duel, Sloan and Pearce, 1942), p. 781 ff.

16. I have not been able to rediscover the volume in which the sleeping man in the shoe is located.

17. Colin Turnbull, *The Forest People* (New York: Simon and Schuster, 1963).

18. Gloria Steinem, *Outrageous Acts and Everyday Rebellions* (New York: Holt, Rinehart and Winston, 1983).

19. *Our Future Selves: A Research Plan Toward Understanding Aging* (U.S. Dept. of Health, Education & Welfare, Washington, D.C. National Institutes of Health, 1980), p. 5.

Chapter Seven

1. *Our Future Selves: A Research Plan Toward Understanding Aging* (U.S. Dept. of Health, Education & Welfare, Washington, D.C. National Institutes of Health, 1980), p. 5.

2. Avodah K. Offit, M.D., "Sexuality: The Facts of (Later) Life," *Ms.* Magazine (January 1982), pp. 32–34.

3. *Ibid.*

4. *Ibid.*

5. Lila Nachtigall, M.D., *The Lila Nachtigall Report* (New York: G. P. Putnam, 1977), p. 48.

6. *Ibid.*

7. Zev Rosenwacks, M.D., "Estrogen Replacement Therapy: Two Views," *Health Issues of Older Women: A Projection to the Year 2000,* Conference Proceedings: The School of Allied Health Professions, S. U. N. Y. at Stony Brook (April 1–31, 1981), p. 55. Nachtigall, *op. cit.,* 213.

8. Saul B. Gusberg, M.D., quoted in Rosetta Reitz, *Menopause, A Positive Approach* (Radnor, Pennsylvania: Chilton Book Company, 1977), pp. 193, 198.

9. Bernard D. Starr and Marcella Bakur Weiner, *The Starr-Weiner Report on Sex & Sexuality in The Mature Years* (New York: Stein & Day, 1981).

10. Myrna M. Weissman, Ph.D., *The Myth of Involutional Melancholia.* Unpublished ms. (n.d.), 7. See also Malkah Notman, M.D., *Midlife Concerns of Women: Finiteness & Expansion, Implications of the Menopause.* Unpublished ms., 1978.

11. Helene Deutsch, *Psychology of Women. Motherhood* (New York: Grune & Stratton, 1945), pp. 2, 457.

12. Quoted in Mary Ann P. Sviland, "A Program of Sexual Liberalism and Growth in the Elderly," Robert L. Solnick, ed., *Sexuality and Aging* (Berkeley: The University of Southern California Press, 1978), p. 102.

13. Quoted in Nachtigall, *op. cit.,* p. 139.

14. Starr and Weiner, *op. cit.,* p. 177.

15. Buck Brown, in *Playboy* (February 1972).

Chapter Eight

1. John Kenneth Galbraith, "Corporate Man," *The New York Times,* January 22, 1984.

2. Paul Theroux, "The Male Myth," *The New York Times,* December 25, 1983.

3. Phil Gailey, "A Nonsports Fan," *The New York Times,* December 18, 1983.

4. *American Journal of Public Health* (August 1981), reported in *The New York Times,* January 31, 1982.

5. Jesse Bernard, *The Future of Marriage,* quoted in Nancy Chodorow, *The Reproduction of Mothering.*

6. Jules Feiffer, "Bernard & Huey," *Playboy* (July 1984), p. 125.

7. Erik H. Erickson, "The Human Life Cycle," (New York: *International Encyclopedia of the Social Sciences,* 1968).

8. "Hers," *The New York Times,* October 6, 1983.

9. Theroux, *op. cit.*

10. Bernie Zilbergeld, *Male Sexuality* (New York: Bantam Books, 1979), p. 328.

11. Reported by Gordon D. Jensen, M.D., in *Human Sexuality,* V. 4, #9 (September 1980).

12. Zilbergeld, *op. cit.* Jane E. Brody, "Personal Health," *The New York Times,* July 5, 1978.

13. Jane E. Brody, "Personal Health," *The New York Times.* February 2, 1980.

Chapter Nine

1. Glasberger, in *Penthouse* (October 1978).

2. Robert Coles, *Entitlement. Privileged Ones. The Well-Off and the Rich in America. V. 5. Children in Crisis* (Boston: Little Brown & Co., 1977), Part 6, p. 363.

3. *The New York Times,* July 6, 1984.

4. Germaine Greer, *Sex and Destiny* (New York: Harper & Row, 1984), quoted in *Ms.* Magazine (April 1984), pp. 53–96.

5. Otto Kernberg, M.D., "Normal Narcissism in Middle

Age," in *Internal World and External Reality* (New York: Jason Aronson, 1980), p. 128.

6. Joseph D. Lichtenerg, M.D., "The Development of a Sense of Self," *Journal of the American Psychoanalytic Association*, V. 23, #3 (1975), p. 454.

7. Roy Schafer, Ph.D., "Men Who Struggle Against Sentimentality." Symposium: *The Psychology of Men: New Psychoanalytic Perspectives* (New York City: The Association for Psychoanalytic Medicine in collaboration with The Columbia University Center on Psychoanalytic Training and Research, January 26, 1985).

8. Dan Kiley, M.D., *The Peter Pan Syndrome: Men Who Have Never Grown Up* (New York: Dodd Mead & Co., 1983), pp. 8, 37.

9. Joyce McDougall, Ed.D., "On Addictive Relationships," The New York Freudian Society, November 16, 1984.

10. Kernberg, op. cit., p. 144.

11. Ethel S. Person, M.D., "Two Male Sexual Fantasies: Their Relationship to Psychosexual Development." Symposium: *The Psychology of Men: New Psychoanalytic Perspectives* (New York City: The Association for Psychoanalytic Medicine in collaboration with The Columbia University Center for Psychoanalytic Training and Research, January 26, 1985).

12. David Guttmann, Ph.D., "Individual Adaptation in the Middle Years, Developmental Issues in the Male Mid-Life Crisis," *Journal of Geriatric Psychiatry*, V. 9, #1 (1976).

13. William A. Nolen, M.D., *Crisis Time! Love, Marriage and The Male at Midlife* (New York: Dodd, Mead & Co., 1984), p. 32 ff.

14. Helen Gurley Brown, *Having It All* (New York: Linden Press, Simon and Schuster, 1982).

15. Evelyn Fox Keller, *Reflections on Gender and Science* (New Haven: Yale University Press, 1985), pp. 104–106.

Chapter Ten

1. Helen Gurley Brown, *Having It All* (New York: Linden Press, Simon and Schuster, 1982).

2. Linda Tschirhart Sanford & Mary Ellen Donovan, *Women & Self-Esteem* (New York: Penguin Books, 1984) Chapter 6, "Women In a World of Mirrors and Images: The Impact of Technology on Imagery," p. 229.

3. William E. Geist, "In Battle Against Aging The Trenches Are Muddy," Column: "About New York," *The New York Times*, November 8, 1986.

4. Brown, *op. cit.*, 150.

5. Alice Miller, *Prisoners of Childhood: The Drama of the Gifted Child* (New York: Basic Books, Inc., 1981), pp. 8–14.

6. *Ibid.*

7. I am indebted to Dr. Robert Anderson for his concept of envy. From his ms. on "Envy and Jealousy."

8. Otto Kernberg, M.D., *Internal World and External Reality* (New York: Jason Aronson, 1980), "Pathological Narcissism in Middle Age." Chapter 8.

9. Margaret Mitchell, *Gone With the Wind* (New York: The Macmillan Co., 1936, Avon Books, 1964).

10. Edith Wharton, *The House of Mirth* (1906), *The Reef, The Custom of the Country, The Age of Innocence* (New York: The Library of America, 1986).

11. Tennessee Williams, *A Streetcar Named Desire* (New York: Signet Books; New American Library, 1947).

12. Joseph Heller, *Something Happened* (New York: Ballantine Books, 1966) p. 424.

Chapter 11

1. Otto Kernberg, M.D. *Internal World and External Reality* (New York: Jason Aronson, Inc. 1980), p. 128.

2. Philip Blumstein, Ph.D. and Pepper Schwartz, Ph.D. *American Couples: Money, Work, Sex* (New York: William Morrow & Co. 1983), p. 268.

3. *Ibid.*, p. 274.

4. Edward M. Brecher, *Love, Sex, and Aging* (Boston: Little Brown & Co. 1984), p. 104.

5. Augustus Y. Napier, Ph.D. "Couples on the Couch," *Vogue* Magazine (February, 1987), p. 460.

6. Kernberg, *op. cit.*, p. 144.

7. *Ibid.*, p. 129.

8. Edith Atkin, *In Praise of Marriage* (New York: The Vanguard Press, 1982), Chapter 16.

9. Francine Klagsbrun, *Married People. Staying Together in the Age of Divorce* (New York: Bantam Books, 1985), p. 99.

10. Roger L. Gould, M.D., *Transformations. Growth and Change in Adult Life* (New York: Simon and Schuster, 1978), p. 271 ff.

11. *Ibid.*, p. 217 ff.

12. Wayne A. Myers, *Dynamic Therapy of the Older Patient* (New York: Jason Aronson, Inc.), Chapter 2.

13. Kernberg. *op cit.*, p. 149.

14. Pearl King, "The Life Cycle as Indicated by the Nature of the Transference in the Psychoanalysis of the Middle-Aged and the Elderly," *International Journal of Psychoanalysis,* 61: 153–160 (1980) p. 159.

15. *Ibid.*, p. 156.

16. The American Academy of Psychoanalysis Conference. Ian Alger, M.D., Helen Singer Kaplan, M.D., Jean Baker Miller, M.D., Theodore Isaac Rubin, M.D., Leon Saltzman, M.D., Panelists. Alexandra Symonds, M.D., Moderator. New York. November 8, 1986.

17. *Ibid.*

18. *Ibid.*

19. *The American Heritage Dictionary of the English Language.* New York. American Heritage Publishing Co., Inc. 1969.

20. Margaret S. Mahler, Fred Pine, and Anni Bergman, *The Psychological Birth of the Human Infant* (New York: Basic Books, Inc. 1975), p. 49.

21. Kahlil Gibran, *The Prophet* (New York: Alfred A. Knopf, 1923).

22. Fred Pine, *Developmental Theory and Clinical Practice.* (New Haven: Yale University Press, 1985), Chapter 4.

23. Carol Gilligan, *In a Different Voice* (Cambridge: Harvard University Press, 1982), pp. 108–109.

24. Phyllis Rose, *Parallel Lives. Five Victorian Marriages* (New York: Alfred A. Knopf, 1984), p. 19.

Chapter Twelve

1. W. Somerset Maugham, "Rain," in *Cakes and Ale* (New York: Arno Press, 1977).

2. "Rain," directed by Lewis Milestone. A United Artists Picture, 1932.

3. Nina Auerbach, *Woman and the Demon, The Life of a Victorian Myth* (Cambridge, Massachusetts: Harvard University Press, 1982).

4. Christopher Bollas, "The Transformational Object," *International Journal of Psychoanalysis*, V. 60 (1978), pp. 97–107.

5. "The Single Experience, 1986," sponsored by the Volunteer Counselling Service of Rockland County, Inc., Nyack, New York, November 23, 1986.

6. Sue Miller, *The Good Mother* (New York: Harper & Row Publishers, 1986).

7. Mark Twain, *The Adventures of Huckleberry Finn* (New York: Harper & Bros. Publishers, 1903), p. 63. (Dialect altered by Rita M. Ransohoff.)

Chapter Thirteen

1. Stephen Vizingzey, *In Praise of Older Women* (New York: Ballantine Books, 1965).

2. For all the material that follows on Jane Digby el Mezreb,

I am indebted to Leslie Blanch, *The Wilder Shores of Love* (New York: New American Library, 1954), Chapter Two.

3. *Ibid.*, p. 189.

4. *Ibid.*, p. 203.

5. Lily Harmon, *Freehand* (New York: Simon and Schuster, 1981).

6. I am indebted for this material to H. F. Peters, *My Sister My Spouse. A Biography of Lou Andreas-Salomé* (New York: W. W. Norton and Co., 1962).

7. *Ibid.*, pp. 119, 120.

8. *Ibid.*, p. 208.

9. *Ibid.*, p. 237.

10. *Ibid.*, p. 293.

11. Mary Kathleen Benet, *Writers in Love* (New York: Macmillan and Co., 1977), p. 228.

12. *Ibid.*, p. 230.

13. *Ibid.*, p. 251.

14. Arlene Derenski and Sally B. Landsburg, *The Age Taboo. Younger Men-Older Women Relationships* (Boston: Little, Brown and Co., 1981), p. 230.

15. Marcia Davenport, *Too Strong for Fantasy* (New York: Charles Scribners Sons, 1967).

16. *Ibid.*, pp. 376, 377.

17. *Ibid.*, p. 380.

Acknowledgments

Grateful acknowledgment is made to reprint previously published material:

"Gladys, is it really you?" by Buck Brown. Reproduced by special permission of *PLAYBOY* magazine. October 1964. Copyright © 1964.

"Willie!" by William Steig. Copyright 1950 by William Steig. Reproduced by permission of the author. Illustration from *The Agony in the Kindergarden.*

Drawing by Claude. Copyright ©1957, 1985. *The New Yorker* magazine, Inc.

"And they told me it would be lonely at the top." Cartoon by Randy Glasbergen. *Penthouse* magazine. Reprinted by courtesy of *Penthouse* magazine © 1978.

"Adieu mon cher, je vais chez mes editeurs . . ." Honoré Daumier. *Lib Women. Bluestockings and Socialist Women.* Paris-New York: Leon Amiel, Publisher, Inc. 1974. Permission to print by Leon Amiel, publisher.

"I am at one with the universe." William Steig. Reproduced by permission of the author. Illustration from *The Lonely Ones.* Copyright 1950 by William Steig.

"Madam, on behalf of the other patrons I must ask you to stop cheering." Buck Brown. *PLAYBOY* magazine. February, 1972. Reproduced by special permission of *PLAYBOY* magazine. Copyright © 1972.

"Now, don't get panicky, I'll have you looking ten years younger in no time." Drawing by O'Brian. Copyright © 1961. *The New Yorker* Magazine, Inc. October 7, 1961, p. 190.

"Your Feet's Too Big." (Refrain) Ada Benson and Fred Fisher. Permission granted Fisher Music and Morby

Venus After Forty